visit sunday church service -

MW00808175

CULTURE, PLACE, AND NATURE

STUDIES IN ANTHROPOLOGY AND ENVIRONMENT

Devon Peña and K. Sivaramakrishnan,

Series Editors

what do they gain from transitioning?

why did Akha abandon zomian values
and embrace christianity and buddhism

Akha Zauh - post 1971

why Akha are targeted by coffee, cash

crops
~~police~~

central question: an
3 dimensions
subsistence ethic, economic, identity
does the zomian of state   is ethnic
ethic remain   and Akha   hill tribe
Association of Christians people
village has a member   thailand - every

read Thai constitution. chapter 1 and 2
charles keyes. religion study ~~Aa~~ - how is
chainess defined, how is it imposed on
villagers, headman is medium between people
and state

ask whether different groups have changed
their religion   old belief system still intact
chineese family still maintaining confiscuism?

CULTURE, PLACE, AND NATURE

Centered in anthropology, the Culture, Place, and Nature
series encompasses new interdisciplinary social science
research on environmental issues, focusing on the intersection
of culture, ecology, and politics in global, national, and local
contexts. Contributors to the series view environmental
knowledge and issues from the multiple and often conflicting
perspectives of various cultural systems.

*The Kuhls of Kangra: Community-Managed Irrigation
in the Western Himalaya* by Mark Baker

*The Earth's Blanket: Traditional Teachings
for Sustainable Living* by Nancy Turner

*Property and Politics in Sabah, Malaysia: Native
Struggles over Land Rights* by Amity A. Doolittle

*Border Landscapes: The Politics of Akha Land Use
in China and Thailand* by Janet C. Sturgeon

BORDER LANDSCAPES

The Politics of Akha Land Use in China and Thailand

JANET C. STURGEON

UNIVERSITY OF WASHINGTON PRESS

Seattle and London

THIS PUBLICATION WAS SUPPORTED IN PART
BY THE DONALD R. ELLEGOOD INTERNATIONAL
PUBLICATIONS ENDOWMENT.

Material drawn from chapter 4 was first published in "Border
Practices, Boundaries and the Control of Resource Access:
A Case Study from China, Thailand and Burma," *Development
and Change* 35, no. 3 (June 2004): 463–84. Material drawn from
chapters 4 and 6 was first published in "Post-Socialist Property
Rights for Akha in China," *Conservation and Society* 2,
no. 1 (January-June 2004): 137–61.

University of Washington Press
PO Box 50096, Seattle, WA 98145, U.S.A.
www.washington.edu/uwpress

Library of Congress Cataloging-in-Publication Data
can be found at the back of this book.

The paper used in this publication is acid-free and 90 percent
recycled from at least 50 percent post-consumer waste. It meets
the minimum requirements of American National Standard
for Information Sciences—Permanence of Paper for Printed
Library Materials, ANSI z39.48–1984. ♾♲

For my parents,

Anna and Galen Sturgeon

CONTENTS

ACKNOWLEDGMENTS

IN CONSIDERING MY DEBTS, MY DEEPEST THANKS GO TO THE AKHA VIL-
lagers in Xianfeng (China) and Akhapu (Thailand) who submitted patiently
to hours of interviews, treks through their land, and repeat conversations
on complicated issues. Their tenacity and intelligence inspired this book.

Xu Jianchu, then deputy director of the ethnobotany department of the
Kunming Institute of Botany (KIB), served as host for my research in China.
Beginning in the late 1950s, researchers at KIB carried out pathbreaking eth-
nobotanical work in Xishuangbanna. An heir to this tradition, Professor Xu
moved beyond it to establish one of the first nongovernmental organizations in China, the Center for Biodiversity and Indigenous Knowledge in
Kunming. He also introduced me to Mengsong. Others who generously facil-
itated field research in China included, among others, Long Chunlin, Su
Yongge, Wang Jieru, and Liu Yitao at KIB; Zuo Ting at the Yunnan Academy
of Social Sciences; Lu Xing and Cai Kui at the Yunnan Institute of Geography;
and Liu Hongmao of the Xishuangbanna Tropical Botanic Garden. Tao
Guoda, forest taxonomist at the Botanic Garden, identified all my tree and
plant species in China. My able research assistant/interpreter was Wang
Jianhua (Ayu), an Akha master's student at KIB.

My host in Thailand was Chayan Vaddhanaphuti, then director of the
Social Research Institute at Chiang Mai University (CMU). Ajarn Chayan,
a renowned scholar/activist in Thailand, welcomed me into his lively community of researchers and gave skillful advice on how to proceed. The most

important among those advising on field research in Thailand were Kanok and Benjavan Rerkasem at the Multiple Cropping Center at CMU; Uraivan Tan-Kim-Yong, Chusak Wittayapak, and Anan Ganjanapan of the Faculty of Social Sciences at CMU; Kwanchewan Buadaeng at the Social Research Institute at CMU; Pinkaew Laungaramsri, then a Ph.D. student in anthropology at the University of Washington (now CMU faculty); and Leo Alting von Geusau, an independent anthropologist of Akha based in Chiang Mai. J. F. Maxwell of the Chiang Mai Herbarium identified my botanical specimens in Thailand, and Simon Gardiner and Pindar Sidisunthorn helped with specimen collection. My research assistant/interpreter in Thailand was Hu Anquan (ethnic Chinese), who spoke fluent Akha.

Many friends, colleagues, and mentors helped sort out my thinking through chapter readings and discussions. These include (in alphabetical order) Arun Agrawal, Ann Anagnost, Jackie Armijo, Hal Conklin, Walt Coward, Sara Davis, Amity Doolittle, Michael Dove, Emily DuPuis, Magnus Fiskesjö, Tim Forsyth, Luin Goldring, Elisabeth Grinspoon, Jane Hanks, Inga-Lill Hansson, Jim Harkness, Stevan Harrell, Emily Harwell, Melinda Herrold-Menzies, Philip Hirsch, Sandra Hyde, Nina Kammerer, Charles Keyes, Ben Kiernan, Margery Lazarus, Ralph Litzinger, Susan McCarthy, Stephen McGurk, Christine Padoch, Judy Pine, Simone Pulver, Hugh Raffles, Jesse Ribot, Mark Ritchie, Jeff Romm, Vasant Saberwal, Suzana Sawyer, Thomas Sikor, K. Sivaramakrishnan, Elena Songster, Jennifer Sowerwine, Gary Suwannarat, Marina Svensson, Pat Symonds, Nicola Tannenbaum, David Thomas, Deborah Tooker, Thongchai Winichakul, and Emily Yeh. Among my friends, my deepest thanks go to Jake Kosek and Celia Lowe for enormous personal and intellectual support.

John Battles and Kevin O'Hara at UC Berkeley, and Steve Hamburg at Brown University, patiently advised on forest data analysis. At Brown, Rick Wetzler guided the final number crunching, and Justin Fried prepared the figures summarizing the forest data. Lynn Carlson at Brown University and John Ng at Simon Fraser University created all the maps for the book.

Border Landscapes grew out of graduate school research I did for the Yale School of Forestry and Environmental Studies. There is a special place in my heart for my doctoral writing group (at UC Berkeley): James McCarthy, Sharad Chari, David McDermott Hughes, and Melanie Hughes McDermott. I also hold in high regard my academic committee: Nancy Peluso (chair), Kristiina Vogt (administrative chair), James Scott, Mark Ashton, and Nick Menzies. Equally important was Peter Vandergeest, who advised on this project from early proposals through its completion. Administrators whose help was invaluable included Kay Mansfield and Elizabeth Barsa at Yale, Mary Graham at UC Berkeley, and Laura Sadovnikoff at Brown University. James Scott and Charles Keyes have been exceptional mentors during the writing of the book.

Research funding was provided by the East Asian Studies Council, the Agrarian Studies Program, and the Tropical Resources Institute at Yale University; the Committee on Scholarly Communication with China; and the Ford Foundation/Bangkok. The National Research Council of Thailand kindly granted permission for my fieldwork. Much of the book was completed during a postdoctoral fellowship in Sweden at Lund University's Centre for East and Southeast Asian Studies, then directed by Michael Schoenhals. The first draft was finished while I was a visiting scholar in the anthropology department at the University of Washington. Revisions were completed during a Freeman postdoctoral fellowship at Brown University co-hosted by the Watson Institute for International Studies and the East Asian Studies Department.

At the University of Washington Press, Lorri Hagman expressed interest in the manuscript long before it was written and offered sustained support during the writing of the book. K. Sivaramakrishnan and Devon Peña encouraged me to submit the manuscript to the series on Culture, Place and Nature. Three anonymous reviewers provided comments crucial to the book's final shape, and Mary Ribesky guided the book skillfully into production.

My brother Nick and my nephew Kit helped in various ways during field research. My mother, to my surprise, knew all along that I could do it. In all, I have received help from hundreds of people, some of whom I have surely failed to remember. For all this generous support, I offer heartfelt thanks. I alone bear responsibility for any shortcomings in the final product.

In 1938, my father, a petroleum geologist, was sent to look for oil in Borneo in what was then the Dutch East Indies. In 1939, my mother joined him in Balik Papan, a town on the east coast of Borneo, where they lived until the approach of the Japanese military in 1941 forced them to leave. During my childhood my parents' Borneo stories enchanted me. For drawing me to Asia, and for their extraordinary love and encouragement for all my Asia adventures, I dedicate *Border Landscapes* to my mother and to my late father.

BORDER LANDSCAPES

INTRODUCTION

THE JEEP LUMBERS UP A DIRT ROAD FROM THE XISHUANGBANNA VALLEY, a tropical site in southern Yunnan in China, to Mengsong, an Akha settlement at the top of the ridge. We pass villages half hidden in the trees and large forests that look good from a moving vehicle. At last we arrive, emerging from the forest onto a spectacular plain atop the mountain that separates China from Burma. Wooded hills ring the plain, with Akha hamlets nestled in the folds where slopes meet the level land. This is an old settlement, with clans that have lived here for more than 250 years. An Akha man dressed in faded army green welcomes me and points out the lone tree in the distance that marks the Burma border. In the main hamlet, adults and children throng the market. A few soldiers from one of the Burmese rebel armies amble with their purchases back toward the border. Since Mengsong is also home to a Chinese military post, I assume that the soldiers from Burma are tolerated. My guide leads me to a large old-growth forest, woods where Akha elders have forbidden cutting for many generations. In the evening, over a lavish meal of wild game and many unfamiliar vegetables, villagers complain that agricultural extension agents from the valley introduce varieties of fruit trees and grains suitable for the tropics, but not for Mengsong at 1,600 meters. Mengsong is firmly enclosed within China, yet is right on the border. Even in this first visit, I decide that this will be the site for the China half of my research.

Two months later, in another jeep on a dirt road severely rutted by monsoon torrents, I approach another Akha village, this one in Thailand. After passing hamlets with extensive fields and scant clumps of trees, the jeep suddenly turns onto a ridge carpeted in dense forest, reputed to be the largest contiguous wooded area in Mae Faluang District of northern Chiang Rai Province. I am about to arrive in Akhapu, settled four generations ago by ancestors of current residents.[1] Akhapu is thought to be the oldest and one of the largest Akha settlements in Thailand. Over dinner, the heads of Loimi and Ulo Akha villages extol the harmony between the two Akha groups living beside one another in Akhapu. I later discover that this harmony was manufactured for my visit—Loimi and Ulo Akha, who migrated here from Burma at different times, have serious conflicts as a result of declining access to land. The village heads also carefully point out that no one here uses heroin, implying that this would be a safe place for me to live. I am intrigued with this locale an hour's walk from the Burma border, with Taiwan-funded tea plantations, large forests, and numerous villagers who speak Chinese. There are obvious signs of wealth—people with trucks, large houses, and cell phones—as well as farmers with tiny, fragile houses and shredded clothing. For the Thailand half of my research, I have found my site.

I had arrived on the geographic peripheries of two major nation-states, China and Thailand (see fig. 1) to investigate border landscapes. China and Thailand represent dramatically different political regimes, yet they share a common set of upland peoples along the borders with Burma. I chose one of these peoples, who call themselves Akha, for a comparative study of border landscapes in two distinctly different settings.

I was interested in "border" in two senses. The first sense means the margin or edge of a nation-state. From the vantage point of Beijing or Bangkok, the two national capitals, these two Akha villages are on the extreme periphery (see fig. 2). In both capitals, modernizing policies over the past several decades have sought to enclose these border areas within the national realm. Using border in this sense, as margin or periphery of a large political entity, I wanted to trace how Akha access to resources and land management had evolved as they and the forests around them became incorporated within the national boundaries and state imaginations in China and Thailand.

The second sense of "border" is as a dividing line that links as well as separates people in two nation-states, including the social relationships surrounding that line. Each village chosen for my research was located within walking distance of the Burma border. In both Mengsong and Akhapu, some villagers had moved back and forth between the adjacent Shan State of Burma and their current location. Taking border as boundary line, I set out to

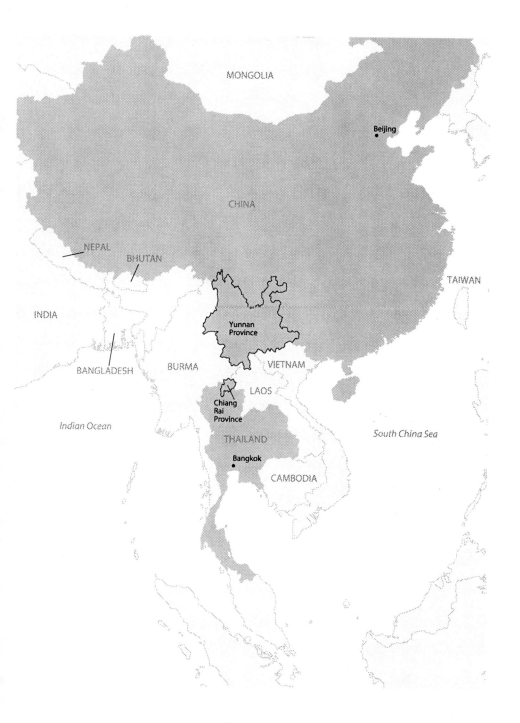

FIG. 1. China and Thailand

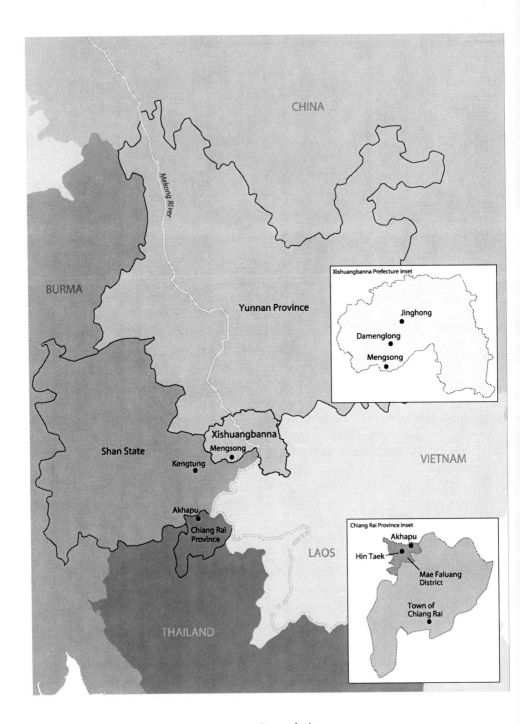

FIG. 2. Research sites

[handwritten annotations in top margin:
China
— citizens
— property rights
— forest as subsistence   resources

Thailand
— mixed levels of citizenship
— legal rights to land?
— forests as state resources

left margin: exporting pollution/heavy use of international resources elated?]

discover how border dynamics and cross-border relationships had shaped Akha access to resources and land use in each case.

Farmers in both Mengsong and Akhapu have experienced the first meaning of border, as periphery, through processes of incorporation that had occurred over the past fifty to sixty years, within the life experience of older villagers. In both nation-states, Akha have been marginalized by their ethnicity, their form of land use, and their upland location removed from mainstream lowland societies. I already knew that in China, Akha were citizens with formal property rights in land and forests, while Akha in Thailand were "hill tribes" and mostly not citizens, without legal rights to land or trees. What was less clear was how Akha in these two places had arrived at this point of inclusion in one nation-state and exclusion from the other. I also knew that the bulk of forests in China had been designated as subsistence resources for villagers, while in Thailand forests had been claimed as state resources to be used for national purposes. The distinction was clear—in Thailand and China, Akha and forests were defined remarkably differently.

The second meaning of border, as a dividing line with dynamics across it, has an intriguingly complex history in both village sites. In premodern eras in each village, before their enclosure in China and Thailand, these upland farmers had been clients of lowland Tai or Shan princes, rulers of small principalities that in turn paid tribute to larger kingdoms and empires.[2] These small principalities constituted the frontiers or border realms between larger political entities. I wanted to find out how premodern border dynamics, with border reaches comprised of tributary principalities, had been translated into modern border practices surrounding clearly delineated lines separating major nation-states. Had the patron-client relationships that characterized principalities disappeared under modernizing regimes? And how had Akha villagers, who surely had relatives and trade relationships in Burma in each case, negotiated the transition to being divided from them by a national line? My questions, then, focused on processes of Akha enclosure within China and Thailand, as well as the changing border dynamics resulting when clear boundaries were drawn between upland peoples related by common social and land-use histories. My overall question concerned how these processes had combined to produce border landscapes in the distinctly different realms of China and Thailand.

[handwritten right margin: tributaries in packet reading re: border war of China & Burma. Yunnan as almost buffer zone]

In addition to looking at processes, I also wanted to assess current outcomes. As of the time of my stay (1996–97), how were Akha livelihoods faring under these very different processes of incorporation? Similarly, what was the condition of Akha forests under these distinct policy regimes? Based

on the initial dichotomy of conditions in China and Thailand, I expected
to find Akha in Mengsong doing reasonably well under China's drive for
economic development, and Akha in Akhapu rapidly losing land and sliding into poverty, as they were elsewhere in Thailand. I also anticipated that
Akha forests in China would be in good condition, while those in Thailand
would be shrinking rapidly and declining in quality. My initial impressions
of both villages suggested that the outcomes were not so clear-cut. So what
was going on?

Over many months in each village, I began to untangle the ways that
Akha farmers—men and women of differing ages and political positions—
made use of their upland, border locales. Their daily lives involved producing food and other products in mountainous terrain, engaging with
state agents and traders, and crossing the border for a variety of purposes.
For Akha in Mengsong and Akhapu, border as margin and border as dividing line often intersected in daily activities, although villagers understood
the difference. For much of the past two thousand years, Akha farmers have
lived in the mountains that now link China and mainland Southeast Asia
and have relied on shifting cultivation in hilly, wooded sites to grow upland
rice and a rich array of vegetables. As of 1996, in addition to cultivating
upland rice in swiddens (shifting-cultivation fields), Akha in both villages
also managed wet rice fields, raised large numbers of livestock, hunted wild
game, and collected many kinds of wild fruits, vegetables, and medicinal
herbs in surrounding fields and forests. Akha cultivation practices revolved
around complex upland environments that varied greatly in elevation and
microclimate. Akha farmers exploited these diverse sites by nurturing an
astonishing array of trees and plants, whether wild or cultivated. Through
practices of shifting cultivation, in which farmers open an area of forest
to plant upland rice for a year or two and then allow it to regenerate into
forest, Akha farmers knew how to take full advantage of products in different
stages of regeneration. In other words, Akha landscapes in both China and
Thailand were complex and mutable, both spatially and temporally, and
produced a great diversity of goods. This diversity and flexibility of production, in fact, constituted Akha strength in engaging with shifting political regimes.

Beyond their understanding of ecological processes, Akha farmers
manipulated their complex environments to meet daily needs, respond to
emergencies, maneuver around state extractions, and to produce for markets. In fact, farmers refashioned their landscapes as a means to negotiate
with both state agents and border patrons. Akha took advantage of the com-

plexity of their land uses and regeneration pathways to deal with state administrators, traders, and diverse political figures. This ability to adjust complicated land uses over time in response to local needs, state plans, and border possibilities is what I call "landscape plasticity."

I first became aware of landscape plasticity and the extent of farmers' use of it early in my field research when I was trekking with a small group of farmers. We were covering all the land areas of Xianfeng, the Akha hamlet in China. At one point, when we had stopped on a ridge, they mentioned that the prefecture government planned to build a reservoir that would inundate much of the hamlet forest we could see stretching out in the valley below. The dam for the reservoir would generate electricity for lowland towns in both China and Burma. This plan was news to me and I reacted with horror. The villagers, however, reacted differently. They pointed to areas of pasture that they would regenerate into trees, because forests were necessary for survival. They would meanwhile move the pastures downslope, taking out some shifting-cultivation fields. They would also open more wet rice fields on their lowest elevation lands. At that moment, I experienced a sudden understanding of these farmers' knowledge and practice of a processual landscape. I also immediately realized the conceptual chasm between their understanding and the usual state vision of set property rights on mapped landscapes for which annual production estimates are made. I began to comprehend the extent and scale at which these farmers could imagine their landscape differently and plan the transition to a new mosaic of land uses. I had previously pictured individuals and households planning on the scale of a swidden and its various stages of regeneration. But here were farmers strategizing on a landscape scale and planning for forests that would not be usable for fifteen to twenty years.

Following this experience, I began to see landscapes not just as topography and land cover, but as sites for maneuvering and struggle. In diverse and sometimes conflicting ways, Akha have produced their livelihoods at the juncture of state actions, border possibilities, and their own sedimented histories in each place. This is the realm of border landscapes.

As of 1997, in each village the possibility for using flexible, plastic landscapes was being undermined. First, state policies for agriculture and forestry had separated cultivated fields from areas of woods, limiting the practice of shifting cultivation. Second, policies had designated property rights in land and trees, mapping out clear areas with known owners or users. Third, policies and development projects had introduced the intensive production of fewer crops on smaller land areas. All three of these steps had reduced landscape plasticity, although in very different ways in China and Thailand.

Another kind of threat to landscape plasticity came from Akha village heads, local chiefs with state appointment to keep order in border realms. These village heads limited landscape plasticity in two ways: (1) by using their connections on both sides of the border to set themselves up as border patrons controlling local resource access and skewing the benefits to themselves; and (2) by introducing state-sponsored simplified land-use practices in ways that linked these border heads to lowland planners and sources of money. In other words, Akha village heads used the border in both senses, manipulating the border-as-line with relations across it to control resource access and collaborating with state agents to include other villagers more securely in the realm of border-as-margin of the nation-state. Through combining their use of border in both senses, village heads colluded with elite actors on both sides of the border to enhance their own roles as border guardians and to further marginalize other Akha. These practices played out in dramatically different ways in China and Thailand, with distinct outcomes for Akha farmers and the practice of plastic landscapes.

In sum, border landscapes encapsulate the conjuncture of two interrelated processes: the intersection of Akha practice and state plans under two very different regimes (China and Thailand); and the mediation of these intersections by border dynamics.

In each country, the Akha hamlet of study is situated within a region that comprises numerous ethnic groups, with Tai in the lowlands and a similar, but not identical, set of hill groups in the uplands. This political and spatial arrangement of lowland and upland ethnic peoples is common in adjacent parts of Burma and Laos as well.[3] The regions of study are Xishuangbanna Prefecture in China and Chiang Rai Province in Thailand (see fig. 2). Each has been the target of a complex array of efforts by state agents, and recently by development experts and entrepreneurs, to integrate it into economic development.

Until the Chinese revolution, Xishuangbanna Prefecture was a Tai Buddhist principality, Sipsongpanna, with strong links to what is now Southeast Asia. The principality was inhabited primarily by Tai wet-rice cultivators in the valley and an array of peoples who practiced shifting cultivation in the hills. Following the revolution of 1949, the central government changed the area's name and sent thousands of Han Chinese to Xishuangbanna to open and run state rubber farms to make China self-sufficient in rubber. These state farms have taken out most of the lowland tropical forest that once carpeted the valley. In the economic reform period since 1982, state extension efforts have promoted cash crops for farmers at all altitudes, and policies have encouraged villager participation in markets. In the late 1990s, Akha and other hill farmers at low to midslope elevations planted high-value fruits, vegetables, and medicinal herbs, as well as rubber trees in their former shifting-cultivation fields. Upland farmers opened areas for wet rice as well as fruit orchards and sugar cane, and state policies were slowly bringing shifting cultivation to an end.

Over the past fifty years, state projects have also seriously reduced forest cover. From 1949 until the early 1980s, central planners considered forests to be an inefficient land use. Agricultural policies from the 1950s through the 1970s ensured that huge expanses of forest were cut to make room for grain production. With China's opening up to outside influences in the early 1980s, international advisors persuaded policy makers to manage forests for both protection and use. These advisors also introduced the understanding, common in environment and development circles, that shifting cultivation was destructive to forests and watersheds. Accordingly, over the past twenty-some years, agriculture and forestry departments have moved to stop shifting cultivation, including in Mengsong. To the extent that they have succeeded, Akha scope to use flexible landscapes has also been greatly curtailed.

Akha send their children to school, some of them through middle and high school, and a handful through university. As a consequence, Akha can be found throughout Xishuangbanna on the staff of every government office, school, bank, and business. As the head of one Akha hamlet put it, "In the next generation, we will be Chinese." In fact, Akha are already Chinese citizens, as they have been since the revolution. In another sense, however, they will not be Han: each ID card identifies the bearer's minority nationality, a marker of backwardness.

Life in lowland Xishuangbanna reflects the rapid transformations of the landscape and livelihoods of Tai, Han, Jinuo, Lahu, Akha and other residents in response to a bustling economy, as well as the ambition on the part of many young people of whatever ethnicity to become "urban," "modern," and "rich." Xishuangbanna has been a provincial target for tourist development, luring foreign and Chinese visitors to view China's colorful minority nationalities in one of the country's few tropical areas. Although not entirely successful, this tourist business has produced numerous hotels, restaurants, and fly-by-night tour guides in Jinghong. As the capital of Xishuangbanna, Jinghong is a frontier town, complete with prostitution, gambling, and growing use of drugs such as heroin and amphetamines.

FIG. 3. A Mengsong hamlet

Unsurprisingly, there is an increasing incidence of HIV/AIDS in Jinghong and surrounding villages, one of the high costs of "modernity," especially in a border town close to Burma, the source of many drugs.

In Xianfeng hamlet in Mengsong, 1,000 meters above Jinghong on the ridge separating China and Burma (see fig. 3), villagers are aware of changes in Jinghong and the threat of AIDS. Problems of drugs and gambling seem distant from their daily concerns, however, as they struggle to increase their incomes, produce grain and vegetables, and send their own children to school. People on the ridge still live within the forest, an entity that both enfolds Akha ancestors and represents a site of contention with state landscape visions. The forest, as well as 250 years of Akha history embedded in the landscape, keep many villagers in the mountains and right on the border.

In neighboring parts of Burma, a complicated civil war has been going on for half a century. When Burma gained independence from Britain in 1948, the new government in Rangoon wanted to take control of the Shan States, tiny Shan (Tai) principalities with an array of upland and lowland ethnic groups similar to those in nearby China and Thailand.[4] In the 1950s, several of these ethnic peoples organized armed political movements to fend off inclusion in Burma. To add to the complexity, some of these so-called rebel armies, together with Nationalist troops escaping from China, were supported by Taiwan and Thailand, while others, including the Communist Party of Burma, were funded by China. In a mini–Cold War arena, these rebel armies sometimes fought against each other as well as against the Burmese army. In this highly contested and violent milieu, in which all parties sold opium to fund their efforts, so-called drug lords introduced large-scale collection of opium, and later heroin and amphetamines, to sell to the international drug cartel. Often caught in the middle of battles, or forced to be unpaid porters for the Burmese army, upland farmers began to flee in large numbers over the border into Thailand. Those who stayed behind use shifting cultivation to produce opium and grain in what are still reputed to be vast stretches of primary forest.

On the Thailand side, Chiang Rai Province, another former Tai principality, is experiencing economic development through tourism and a dynamic real-estate market, a market somewhat variable and muted since the economic crisis beginning in 1997. For Thais, the good life is urban, or urbanlike, and part of the urban experience is to retreat occasionally to resorts in the mountains amid nature tamed into golf courses. Overseas tourists come to see the town of Chiang Rai, to tour colorful hill tribe villages, and until recently, to smoke a little opium. Chiang Rai and the far north have a reputation as being slightly dangerous and wonderfully exotic, qualities attractive to urban foreigners.

Much of Chiang Rai Province was forested until fairly recently, when a combination of government-approved logging operations, lowland Thais moving into the hills, and a sudden influx of people fleeing the violence in Burma rapidly took a toll on the forests. In the 1980s, there were a cluster of major international highland development projects across northern Thailand to end opium cultivation and substitute other cash crops, such as cabbages. A general outcome of the projects was agricultural intensification on much-reduced areas of land. More recently, the Royal Forestry Department has been reclaiming both forests and shifting-cultivation lands. In the late 1990s, Akha villages at all elevations were losing their land, whether to state reforestation efforts and protected areas or to enterprises such as golf courses and resorts. The loss of land, together with sedentarized production of cash crops, has nearly eliminated Akha flexible land uses.

In Akha villages across the north, people sense uneasily that government efforts are pushing them out of the hills to work in towns, where with a hill-tribe ID card they cannot own a house or work at any but low-end jobs.[5] There are no Akha in Thailand's government offices, schools, or large businesses. For Akha in towns, two avenues beckon with a promise of wealth: prostitution and the drug trade. Through either route, many Akha and other highland people wind up HIV positive. Although statistics vary widely, the incidence of HIV/AIDS among hill-tribe populations in the north is staggering.[6]

is this still true?

In Akhapu (see fig. 4), drug use is limited and cases of AIDS have been few. For this reason, the devastating effects of AIDS are not included in this analysis. To understand the context of this hamlet, however, it is important to realize the implications of the limited prospects for Akha in towns, as well as the increasing poverty and insecurity for many Akha in the hills. Most Akha in Akhapu are anchored in the hills by the remaining forest, the tea planted within it, and connections across the border.

protected by royal project?

and coffee?

Both Xianfeng and Akhapu are at high elevations, with a longer history of residence than other Akha hamlets in their respective states. For each hamlet, its location right on the border makes it a site of heightened state concern, as well as a place with easy access to people and goods in Burma. In comparison with other Akha hamlets, both Xianfeng and Akhapu benefit from their altitude, border location, length of residence, and particular social history. They are also among the few hamlets with sizeable remaining forests.

Among the various mountain peoples who practice shifting cultivation, I chose Akha because of their dispersal across this mountainous region and the disparity between their reputations in China and Thailand. In China, state administrators think Akha (Hani[7]) are good managers of the environment. Local officials in Xishuangbanna rate Akha as the "most developed" among the hill groups. In Thailand, by contrast, state officials consider Akha to be forest destroyers. When officials rank highland peoples, Akha are always at the bottom, those with the most entrenched "backwardness," the opposite of "developed." How did these different narratives come about, and what relation do they bear to Akha livelihoods and land uses? Are Akha management practices, especially of forests, significantly different in these two places? Or do state officials read in the landscape what they expect to see based on strong preconceptions about what Akha and forests are in relation to state plans? Or are these two possibilities somehow combined? Additionally, what role does their border location play in Akha reputations and forest practices?

weird rating system... ranking ethnic minorities?

Akha are variously thought to have originated in northern Yunnan or in

FIG. 4. Akhapu hamlet

Tibet (Alting von Geusau 1983; Bernatzik 1970:33; Sturgeon 1996 field notes).[8] In either case, these are now parts of China. Akha speak a Tibeto-Burman language related to Lahu and Yi (Matisoff 1983), other mountain peoples in this same region. Chinese documents from the twelfth century refer to Woni (Hani) (Armijo-Hussein 1996), although Akha genealogies suggest that they have lived in what is now China for at least two millennia. In recent centuries, some Akha have migrated south into Laos and Burma, and some farther into what are now Thailand and northern Vietnam. From the Thai point of view, Akha are newcomers and indeed intruders in the realm of northern Thailand. Akha are now spread across mountainous mainland Southeast Asia, including the part of China (Xishuangbanna) historically most closely related to other Southeast Asian kingdoms. While I make no claim that Akha in China are "the same" as Akha in Thailand, these peoples are historically related and share genealogies reaching back fifty-five to sixty-five generations to the first Akha.[9] In my two research sites, Akha live in similar evergreen oak forests, and until the early 1950s, land uses in both locations were almost identical. These similarities from the time before major state making took hold made possible a comparative study of Akha access to resources and land use as they and their forests became enclosed within China and Thailand. The similarities also allowed an exploration of the workings of border landscapes, as Akha, in various and sometimes contested ways, engaged with an array of new policies and markets in modernizing states, as well as with the violent and at times lucrative world of Burma.

While doing this study, I tacked back and forth between China and Thailand several times to trace the comparison. Each time I arrived in either hamlet, the experience was dizzying. In the two hamlets, Akha spoke a common dialect of Akha, recited almost identical genealogies, managed forests with many overlapping species, and lived along the Burma border—these peoples and their environments were clearly related. But the worlds they inhabited were dramatically different. I attempt here to capture both the remarkable similarities, and also the vast differences, in the constitution of these two worlds in terms of access to resources and land use among Akha in China and Thailand. I also explore how the manipulation of complex, flexible landscapes, enhanced by border dynamics, strengthened Akha hands in managing their environs. This book is situated on the boundary joining these two processes: the intensification of rule of two modernizing states and Akha land-use practices along the border.

Before I had ever imagined doing this research, I worked for seven years as a program officer in natural resource management programs related to Asia. From activities that I oversaw in China and Thailand, I knew that there were numerous upland ethnic minority peoples who spanned the mountains linking southwestern China, Burma, Thailand, Laos, and Vietnam. My strong interest in upland peoples and mountainous border realms had been sparked earlier during a five-year stretch living in Nepal. The desire for a better conceptual understanding of property rights in natural resources and upland livelihoods propelled me back to school in 1993, where I embarked on doctoral study at the Yale School of Forestry and Environmental Studies. An earlier master's degree in Chinese Studies, plus many extended visits to China, had fostered my fluency in Mandarin Chinese. By the time I arrived in Xianfeng and Akhapu,[10] I was a middle-aged Caucasian woman with years of experience in Asia, able for the first time to do extended research in mountain villages.

I studied Akha language during my village stays, but worked with an interpreter fluent in both Chinese and Akha in doing interviews in both Xianfeng and Akhapu. In China, this was an Akha master's student at the Kunming Institute of Botany. In Thailand, my interpreter, who spoke excellent Akha, was an ethnic Chinese from the Chinese village adjacent to Akhapu. To my surprise, I found myself doing research in both sites in Chinese, one of the *lingua francas* in this frontier region of China, Burma, and Thailand.

The terms for administrative units in both research sites deserve a bit of clarification. In China, Xianfeng is one of eleven hamlets in the administrative village of Mengsong. Since "administrative village" is cumbersome, I sometimes refer to "Mengsong village." In Thailand, the units are not as clear-cut. "Akhapu" is the name for both the three-hamlet settlement as well as for the research hamlet. To avoid confusion, "Akhapu settlement" means the three-hamlet unit and "Akhapu" means the research hamlet. There are other potentially confusing names in Thailand as well. The town of Chiang Rai is located in Chiang Rai Province, and the city of Chiang Mai is located in Chiang Mai Province. For clarity, references to "Chiang Rai" and "Chiang Mai" mean the cities. References to the provinces specify "Chiang Rai Province" and "Chiang Mai Province."

To begin the research, first in Xianfeng, then in Akhapu, I gathered detailed information on hamlet and land-use history through semistructured interviews with older villagers, male and female. In both hamlets, this history reached back to a time before China or Thailand was a major presence in their lives. To get diverse perspectives and bring narratives up to the present, these interviews were repeated with middle-aged and younger men and women. The second stage of interviewing, again carried out in both villages, focused on moments of change in land use and corresponding access rights, supplemented with timelines and group mapping exercises for land use at specified times. I also worked alongside farmers in fields and forests and questioned them about present and past uses in these sites.

I was able to make limited trips across the border into Burma, at least from the China side. The administrative village head and the Xianfeng hamlet head each separately accompanied me to nearby villages in Burma. From Akhapu in Thailand, it was not safe to cross the border because the Wa and Shan armies were active on the other side. Most information about relations with Burma came from interviews, either with residents of Xianfeng or Akhapu, or with Akha visiting from Burma.

In both China and Thailand, I supplemented extended hamlet stays with visits to officials and researchers at different administrative levels. In China, this included interviews at township, county, prefecture, province, and national levels to gain the perspectives of government administrators, researchers, and university faculty. In Thailand, this comprised interviews at the subdistrict, provincial, regional, and national levels with government personnel, nongovernmental-organization (NGO) workers, private and state researchers, and university faculty to get diverse points of view about forests, land management, and ethnic minority peoples.

Traveling from Xianfeng to Akhapu entailed a four-hour bus ride to Jinghong, a flight to Kunming, a flight to Chiang Mai, and a five- to six-hour jeep ride up to Akhapu. Traveling in the opposite direction meant, of course, reversing this procedure. I made these journeys at least six times. Through scores of interviews in China and Thailand, and a few in Burma, I traced processes related to resource access, land use, and border livelihoods in Xianfeng and Akhapu. Altogether, my field research lasted twenty months.

In the spring of 1997, just before concluding research, I conducted a social survey on landholding and incomes. By then I had a good understanding of the complicated dynamics surrounding changes in land use and resource access in the two villages. I also carried out forest measurements on the various kinds of wooded sites, including regenerating swiddens, managed by Akha in each village. Maps of the two locales summarize my overall findings. The first (fig. 5) is a schematic map of land use in the early 1950s, when land uses were almost identical in the two hamlets. The subsequent maps (figs. 6 and 7) are schematic depictions of Xianfeng and Akhapu as of 1997.

In the early 1950s, when land management was similar enough that the hamlets can be described together (see fig. 5), Akha farmers kept an area of forest around the village large enough that it took about an hour to walk from their houses out to their shifting-cultivation fields. They also kept an area of protected forest right around the village, as well as a cemetery forest and a watershed protection forest where cutting anything was prohibited. Along a river, farmers opened areas for shifting cultivation. Households could open swiddens (shifting-cultivation fields) wherever they wanted, making them large enough to meet household needs for grain. When that field regenerated to forest in thirteen to fifteen years, any household could open that field the next time. In other words, in terms of resource access, Akha villagers had rather set, enduring rules for areas of forest, and flexible rules for areas of shifting cultivation.

The next schematic map shows land use in Xianfeng in China in 1997 (see fig. 6). The area of forest surrounding the village is still in place, now

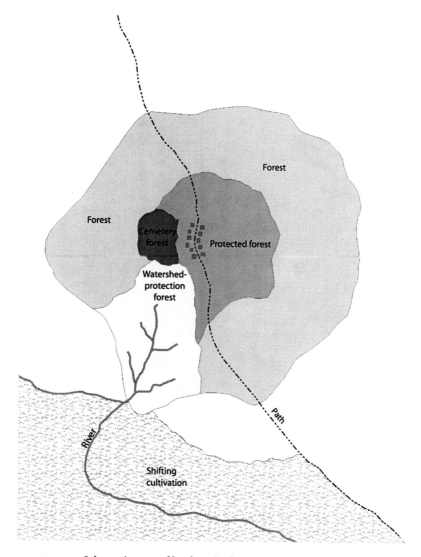

FIG. 5. Schematic map of land use in the 1950s, Xianfeng and Akhapu

divided into sites designated as collective forest and household fuel-wood forest. The protected forest around the village, the cemetery forest, and the watershed protection forest are still there. Along the river, much of the shifting-cultivation land has been terraced for wet rice. Upper-elevation shifting-cultivation fields have been turned into pastures. A new area for

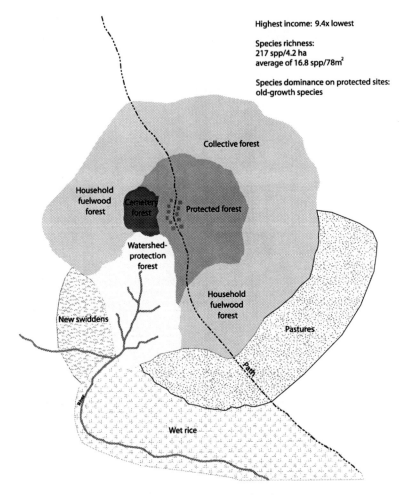

FIG. 6. Schematic map of Xianfeng in 1997

swiddens has been opened. The point to notice in this map is how similar land uses and the sites designated for them are to the map from the 1950s. Areas for forests and the production of grain are still the same.

The data to the right of the maps are condensed versions of the most important outcomes as of 1997.[11] In Xianfeng the household with the highest income earned almost ten times more than the poorest household. Disparities in income were noticeable but not pronounced. In general, household incomes were gradually rising. No one was really rich, but no one was desperately poor, either. Landholding in Xianfeng was relatively equitable. On wooded sites, the species richness overall was 217 different species per 4.2 hectares of sampled plots, with an average of 16.8 species for 78 square meters of sampled area. Considerable species richness, or biodiversity, together with the presence of numerous old-growth species in protected forests, shows that some of the forests were of notable age and diversity, indicators of forests in reasonably good condition for an area of shifting cultivation.[12]

The next schematic map shows land use in Akhapu in Thailand in 1997 (see fig. 7). The area of forest around the village has been planted in tea, displacing the primary forest. There is still a cemetery forest and a watershed protection forest designated by Akha, but there is an additional watershed protection forest in a new site chosen by the Royal Forestry Department (RFD). As in China, there are now wet-rice terraces along the river. On either side of the river, what used to be shifting-cultivation lands have been taken over by the RFD for reforestation. The point to notice here is how much this map differs from the map from the early 1950s. The primary forest around the village is being replaced by tea, while a new forest, claimed by the RFD, has been planted in the old shifting-cultivation fields. In other words, the location and owner of the forest has changed completely. Akha are losing their forest to tea, and the new forest belongs to the forestry department. Farmers have also lost their shifting-cultivation lands.

In Akhapu, the highest-earning household earned nine hundred times more than the poorest household, showing extreme economic stratification in the village. A handful of people were really wealthy, while those on the bottom were falling through the cracks. Wealthier villagers owned the wet-rice fields, while poorer villagers (the majority) had recently lost their shifting-cultivation fields to the RFD. As for forests, the species richness was 87 species for the 9.4 hectares of sampled plots, with an average of 7.4 species on the 78 square meters of sampled area. Species richness was considerably less than in China (87 as compared to 217 species). The relative lack of species diversity, together with the presence of many more pioneer species on protected sites, indicated that forests in Thailand were frequently cut and sometimes burned, and not in very good condition.[13]

Xianfeng and Akhapu had almost identical land uses in the early 1950s. At that point large areas of primary forest surrounded both hamlets, with extensive swiddens beyond the forest. By 1997 in Xianfeng, the forest around the hamlet had been divided into collective and household forests. Additionally, there were now large areas for wet rice and pastures. Overall, though, the land area for Xianfeng was much the same as in the 1950s, and sites for

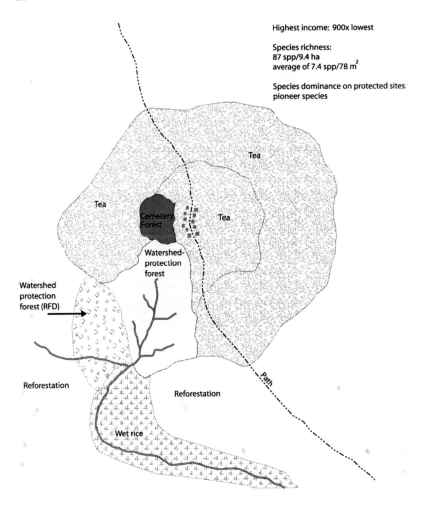

Highest income: 900x lowest

Species richness:
87 spp/9.4 ha
average of 7.4 spp/78 m^2

Species dominance on protected sites:
pioneer species

Tea

Tea

Cemetery
Forest

Tea

Watershed-
protection
forest

Watershed
protection
forest (RFD)

Reforestation

Reforestation

Wet rice

Path

FIG. 7. Schematic map of Akhapu in 1997

forest and grain production were still the same. In contrast, by 1997 in Akhapu, farmers were losing their primary forest to tea production. Their shifting-cultivation fields were gone, replaced by new forests for the RFD. The land available to farmers had shrunk dramatically, especially considering that wet-rice fields belonged to the wealthy few. There were large disparities in household landholding as well as income.

How did these divergent outcomes come about when land uses in the 1950s were very similar? Through what processes had Akha in China continued to manage forests with considerable biodiversity, including old-growth forests, while Akha in Thailand used forests with declining biodiversity and many pioneer species? Beyond what is visible on the maps, how did Akha become peripheral peoples in such different guises in these two places? How did state policies for ethnic minorities, forests, and land use reshape Akha land uses? In each case, how did the proximity of the violent, drug-producing Shan State of Burma play into local power relations, access to resources, and flexible landscapes? And finally, how did Akha practices of plastic landscapes mediate their political relations at various scales, including across the border? Examining border landscapes for Akha in China and Thailand addresses all of these questions.

THE PRODUCTION
OF BORDER LANDSCAPES

One morning in Mengsong I found Akheu, the administrative village head, nailing a leopard skin to the doorframe of his house to dry. Akheu was smiling to himself as he worked, clearly pleased with this leopard skin. I admired the skin and asked how he got it. He had shot the leopard in Burma in a wooded site some ten kilometers south of Mengsong. As he explained, many Akha men from Mengsong hunted in Burma, since the Chinese government prohibited shooting certain wildlife, including leopards, within its borders. The solution was to hunt in Burma, where state agents imposed no such restrictions.

For Akheu, the hunting landscape extended into Burma for quite a distance. Akheu could cross the border by the road or numerous footpaths, thus extending the scope of his hunt well beyond the domain of Mengsong. He could also escape from the Chinese regulations, which he, as a state agent, enforced in Mengsong. In his hunting, Akheu transgressed the usual meanings of border and landscape, moving beyond not only Mengsong "property," but outside his home nation-state as well. Akheu was familiar with the nearby terrain in Burma, as well as with family and friends there with whom he could share a meal. His hunting routinely crossed the border and back again, producing a landscape that was in China and not in China, procuring game that was illegal in one place and not in the other, allowing him to navigate between the realms of China and Burma in ways that played out to his advantage. He could also share wild game with township administrators, nurturing his good offices with them. This is an instance of producing a border landscape through livelihoods that combine border-as-margin and border-as-line between nation-states.

THREE RELATED PROCESSES COMBINE TO PRODUCE BORDER LANDSCAPES: the production of marginal peoples and landscapes; the production of borders; and the encounter between state and Akha landscape visions under different state regimes. Resource access and control are entwined in all three processes.

The production of marginal peoples and landscapes on the margins of China and Thailand and along their borders with Burma has occurred primarily at a national scale, with long historical roots. State definitions of peoples and forests have been of overriding importance in determining current outcomes for both.

The production of borders in this mountainous, frontier region has been constituted in both premodern and modern contexts through the accumulation and distribution of resources. Border chiefs today continue to mediate the border through the control of resource access. Borders are sites of negotiation between local border chiefs and state agents, with the state implicated in the production of both predatory border chiefs and their border-mediating role. *are most?*

The third process in forming these border landscapes has been the encounter between state and Akha landscape visions under two very different state regimes. A combined spatial and temporal knowledge, "landscape plasticity," gives Akha a certain resilience in negotiating with state agents and extending land uses across the border. State policies in China and Thailand have sought to reduce the scope for Akha practice of landscape plasticity, but through different processes and with different outcomes. Flexible, plastic landscapes are sites of agency, negotiation, and conflict, as farmers maneuver between border-as-margin and border-as-connecting-line in engaging with the state.

These border landscapes, then, have been constituted through state definitions of upland peoples and forests, the negotiation of borders through resource access and control, and encounters between Akha and state landscape visions. Practices of resource access and control are threaded through all three processes forming border landscapes. In fact, a focus on resource access reveals that small border chiefs, having accumulated clout through cross-border maneuvering, maintain resource control by introducing the clarified, simplified landscapes promoted by the state. Border landscapes may be understood as sites of accumulating influence and riches for village heads and local elites, and as sites of increasing marginalization for local farmers. *is state sponsored model of land beneficial for heirarchies?*

These processes—the production of marginal peoples and landscapes, the production of borders, and the encounter between state and local landscape visions—played out very differently in China and Thailand. The conceptual underpinnings of these three related processes, and the resource access that knits them together, are explored below.

THE PRODUCTION OF MARGINAL PEOPLES
AND LANDSCAPES: RESOURCE ACCESS ON THE PERIPHERY

In both China and Thailand, Akha are peripheral in several senses. They live on the geographic edges of both nation-states. They are regarded as socially different from mainstream peoples, whether those are Han or Thai, and "backward" in either case. Their location in upland areas is marginal to the lowlands, where majority peoples live. And their land use, shifting cultivation, is considered in both places as different from and inferior to lowland agriculture. Akha in each country have also become located on political-economic peripheries, but in ways that have spun out differently in each case. How do certain peoples become peripheral or marginal? In relation to modernity, how do some people become backward? The answers lie largely in how various peoples were incorporated into modern nation-states, through processes that have been simultaneously cultural and political.

In much of Asia, the imposition of citizenship in the twentieth century entailed identifying and categorizing peoples inhabiting national territory. Although citizenship created an "imagined political community" of people who came to see themselves as having a "deep, horizontal comradeship" (Anderson 1991:6, 7), the classification of people into "races" or "ethnic groups" undercut the presumed equality of citizenship. These practices were modeled on European racial classifications based on biological, linguistic, or cultural differences (Keyes 2002). Unlike Asian typologies in the past, these purported to be based on "scientific" criteria (1164). In effect, such state classifications were a technology of power (Keyes 1994) that enclosed peoples into a new nation in marginalized and disempowered positions. These classifications, while seeming to be bureaucratic, neutral procedures, were "exercises in social engineering which [were] often deliberate and always innovative" (Hobsbawm 1983:13). Ethnic groups discovered through scientific criteria were in effect invented traditions that gained their power by seeming primordial. Named and evaluated ethnic groups seemed natural, as if they had always been there.

In some cases the categorization was done by colonizing states, but in forms that persisted into independence, such as the division of peoples into castes and scheduled tribes in India (Guha 1999). In precolonial India there had been named occupational groups, and members could sometimes

[margin handwritten notes:]
Nation as socially constructed, imagined community. -democ. & dictatorship list -Film hist 111

Myanmar's official list of ethnic groups is very confusing

Fluid ethnicity

change their occupation or residence and make claims to higher status. The British-allocated caste system hardened the boundaries between castes and relegated some peoples to "primitive" status based on their "isolation" since time immemorial. Sumit Guha demonstrates that one group named "primitive isolates" had earlier been upland militants who inspired considerable fear in the lowland farmers paying them tribute (Guha 1999:83–105, 130–145). The Dutch in Java in the early twentieth century identified difference among peoples as "cultural divergence" (Kahn 1999:79), a mechanism that continued after Indonesian independence. The idiom of cultural divergence erased the power differentials between centers and emerging peripheries. It also obscured the processes through which social differences were being created by colonial and regional political economies. Whether done by colonial or modern states, the new categorizations imposed "ethno-racial hierarchies" (Anderson 1991:169) that slotted some people into the nation as "mainstream" and others as "minorities" in varying degrees of inferiority. Certain peoples became marginal within the nation in part because they were defined as such during classificatory moments.

In both China and Thailand, an evolutionary model of human society influenced how policy makers and urban elites conceived of upland peoples. Lewis Henry Morgan, an American anthropologist, propounded the theory that human society developed from savagery, to barbarism, to civilization (Morgan 1964 [1878]). The socialist regime in China fully adopted the evolutionary view, with direct lineage from Morgan to Engels to Stalin to Mao (Gladney 1991:72). In the modes of production theory, which Mao Zedong adopted from the Soviet Union, societies were thought to evolve from primitive to slave, feudal, capitalist, and socialist modes of production. In China, Akha (as Hani) were rated at a primitive mode of production, meaning that at the point of entering China as citizens, they were seriously "behind" and backward in their social development. This rating was derived from their property system, which Communist cadres saw as communal, and their land use, shifting cultivation. Especially for hill peoples, such as Akha, their state-allocated identities have also been constructed in relation to their forested upland location and their land use, which often includes shifting cultivation. In evolutionary models, shifting cultivation was imagined to evolve naturally over time into settled "intensive" agriculture. From the 1950s to the late 1970s, Chinese state planners were not concerned about protecting forests, which they saw as resources to either exploit or move out of the way for agriculture. They regarded shifting cultivation as a form of agriculture, but a backward and unproductive way to

LAND AS FREE GIFT OF NATURE

↓

"civilization" in western minds linked to property

produce grain. The state project, dominated by Han, was then to "help" Akha farmers learn to be productive and advance into socialist modernity.

In Thailand, the adoption of an evolutionary model was more diffuse, arriving with Thai scholars who had studied in Europe and the United States, as well as with Western development project staff beginning in the 1960s. As early as the 1940s, staff from the Food and Agriculture Organization of the United Nations (FAO) convinced Thai foresters that shifting cultivation was damaging to the environment (FAO 1948). Influential Western scholars in the 1960s and 1970s doubted if Akha had a property regime and judged Akha land use to be destructive to soils and forests (Kunstadter et al. 1978:201–202). In the 1970s, Akha backwardness was equated with being threats to the forest. In contrast to China, the meaning of forests in Thailand at that time was as state capital assets to be exploited to fund industrialization. Since Akha land use was perceived to damage the nation's wealth and threaten its development, they and other "hill tribes" were defined in relation to Thai society as "not Thai" and not citizens. The state project was therefore to protect state assets, the forests, by keeping hill tribes out of them.

China and Thailand have recently experienced dramatic economic transformations and rapid incorporation into global economies. In contrast to these dynamic changes, largely experienced by urban populations, central state planners have tended to see peoples such as Akha as even more backward than before. Newly industrializing state regimes in Asia have responded to the exigencies of late capitalism by instituting graduated sovereignty (Ong 1999). Some kinds of citizens have become transnational employees of global enterprises, while others have turned into low-wage workers, illegal immigrant laborers, and what Aihwa Ong refers to as the "aboriginal periphery." Different kinds of citizens become located in "zones that are . . . subjected to different kinds of surveillance and in practice enjoy different sets of civil, political, and economic rights" (Ong 1999:216). Her category of "aboriginal periphery" is where Akha are located, a zone subject to frequent redefinition depending on what development means. Although the Chinese regime is quite different from the Thai one, the zone of sovereignty for Akha in either case is geared for peripheral, marginal, and backward peoples. In China the zone of aboriginal periphery is for upland minority nationalities whom the Han can modernize, whereas in Thailand the zone is for hill tribes who do not qualify to be Thai. Although there are important differences in these state-given Akha identities, the zone in each case is clearly marginal and distant from urban entrepreneurs.

In sum, state representations of peoples, upland land uses, and forests

have been fundamental in determining modes of citizenship, official property rights in rural resources, and the degree of maneuvering room available for local people's customary land uses. Chapter 2 traces the contours
of this process in China and Thailand through the longer-term history of
peripheral peoples and spaces and through the twentieth century development of policies for citizenship and ethnic minorities, property rights in
land and forests, and state claims on rural resources.

THE PRODUCTION OF BORDERS: SITES
FOR THE ACCUMULATION AND DISTRIBUTION OF RESOURCES

The two Akha hamlets are located right next to the Burma border. In each
state, the border could be considered as both the end of the state's margin
and as a line to step across. But what difference does the border make, in
either sense, for access to resources and the production of border landscapes? Answers to these questions depend on how we conceive of national
borders and on what practices produce and maintain them.

Richard Muir, a contemporary geographer, gives a technical definition
of a border: "Located at the interfaces between adjacent state territories, international boundaries have a special significance in determining the limits of
sovereign authority and defining the spatial form of the contained political regions. . . . Boundaries have been loosely described as being linear; in
fact they occur where the vertical interfaces between state sovereignties inter-
sect the surface of the earth" (Muir, *Modern political geography* [London:
Macmillan, 1975], 119, cited in Thongchai 1994:74).

In a similar definition, boundaries of modern states are "the point at
which a state's territorial competence finds its ultimate expression" (Sahlins
1989:2). In these rather static formulations, boundaries define the limits of
state territory and sovereignty, as if these projects had already been completed. These definitions emphasize the vantage point of centers, where border areas are imagined as margins of the nation-state rather than as sites of
cross-border relations.

Recent studies of borders emphasize the need to look from the border
vantage point, discovering how states bring border peoples and territories
under central control. M. Baud and W. van Schendel feature borders
between nation-states as political constructs, "imagined projections of territorial power" (1997:211). They conceive of borders as state creations that
are separate from local life, artifacts that border people might "challenge,"
"take advantage of," or subvert (211, 212). From their perspective, the state

tries to eliminate cross-border networks established by local elites, since these networks give elites "leverage with regard to the state" (226). In a related way, Hastings Donnan and Thomas Wilson conceptualize boundaries as "the expression of the spatial limits of state power, the manifestations of polit- ical control" (1999:46). At the same time, however, they see borders as socially constructed sites of power, an "interface . . . between two systems of activ- ity, of organization, or of meaning . . . liable to be characterized by ambi- guity and danger" (22). People who live in borderlands, as a result of their location at the intersection of multiple systems, "draw strategically on mul- tiple repertoires of identity" (39). While differently argued, these recent stud- ies present borders as process and sites of negotiation. They take into account social relations across the border, but expect that the state would seek to curtail or control cross-border relations.

high self-monitors?

Regarding upland peoples and borders in Southeast Asia, John McKinnon and Jean Michaud maintain that the state has ushered "isolated highland societies into the World System," and that ethnic minority societies are dis- tant "from the seat of power" (2000:5, 8). They conceptualize border regions as margins of the nation-state. Analyzing the border between Thailand and Laos, Andrew Walker critiques the center-periphery approach. He advocates analyzing "the active involvement of local communities in creating and main- taining trans-border connections," noting that "state regulatory practices are intertwined with those of local communities" (1999:13, 17). Walker depicts "nodes" of power where border transactions occur, sites of local agency in "benign" interactions with states and markets. He emphasizes border in the sense of cross-border relations in which local people can benefit. His analy- sis underplays the importance of border as national margin.

Understanding the extent to which these border conceptions help explain dynamics along the Burma border requires a brief sketch of borders and boundaries in premodern Southeast Asia. During the era of Southeast Asian kingdoms, lords in small principalities between kingdoms maintained their relative autonomy by both accommodating and fending off the interests of major kings (Thongchai 1994:84–88). To do this, small princes accumulated resources and controlled their distribution. They extracted products from people under their rule, as well as corvée labor. They sent tribute to over- lords, whether voluntarily or under duress, both to ensure protection from mightier kingdoms and also to prevent takeover. Small princes often main- tained ritual and kin links in multiple directions, sending tributes of alle- giance to various larger and smaller entities (Steinberg 1987; Tambiah 1976; Thongchai 1994; Wyatt 1984). Political relations were enacted through the collection and distribution of resources, and networks of patronage and alliance constituted the border regions between larger kingdoms and empires. In other words, these borders were created and maintained through the collection and distribution of resources.

In relation to borders with Burma, E. R. Leach argued that Burma itself was a frontier between China and India, meaning a border region with people of multiple ethnicities. Burma was distinct from European notions of a nation comprised of people with a common culture and language (Leach 1960:49). Leach (1954) described political systems in highland Burma involving complicated patronage relations between lowland and upland peoples of differing ethnicity. These political systems, known elsewhere as principalities (cf. Hill 1998; Thongchai 1994), were separated from one another and larger states not by boundaries but by "zones of mutual interest" (Leach 1960:50). Critiquing Leach, Gehan Wijeyewardene (1992) claimed that by 1960, when Leach's article on borders was published, Burma had delineated clear national boundaries and some of the ethnic groups mentioned by Leach had defined themselves as political units in opposition to Burma. Indeed, in the frontier region that extended into adjacent parts of China and Thailand, policy makers had been working to extend control over people and resources in ways leading toward territorial sovereignty. In part, their efforts were intended to protect the homeland from the political violence and drug trade in the neighboring Shan State of Burma.

The state policies in question delineated borders and defined peoples (citizens and ethnic minorities) and property rights in rural resources. An unexpected spin-off from state building in the border areas of Thailand, China, and Burma has been the production of small polities much like the premodern principalities referred to by Leach. Small political entities based on patronage have been revised in diverse ways to suit the emerging needs of their rulers. In Burma these entities included Chinese Nationalist forces, ethnic rebel armies, and drug-lord realms. In the late twentieth century, these borders continued to be sites of negotiation with a degree of autonomy. China and Thailand faced an array of political, economic, and ideological adversaries across the border in Burma. Agents of the Chinese and Thai states sought to keep out these enemies, get information about them, and sometimes to form covert alliances with them. The ambiguity or conflict among these desires recreated the need for border-mediating figures.

Among these figures have been Akha village heads who claimed loyalty to the state, but meanwhile, through connections (and loyalties) across the border, provided useful information and at times illicit goods from the other side. With their role enhanced by state approval, Akha village heads as small border chiefs have reworked patronage practices, serving larger state interests while controlling local resource access. By maneuvering among multiple affiliations in more than one state, border chiefs have in fact constituted the border, much as princes did in the past. Territorial sovereignty, local resource control, and the meaning of "citizen" and "ethnic minority" have all been mediated by these border chiefs as patrons and negotiators, and borders are sites of ambiguity, negotiation, transgression, and the concentration of power.

State agents and Akha village heads are linked together in a complicated dance to both protect the border and to enable transgressions across it. This perspective rejects a characterization of borderlands as "distant from power," as portrayed by McKinnon and Michaud, although it accepts the view from the periphery advocated by both Baud and van Schendel and Donnan and Wilson. Unlike all of these authors' assessments, in the cases portrayed here the state is not entirely separate from border chiefs, nor would state agents seek to eliminate networks cultivated by Akha village heads. Like in Walker's view, state agents and village heads are involved in border regulation. But in contrast to Walker, the picture here is of predatory border chiefs, whose growing control of local resource access is not "benign." A focus on resource access allows a conception of border practices different from what these scholars describe. Borders are nodes for the collection and distribution of resources, and the role of small border chiefs is implicated in and even produced by state making. Border practices are intimately entwined with the control of resource access. Chapter 3 explores how borders have been produced, historically and currently, in the Akha hamlets of Xianfeng and Akhapu.

STATE AND AKHA LANDSCAPE VISIONS:
PRODUCTIVITY AND RULE VERSUS PLASTICITY

As James Scott argues, modernizing states have imposed a "legible property system" of freehold tenure that produced legible landscapes, those that state agents could "read" and tax appropriately (1998:33ff.). He contrasts this with customary tenure arrangements that are "illegible" to state agents but readable by local inhabitants. Tania Li questions Scott's notion of legibility, especially its assumption that the state and local people are separate and that local people resist, reject, or flee from state control and extractions (Li 2001:43–44). Li points to upland people who desire the security and market goods that connection with a state can bring. In conformance with Li's assertion, Akha in China and Thailand welcome property rights and recognition from the state. But they have a complicated relationship with landscape legibility, sometimes seeking and sometimes evading it, in dramas that have generally played out among Akha rather than directly between Akha and state agents. Legible landscapes in Scott's sense, though, inform the language and goals of state administrators. In fact, state goals of legible landscapes are reinforced by understandings from international development projects, which promote clear and secure tenure as fundamental to economic development (see, for example, Feder and Feeny 1991; Meinzen-Dick et al. 1997; World Bank 2001:35–37). State administrators promote clearly demarcated landscapes under coded and quantifiable uses, whether the reality on the ground reflects that desire or not. Indeed, state agents use the call for clear, simplified land uses whenever they chastise Akha for messy landscapes and backward practices. The discourse of legibility is founded on landscapes of productivity and rule.

Roderick Neumann focuses on the visible aspects of landscape in describing what he calls "landscapes of production" (1998:19). In Neumann's formulation, landscapes of production are where people labor, in contrast to landscapes of consumption, those bounded areas of nature, such as national parks, that middle-class visitors consume and admire. But like landscapes of consumption, landscapes of production, in the view of central and regional state planners, should look a certain way (cf. Neumann 1998:1). In southern China and Thailand, lowland agriculture should look like wet-rice fields, where the property lines and invested labor are both evident and the combination has produced beautiful, manicured paddies as well as abundant grain. This is a civilized landscape, under the management not only of hardworking farmers, but also of a benevolent state regime. For state agents, the visible landscape reflects an advanced culture derived from centuries of knowledge and experience. It is also a visible reflection of state power. Other kinds of rural landscapes would also qualify as manifestations of productivity and rule, but for Xishuangbanna in China and for northern Thailand, the appearance of well-managed wet-rice fields is the paramount example.

In the eyes of modernizing state agents in the 1980s and 1990s, Akha landscapes were the opposite of legible. Property lines were messy or invisible, productivity was deemed to be low, and the influence of state authority seemed to be missing. When faced with similar landscapes, British colonizers in India realized that the imposition of sovereignty entailed "creating more discernable areas of cultivation, wastes, and forests" (Sivaramakrishnan 1999:45). Similar to state projects in China and Thailand, the work of British colonial agents was to clarify and essentialize categories of people and to link them to landscapes (82). From an official point of view in China and Thailand, Akha landscapes were not only messy but out of control. Both people and land uses needed to be clarified and governed. What is recounted here is the negotiated process through which Akha landscapes became "governed" and somewhat legible.

In the twentieth century, clarifying agricultural landscapes and making them productive meant two things: (1) introducing property rights to identify and secure ownership; and (2) making them simpler: "The great advances in agricultural production of the past fifty years have not been achieved by increasing the diversity of crops and farms, but rather by decreasing the diversity" (Padoch 2002:96). Supported by international organizations as well as states, "the road of ever-increasing simplicity has been well documented, tested, and promoted by agronomists, foresters, and the government and private organizations that they serve" (96). For agricultural scientists, diversity of production supports subsistence livelihoods, while specialization in limited crops promotes engagement with a market where farmers enjoy a comparative advantage. Under this scenario, farmers should be moving toward simpler production systems to increase their incomes.

In the face of this persistent advice, however, small holders throughout the world, including shifting cultivators, often manage for diversity. Small holders, including those in upland areas, make best use of limited land areas through diversity and dynamism: "Theirs is a landscape of great diversity. Small farmers often make detailed use of small local variations in soil, microclimate, and water conditions and often produce a great variety of crops" (Brookfield 2001:21).

In an early study of shifting cultivation, Harold Conklin portrayed upland farmers as almost entirely self-sufficient, intercropping forty to fifty different field crops with upland rice as well as managing multiple kinds of tree crops (1957:85). More recent scholarship has focused on how shifting cultivators have adjusted to changes, whether from markets, development projects, forest policies, resettlement schemes, or climatic variations (Padoch 1982; Dove 1999, 1996, 1985; Rambo and Cuc 1995; Peluso 1996). Upland farmers rarely rely solely on shifting cultivation, but instead engage in "composite swiddening," an array of practices that allows farmers to concentrate energy on different parts of the land-use system at different times (Rambo and Cuc 1995). Shifting cultivators select from among a "portfolio" of activities that may include wage labor (Dove 1999:212). Under new policies and growing markets, some farmers have moved out of shifting cultivation to concentrate on managing elaborate fruit gardens in landscapes that continue to be diverse in both access arrangements and production (Peluso 1996). In other words, shifting cultivators respond to and sometimes take advantage of political-economic transformations but in ways that reproduce the diversity of practices and crops. Participation in markets may change the composition of activities but not necessarily simplify landscapes. State administrators are mistaken in thinking these landscapes show no state or market influence. Often, upland farmers have lost land to state forests (Peluso 1996) and cultivate goods to sell (Dove 1999; Peluso 1996). As a result of their complexity, however, from an official perspective these landscapes remain messy, illegible, and distant from landscapes of productivity and rule.

In addition to making constant adjustments, small farmers "plan their activities over a long time horizon, investing in improvements while continuing production" (Brookfield 2001:xiv). The way shifting cultivators adopt new land uses, such as wet rice, reflects long-term plans (Padoch et al. 1998). Farmers can make quick changes for new markets, policies, or infestations of pests, while keeping an eye on the long-range future. Managing for both diversity and dynamism allows them to do both. This managed diversity is a "flexible system, able to make space for new crops, more people, and new demands and to permit survival in climatically exceptional years" (Brookfield 2001:20). This flexibility, in addition to long-range planning, is inherent in landscape plasticity.

While Harold Brookfield portrays the flexibility as "adaptation" to changing biological, social, political, and economic conditions (2001:21), farmers' use of complex landscapes can be seen as more proactive. Akha in China and Thailand have used their detailed knowledge of the spatial landscape and of regeneration patterns to withstand rapacious political regimes, famine, and war. They have equally well used this knowledge to produce new crops and gather nontimber forest products for complex and dynamic markets. Their understanding of plastic landscapes is a tool for responding quickly to favorable possibilities as well as for retrenching in times of dearth. Their flexible land uses, however, are not mere adaptations to outside stimuli, as Brookfield would suggest. Nor are they totally separate from state plans, as Scott would have it. These landscapes are instead sites of negotiation and struggle among Akha as well as between Akha and outsiders over Akha livelihoods and land uses.

Under modernizing states, the imposition of state-allocated property rights and clearer, simpler landscapes clashed with flexible production practices. Landscapes of productivity and rule intersected with landscape plasticity, with protagonists on unequal terms. State agents and Akha villagers, in complicated and conflicting ways, have struggled over state plans to transform the landscape. These processes have played out very differently in China and Thailand. Most importantly, the amount of available negotiating room has differed greatly for Chinese and Thai state agents. In China, state ideology and policies for minority nationalities and forests recognized Akha forest knowledge and allowed them to manage wooded areas. As a result, Akha landscapes in China reflect both state property lines and Akha complexity—a negotiated legibility. In Thailand, state representations of hill tribes, together with state forest claims, left only a "meager space for negotiation" (Pinkaew 2001:3). The resulting landscape, while somewhat more legible to state authorities, also represents considerable coercion in implementing state plans—an enforced legibility. Chapter 4 explores the encounter between state and Akha landscape visions in China and Thailand and the contrasting outcomes for those who practice processual landscapes.

Fishing land was neighbor's but they don't "own" it

PROPERTY RIGHTS IN NATURAL
RESOURCES: THE KEY TO BORDER LANDSCAPES

The complex story of border landscapes is made legible by a focus on resource access, or property rights. In common parlance, property rights are often thought to be those granted and enforced by the state, and "property" is mistakenly thought to be the thing owned. In legal and political thought, property is defined as an enforceable claim "to some use or benefit of something" and "a political relation between persons" (Macpherson 1978:3, 4). A property claim is enforceable because there is an authority, usually the state, to back it. Equally important, a property claim is enforceable because it represents a "moral claim" recognized within a community (11). Property can also be a form of dominion over others: the owner of financial, intellectual, or material resources has control over people who want to share in the benefits from those resources (Cohen 1927:12).

enforceability allows state to be agent in transactions

The complicated nature of property is reflected in the formulations of John Locke and Adam Smith. Locke supposed that "As much Land as a Man Tills, Plants, Improves, and can use the Product of, so much is his *Property*" (1964 [1704], cited in Macpherson 1978:19). He emphasized the moral claims in property, a right to livelihood and to appropriate land through labor. This view of property is important because it is shared (without influence from

rome stay mom's land - Locke - local agreements
Akha land use reflects a threat to the state
Locke's is illegible

Locke) among farmers across Asia (see Peluso 1996:525) and certainly among Akha in China and Thailand. Smith, by contrast, underscored the political underpinnings of any property regime: "Civil government, so far as it is instituted for the security of property, is in reality instituted for the defence of the rich against the poor, or of those who have some property against those who have none at all" (1986 [1776]:297). Smith had in mind a group of herders, among whom the richest devised property rules to protect themselves against all other herders, with rich herders an example of a proto-state, thus explaining how any property system originates. Property rules, in Smith's view, arose from political elites protecting their economic assets. Putting Locke and Smith together, we get property as political relations with moral justifications for livelihoods and the protection of economic assets.

Property theorists refer to *de jure* (legal) and *de facto* (customary) property arrangements. *De jure* property rules are ordinarily those allocated and protected by the state, while *de facto* property arrangements are enforced by customary sanctions. When state agents implement new property regimes in rural areas, they are often unaware of customary property rules, but state-allocated property rights by no means eliminate customary practices. Often, local people rework formal property rights, ignoring or choosing selectively among them, or turning them to their advantage. Differently positioned villagers may adopt varying strategies with respect to new possibilities, sometimes leading to localized conflict. In any case, the likelihood of a transformation in property based solely on state plans is slim: "The embeddedness of land-holding in ecological, social, cultural, and political life means that one tenure regime can seldom be legislated away in favour of another. To try to do this is to add layers of procedures or regulations on to others unlikely to disappear, and to add possibilities of manipulation and confusion between the multiple opportunities, and conflicting constraints, of older and newer land-holding regimes" (Shipton and Goheen 1992:316).

In this book the term "resource access" has a broad meaning that includes formal property allocations, customary practices of access, and local accommodations to—and reworkings of—state-given property rights. Local property relations turn out to be complicated negotiations between state agents and local farmers, as well as among villagers themselves. These negotiations, sometimes heated, are ongoing, as changing conditions revise local social relations and the valuation of resources.

Studies of landholding in Africa have shown that shifts in political, economic, and cultural factors—seen more simply as changes in power, wealth, and meaning—have overlapping effects on property rights (Shipton and Goheen 1992). Other works have also emphasized the importance of meaning to property contestations. "People may invest in meanings as well as in the means of production—struggles over meaning are as much a part of the process of resource allocation as are struggles over surplus or the labour process" (Berry 1988:66). What is contended over or manipulated is not only the ownership or control of productive resources, but also "control over the human imagination" (Peet and Watts 1996:37). In local conflicts, the meaning of resources and their use is linked to understandings of community and custom, and to struggles to define them among contenders with unequal power (Li 1996:509). The contestations are political, as well as cultural and economic. This view is inherent in the combination of Locke and Smith as well. Recent scholarship has pinpointed that the focal point of conflict may be the notions of morality and community at stake in resource claims.

Studies of property regimes or of access to resources are often fraught with struggle. So how are struggles manifested, and equally, how do people ever cooperate? Carol Rose suggests that storytelling is inherent in both processes: "We tell tales to create a community in which cooperation is possible" (1994:27). Rose argues, in fact, that storytelling is fundamental to property, as exemplified by Locke's extended narrative in the *Second Treatise of Government* about a farmer appropriating land, and gradually more farmers appropriating land, and this somehow leading to the formation of government with rules to protect property. As Rose notes, Locke's "story" has no historical basis, yet his ideas have become the basis for Western property conceptions. To confirm Rose's point, there is no historical basis to Adam Smith's story about herders, either. Narratives about property are basic to any state, but also to any organized group that uses natural resources. Within Akha hamlets, there is general agreement about access rules, but divergence in stories about how those rules play out. Each story reveals something about how power is mediated by culture at a particular moment. Akha tell stories about landholding, either in the past or the present, to create a community of cooperation at various scales. Sometimes the stories about current conflicts are passionately recounted, but often to an audience in agreement. As Louise Fortmann notes, "Stories have the power to frame and create understanding; to create and maintain moral communities" (1995:1054). The stories give clues to the symbolic contestations that entrain a wider field of actors, including local villagers, state officials, and traders—agents of political-economic transformations that prompted the tale.

In addition to property as storytelling, something that one might hear, property can also be visible in the landscape: "One can read the messages of successive generations through the way that property looks" (Rose 1994:269). Rose mentions fences and plowed furrows as markers of entitlement. When Akha farmers walk through their landscape, they can read there the history of many generations—successive (and diverse) uses of various plots of land, former trails, previous forests that were cut and then grew again. With an intimate knowledge of the landscape, Akha can see there the past, the present, and possible trajectories into the future. They also tell stories as they walk, tales embedded in particular sites about past violence, privation, or wealth. These are visual cues to local histories, told somewhat differently by each teller.

Although Akha can read their landscapes easily, the same vistas present a conundrum to most outsiders. A visitor sees areas of forest, but also fields colonized by what look like weeds. Farmers cut and burn patches of forest to open fields on slopes that, from a lowland perspective, seem too steep for agriculture. On these fields farmers plant grains, vegetables, fruits, and herbs all together in seemingly haphazard fashion. There are livestock ambling around, but apparently not fenced in or even herded. Referring to landscapes other than Akha, but under similarly complex land uses, even sympathetic researchers have found such visual displays "bewildering" (Brookfield 2001:4), or "visually confusing" and "disorderly" (Padoch 2002: 98, 100). Agricultural extension agents and state foresters, usually less sympathetic, see in these landscapes forest degradation and soil erosion (cf. Forsyth 1995:881). In other words, these are landscapes that need to be clarified and governed, made into landscapes of productivity and rule.

An understanding of the shifting nature of Akha resource access and use contributes to the scholarship on property rights. In most recent studies of resource rights, access claims are highly contested but the resources in question are stable categories (e.g., Peluso 1992; Moore 1993; Li 2001, 1999, 1996). By contrast, Akha resource access and use keep moving around, sliding across delineated plots, state land-use regulations, and even international boundaries. This complex, malleable quality, in fact, constitutes the strength of these upland land-use practices. The very flexibility of Akha land uses, of course, has been what state policies and development projects have set out to sedentarize.

Clear international boundaries have also resulted in attempts to increase state control over Akha and their landscapes. As in K. Sivaramakrishnan's case study (1999), state control over people and resources was unevenly accomplished and variable over time. In the Akha cases, hamlets located on the border generally drew more state attention and investment than those distant from the border. In each case, though, small border chiefs parlayed these investments to their own advantage. The accomplishment of state rule played out in ways that strengthened small border chiefs and further marginalized Akha farmers. Border dynamics mediated through village heads have tended to undercut villagers' access to resources and scope for the practice of flexible landscapes. Additionally, small border chiefs became state representatives in local domains. At key moments, Akha village heads promoted simplified land uses and clearer property rights if these changes increased their authority, introducing landscapes of productivity and rule if this made the village heads more like rulers. These clearer, simpler landscapes have tended to benefit local elites and outside actors, while other local farmers have tended to lose out.

The practice of landscape plasticity, then, is not merely adaptation to changing conditions. It is a knowledge and practice that enabled Akha to live in complex environments, engage in trade, and pay tribute to premodern princes. Modernizing states in both China and Thailand reduced the scope for flexible landscapes, but did so differently. Landscape plasticity allowed Akha farmers to engage both proactively and defensively with a variety of predatory rulers and exploitative economic conditions, as well as to respond productively to new policies, enterprises, and markets. Where state policies and practices enabled landscape plasticity, both Akha and their forests fared well. This was the case in China. Where state policies disabled landscape plasticity, Akha and their forests fared poorly. This was the case in Thailand.

Understanding Akha access to resources and land uses as Akha and their forests became bounded within national territory and state plans requires tracing how the practice of landscape plasticity was reformed and curtailed under national policies, growing economies, and new border practices. State representations of Akha as backward shifting cultivators on the borders of the realm ensured their encapsulation on the aboriginal periphery, on the border-as-margin in both China and Thailand. The border-as-line with social relations across it, meanwhile, opened up cross-border possibilities for Akha village heads as well as local farmers. Akha village heads had more scope for taking advantage of cross-border social relations and border mediation than did ordinary farmers. In the name of protecting the border for the state, small border chiefs introduced state landscapes of productivity and rule at moments that strengthened their own stature and resource control. The collusion between Akha village heads and state agents served to further marginalize other Akha, advancing their enclosure within the nation-state on

Is the head man seen as an ally here?

the state's terms. In the face of state plans and village heads' machinations, Akha farmers sought ways to rework complex, flexible livelihoods and landscapes. Farmers' attempts to remake plastic landscapes had differing outcomes in China and Thailand, both for Akha livelihoods and for the condition of their forests. In the two cases, state representations of people, forests, and land uses, together with the political economies that manifested these representations, have produced dramatically different arenas for the practice of border landscapes. The available arenas for negotiation and action, in turn, have meant the difference for Akha between continuing to practice landscape plasticity in China and losing that possibility in Thailand.

we should look at who wants clear property
lines
why   aka who benefits
most

sanctioned
refusal to follow practices means they are
labeled backwards, marganilized further

2

THE PRODUCTION OF MARGINAL PEOPLES AND LANDSCAPES

Resource Access on the Periphery

In Yunnan the barbarians who have yet to be incorporated are many.

FIRST GOVERNOR OF YUNNAN (1253 CE),
"Biography of Sayyid 'Ajall," *Yuanshi, juan* 125, quoted in
J. Armijo-Hussein, *Sayyid 'Ajall Shams Al-Din*

The king's rule is a "variable sphere of influence that
diminishes as royal power radiates from a center."

S. J. TAMBIAH, *World Conqueror and World Renouncer*

IN BOTH PREMODERN CHINA AND SIAM,[1] THE MODES OF CENTRAL RULE
over rural areas were configured around the collection of grain. In each case,
the government extracted taxes in grain from lowland farmers who were
included in mainstream society. Aside from the common concentration on
grain, however, the two modes differed considerably. In China, the official
history of Yunnan indicates that as early as the thirteenth century rulers
exerted control over territory as well as people, with officials organizing territory into prefectures, counties, and plots of land and requiring farmers
to pay taxes in grain based on landholdings (*Yuanshi, juan* 125, quoted in
Armijo-Hussein 1996:167). In Siam, for many centuries rule was arranged
through a hierarchy of patronage relations, with the king at the top. The
king allocated serfs and slaves to nobles, who managed the labor of serfs to
produce grain, against which head taxes were collected and sent to the central court. Rule in Siam sought to control labor rather than land (Feeny
1989:285; Vandergeest and Peluso 1995:392).

Looking outward from the court, scholars and officials in China and Siam also identified those peoples on the periphery, in the distant forested mountains, in relation to state rule. The location of the periphery in each case is centuries old. In China, such definitions created a taxonomy of "barbarians," especially in the southwest, categorized according to their degree of amenability to imperial rule. In the central view, the civilizing influence of the emperor was to bring these peoples as well as their territory into the fold. In Siam, by contrast, mountain people were generally regarded as "wild" people beyond the reach of the king's moral influence. In relation to the king's rule, however, these wild people also constituted potential captives to be brought back to lowland society as slaves. The role of wild people was ambivalent, both outside of society and within it as the lowest rank.

In both China and Siam, these modes of rule and the central definitions of marginal peoples and landscapes were transformed in the twentieth century by state-making efforts to "modernize" rural production, although under very different ideologies and political-economic systems. Central to these transformations in rural areas were the imposition of citizenship, new forms of state-sanctioned property rights, and intensified state claims on rural resources. In relation to peoples on the margins, policies in China over the past fifty years have included so-called minority nationalities in the polity and have linked upland minorities to their mountain (and forested) land through production of grain for the state. In Thailand, meanwhile, policies over a similar period have claimed forests as state assets and national treasures, separating minorities from the forests by identifying "hill tribes" as fundamentally "not Thai" and undeserving of Thailand's land and resources.

How did these disparate outcomes come about? Historical antecedents as well as twentieth-century moments of solidifying state definitions and purposes produced differences in definition and practice. This resulted in distinctly different conditions in these two countries, with greatly differing outcomes for Akha and their forests.

HISTORICAL CONSTRUCTS OF PEOPLES AND LANDSCAPES

Barbarians in Southwest China

The area that is now Yunnan Province in China is mentioned in official documents as early as the first century CE as a place where numerous primitive peoples lived. Court records recount that various groups agreed to pay tribute to the Chinese court, sending salt, rhinoceros, elephants, textiles, and jewelry, in return for gifts of silk from the Emperor of Heaven (Bielenstein, Wang Mang, the restoration of the Han dynasty, and later Han, in *The Cambridge history of China, volume 1, the Chin and Han empires* [Cambridge: Cambridge University Press, 1978], cited in Armijo-Hussein 1996:107). The exchange of gifts implied a connection, probably interpreted at court as an indication of the primitives' recognition of the superiority of Chinese culture. The Chinese notion of a southwestern periphery is very old.

The official history of the Yuan dynasty (1279–1368), *Yuanshi*, from the era following Kublai Khan's incorporation of Yunnan into the Chinese empire, notes that "the customs of Yunnan are without any of the rituals or ceremonies . . . [and farmers] did not have rice paddies, mulberry or hemp" (Armijo-Hussein 1996:22). The customs and land-use practices were different from those of the central, mainstream peoples and were considered barbaric. The work of the first governor of Yunnan, appointed by Beijing, was to impart "civilization," part of which involved instructing barbarians in proper techniques for agriculture. He also set up prefectures and counties and established a civil administration to collect land taxes. Moves to extend the administration of both territory and people were key to bringing this area under imperial control.[2]

Two documents from the early fourteenth century, one from Marco Polo and one from the Chinese scholar Li Jing, describe barbarian groups in Yunnan in some detail. Li Jing traveled throughout Yunnan for two years and mentioned the Bai, Luoluo, Naxi, and Jingpo tribes, as well as the Woni (Hani[3]). Tribes displayed traits such as sexual licentiousness, violent settlement of disputes, and consumption of raw meat. All of these habits implied contrast with the Chinese, who, in idealized Confucian portraits, were sexually proper, given to learned discussion in settling disputes, and ate refined culinary fare. As the first depictions from Yunnan, Li Jing's descriptions of primitive peoples became the model for all future compilations about barbarians in the southwest (Armijo-Hussein 1996:125).

In Yunnan, there were gradations of "primitiveness" among barbarians, depending on their form of livelihood. In general, hunter-gatherers at high elevations were thought to be the most primitive; shifting cultivators at midslope elevations were a step up; and wet-rice cultivators in valleys were well along the path to becoming "civilized" (Fitzgerald 1972:40). Some groups, such as the Tai in Sipsongpanna, had a writing system and Buddhist legal codes. Chinese scholars thought these peoples were more cultured than illiterate groups. Tai farmers also cultivated wet rice in valleys, showing, in

Chinese eyes, a more productive and cultured landscape than that of shifting cultivators in the hills.

Some peoples in Yunnan and neighboring Guizhou were categorized as more open to civilization, as shown by their willingness to learn the Chinese language and to follow laws. These groups were known as *shu*, or "cooked" barbarians. Other groups who fled authority and refused to learn Chinese were described as *sheng*, or "raw" barbarians. A close reading of the records reveals that the distinction between raw and cooked lay in the degree of submission to imperial control (Fiskesjö 1999:150), rather than in degrees of civility, since in many cases different segments of the same non-Chinese group were designated as *sheng* and *shu*.[4] Raw peoples were viewed as unwilling to be civilized (Diamond 1995:100).

Some of the characteristics of barbarian groups persisted into the so-called Miao albums, descriptions of barbarian tribes in Guizhou and Yunnan that were compiled from the eighteenth to the mid-twentieth centuries for the use of administrators posted to areas of Han colonization (Hostetler 2001:6). These albums consisted of written text with an accompanying painting depicting each group and its predominant traits. The Miao albums not only categorized barbarian groups, but also justified Chinese takeover of their territory as a means of offering primitive people the possibility of learning superior ways (Diamond 1995:104). Indeed, the very detail of the Miao albums, covering the characteristics of many different groups, provided a primer for understanding and thus governing each group (Hostetler 2001:6).

Following patterns set in the Yuan dynasty, not only the teaching of proper rituals, but also the imposition of appropriate civil administration and agricultural methods were all part of the Chinese means of including barbarians in the civilized world. These methods also ensured that appropriate taxes would be levied on agricultural production. The ongoing existence of *sheng* people on the frontier represented potential future expansion of imperial territory and civilizing control, as well as justification for imperial rule to maintain that civilizing pressure (Fiskesjö 1999:150).

Chinese culture (*wenhua*) was understood as a civilizing process effected through education or contact with literati (Harrell 1995:13–14). Imbibing classical literature involved a transformation in both knowledge and morality. All Chinese, whether elite or farmer, needed to go through this process to become civilized. For barbarians on the frontier, the distance from civilization was greater, but those barbarians willing to change could, in principle, become civilized, or cooked.

Nicholas Menzies (1992) has argued that during late imperial China (1644–1911) policies of inclusion were deployed in dealing with potentially restive border areas, such as the southwest. In his definition, inclusion means sending people closely linked to the center to peripheral areas to enfold the border region into central political and economic projects. Such "inclusive" policies were designed to bring both frontier territory and the barbarians living there under central control.

Long before the twentieth century, though, the southwestern periphery had been related to the Chinese empire, whether formally included in it or not. The state had defined and categorized the primitive peoples who lived there and marginal peoples and landscapes had been identified. The distinguishing feature of Chinese imperial rule was an impulse to bring uncivilized peoples and territory under central control, whether that desire was fulfilled or not.

The Republican revolution of 1911 ended the two-thousand-year-old imperial system as well as the legitimacy based on the civilizing power of the Son of Heaven. During the Republican period (1911–49), warlords dominated much of China, with Chiang Kai-shek as the warlord claiming to represent the legitimate Chinese Nationalist government. For much of the 1920s and 1930s, the governor of Yunnan Province operated fairly independently of Chiang's government, while at the same time offering verbal alliance with Chiang rather than with the Communists under Mao Zedong (Diamond 1995:106). Following the Japanese invasion of eastern China in 1937, Chiang's Nationalist (KMT) government retreated from Nanjing (Jiangsu Province in the east) to Chongqing (Sichuan Province in the southwest). Chiang's staff issued statements about assimilation of indigenous groups into Chinese society. While not enforced, the statements reflected new understandings of what assimilation or civilization meant, since they described not only the importance of Chinese culture and rituals, but also the need to get rid of "superstitious" practices and adopt "modern" ways (Diamond 1995:106). Even before the Communist revolution of 1949, being "Chinese" already meant being more advanced than the backward mountain groups, who had gotten caught somewhere in history and had not progressed as the Han had. "Modern" and "backward" had replaced "cultured" and "barbarian" as the descriptors used to differentiate mainstream and marginal people. The goal of becoming modern would also dominate the Communist regime beginning in 1949, but with new meanings for both the advanced people as well as those whom history had left behind.

Uncivilized Peoples on the Fringes of Siam

The scholarly conception of Siam before the arrival of the teak-seeking British depicts a central court with a king and nobles in a hierarchical arrangement of rule and production in which urban dwellers, nobles, and the serfs who belonged to them, comprised civilized society. The king and his courtiers saw peoples who practiced shifting cultivation, somewhere in forests on the fringes of known kingdoms, as outside the civilized order (Steinberg 1987:21).

To administer the kingdom and extract revenue, rulers of Siam generally sought to control labor rather than land. All land and life were thought to belong to the king (Kemp 1989:2; Tambiah 1976:110). The king allocated land and the labor of serfs to nobles, who in turn mobilized this labor to produce wet rice. Alternatively, the king conscripted this labor into an army that captured people from neighboring kingdoms or upland forests. The captives brought back from these raids became slaves for the king to allocate to nobles, as a means of demonstrating or extending his influence. In the fifteenth century, the king's allocations to nobles were made in numbers of rice fields, but the meaning of "rice fields" quickly changed into numbers of slaves and serfs to work those fields (Wyatt 1984:73; Kemp 1989:2–3). Wealth was measured in the quantity of serfs under one's control, with nobles ranked according to the numbers of bodies allocated to them by the king. Individual serfs were registered with a noble to whom they owed labor. Individuals or households were also registered for purposes of head taxes, corvée labor for the king, and military conscription (Vandergeest and Peluso 1995:392–93; Wyatt 1984:155). This system, called Sakdina, concentrated on control over labor.

The configuration of the civilized world was of wet-rice farmers clustered around nobles in towns and cities, with the civilizing and moral power of the king radiating from the royal city outward to those who were registered within this hierarchical system of labor and obligation (Kemp 1989:11). On the fringes of this system were shifting cultivators in upland areas. Occasionally military raids would capture upland peoples as slaves, but people at the court did not think of shifting cultivators as integral to Thai society. In fact, if a farming household decided to give up wet-rice cultivation in favor of upland rice, these people lost their lowland identity and were no longer subject to corvée labor or military conscription (O'Conner, pers. comm. 1994).

In Thai, the word for forest (*paa*) has connotations of "untamed" and "uncivilized" (Taylor 1991:107). Forests have historically been and are still associated with "contraband articles, undisciplined and immoral people" and are the "domain of wild animals, demons, spirits, and uncivilized tribal people" (108). Forests were dangerous sites where civilized people would not want to go. Additionally, forests were not seen as beautiful, since they have not yet been civilized or managed into recognizable patterns. In lowland Thai thinking, "the cosmological layout of 'patterned' human settlements corresponds to a hierarchy in which beauty and civilization flows downward from the towns to the villages" (108). Beyond the villages was the forest, but the king's civilizing power seemed to come to earth at the edge of the woods. For rulers and lowland farmers, then, society did not include the people in the forest.

Documents in the Tai language from the sixteenth century refer to "people who lived in *muang* and to people who did not" (Renard 1993:1), with the people in *muang* (a city or political entity) the ones who had been civilized by religious and political practices that had come to Siam from India. The court of Siam had adopted from India the Dharmasastra, the Hindu law books laying out "the natural order of things which kings were obliged to uphold" (Wyatt 1984:137). For crimes related to property, the inability to pay fines frequently led to debt bondage or slavery, reinforcing the hierarchy based on wealth in people or labor (Wyatt 1984:73).

The word "Tai" came to refer to people in the lowland kingdoms of Chiang Rung (extending from Sipsongpanna to Chiang Mai) and other regions. The counterpart of the civilized Tai were the *kha*, a general term for all the uncivilized people living in upland areas (Renard 1993:10). If *kha* were captured as slaves to people in the *muang*, however, *kha* or their descendants could become people of the *muang*. Renard describes the different trajectories for those of the hill group Karen, who entered into tribute relationships with rulers in Chiang Mai and Bangkok and were described as "tame," versus those Karen who stayed in the forest and refused to offer tribute, who were known as "wild."[5] In the two hundred or more years since this initial distinction, the tame Karen have evolved from being subjects of the ruler to citizens of the state and are now Thai. Those Karen who remained in the forest have become members of the hill tribes and not citizens, unless they have managed to go through special procedures to become citizens (Renard 1993:41; Chiang Rai Committee 1994).

Within this dichotomy of valley-civilized/hill-uncivilized, however, there is evidence of relationships between hill and valley people that challenge and complicate the simplicity of this formulation. As early as the six-teenth century, leaders of small states north of Siam had agreements with non-Tai groups that if they settled and provided useful products to the rulers, these groups would be exempt from corvée labor and taxes (Renard 1980:143). Some Karen were in tributary relationships with lowland Tai (Pinkaew 2001:50).

In theory, the distinction between *muang* and *kha* would have been between those who paid taxes and tribute and those who did not. Another marker of difference would have been between those who cultivated wet rice and those who planted upland rice. As described above, however, in practice these distinctions were not nearly so clear. Still, with the *muang/kha* dichotomy, those in the central court could proclaim that people who lived in the forest and paid no tribute or taxes were beyond the benefit of the king's moral influence and were uncivilized. Armed troops went out to cap-ture and bring back *kha* to the center, where known forms of control over slaves would ensure their compliance with civilization.

Before the onset of modernizing policies, then, the periphery had already been defined, as had the primitive peoples living there. Their prac-tice of shifting cultivation was viewed as inferior and uncultured, linking people, place, and land use in a formulation of inferiority. Rule in Siam was imposed through control over labor, including the labor of upland peoples when they had been captured and incorporated into hierarchical lowland regimes.

During the second half of the nineteenth century, threatened by British and French colonial endeavors on either side of Bangkok, King Chulalong-korn (r. 1868–1910) embarked on a series of "self-civilizing"[6] projects in imitation of "modern" governments in the West, including ending slav-ery, instituting property rights in land rather than in people, and trans-forming serfs or slaves into citizens (Feeny 1989:285; Bunnag 1977). The king also maneuvered to incorporate the Lanna States in the north into Siam to protect the British teak concessions there. Chulalongkorn followed Britain and other European nations on a mercantilist and, later, capital-ist path to developing a modern economy and the state apparatus to sup-port it (Bunnag 1977; Mekvichai 1988). His moves to end slavery and insti-tute property rights in land directly led to a free labor force and a land market, where land could be used as collateral for loans. Chulalongkorn and his predecessors had studied Western economics and consciously chose many of the steps in the self-civilizing process they thought would lead to being modern.

TWENTIETH-CENTURY REWORKINGS
OF MARGINAL PEOPLES, SPACES, AND LAND USES

Forms of rule and definitions of marginal upland peoples, spaces, and land uses were transformed in the twentieth century through the institution of citizenship, property rights in rural areas, and state claims on rural resources. These three elements are closely intertwined, as they are all implicated in the intensification of state rule and claims on rural production.

As citizenship was deployed as a means of creating membership in or exclusion from the nation-state, the definitions of upland peoples went through a metamorphosis. Previous understandings of these peoples' role influenced the processes that later shaped their inclusion in China and their exclusion in Thailand. The justification for inclusion or exclusion, however, was defined in terms appropriate for a nation-state. Once citizens became distinct from noncitizens, definitions of minority nationalities, or hill tribes, continued to shift as the purposes and policies of state rule evolved.

State-imposed property rights in land and other rural resources were linked both to citizenship and the definitions of people, but also to state strategies for increasing rural productivity and controlling land uses. These moves also joined property rights and citizenship with state claims on rural resources, the most important of which were grain and timber. The state not only extracted grain or timber to fund industrialization, but also defined particular spaces, such as upland forests, in relation to state needs. All three actions constituted new state landscape visions of progress and modernity, resulting in landscapes of productivity and rule.

The obverse side of these actions reconstituted marginal or peripheral spaces. China and Thailand, from their centers in Beijing and Bangkok, produced very different images of what these spaces represented for the center and correspondingly different plans for how "we Chinese" or "we Thai" should relate to the people and resources there. Pursuing policies influenced by imperial practices, Chinese proclamations included both the territory and the people in marginal regions as objects of state rule. Rural farmers, including ethnic minorities, were to manage land and trees on behalf of the central state. People, land, and trees were kept together, conceptually and materially. In Thailand, resources and people were divided. Since timber served as one of the key resources for financing industrialization, the Thai state claimed forests as state assets and allocated their harvest to timber companies. As a result, forest-dependent peoples became intruders and crimi-

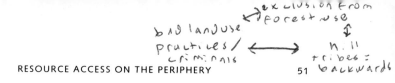

nal users of state property. Framed as hill tribes, these people were excluded from citizenship, or membership in the nation.

China: Marginalization through Inclusion *I skipped*

Socialism and Backward Minorities in China: Citizens of a Different Order.
When instituting citizenship, Chinese policy makers at first adopted whole-sale Marx's formulation regarding ethnic minority groups, identified in Marxist terminology as "nationalities." In addressing the "Nationalities Question" in the early 1950s, Mao Zedong followed Stalin in promising minority nationalities autonomous regions and support for their own cultures, while disallowing secession from the People's Republic of China. Policies for all nationalities, who were all automatically citizens of China, proceeded from this understanding (Grunfeld 1985; Connor 1984).

Regardless of territorial autonomy, however, in the long run minority nationalities were to be assimilated into a new society of "socialist man" (Grunfeld 1985; Connor 1984:201). In like manner, Han were to be transformed by the process of revolution and reeducation into true socialists. During the Long March in the 1930s, from Guangxi in the south, through parts of southwest China, and finally to the revolutionary base in northwest Gansu, Mao came to see that the greater part of Chinese territory was the homeland of the so-called minority nationalities[7] (Connor 1984:73).

Following the revolution of 1949, all residents of China were automatically citizens, and the Constitution of 1954 promised minority nationalities cultural, economic, and political equality with Han in the new China (Connor 1984:208). Citizenship was universal from the beginning, and plans were made to modernize those who lagged behind the vanguard. The formulation of economic equality included an element of "to each according to his labor" plus an attempt to develop backward areas. The original plan envisioned a long period of support for different languages and customs, together with new forms of education, which would eventually lead to assimilation of all into a uniform socialist society (Connor 1984:213).

During the 1950s the government in Beijing launched a campaign to identify all minority nationalities. People all over China were invited to claim minority status, and more than four hundred groups applied, since a legitimated claim would bring autonomous self-rule and support for the group's culture. Teams of researchers, including well-known Chinese anthropologists, went out from Beijing to examine all the claims (Guldin 1994). The

research teams identified fifty-four nationalities, including the Han as a separate nationality (*minzu*). Subsequently, two more nationalities were
included, so that today China officially recognizes fifty-six. The research
teams also rated each nationality according to its mode of production, from
primitive to slave, feudal, capitalist, and socialist stages of progression. Then
plans were made to advance each group to a socialist mode of production
and into modern civilization (Harrell 1995:23; Wu 1990).

While proclamations during the 1950s emphasized equality of all nationalities and a socialist society as the goal for all groups, before the decade
ended the Han became the model nationality, and their level of culture
became the measure of progress (Harrell 1995:26). But unlike premodern
assumptions that anyone could become cultured and civilized through training and contact with the superior Han, the new conception had harder, "scientific" edges: the Communists had evaluated and rated each nationality,
and with the possible exception of Manchus, Muslims, and Koreans, all
groups fell behind the Han by varying degrees (Harrell 1995:27). This categorization represented a state technology of power that marginalized certain peoples at the moment of inclusion (Keyes 1994).

During the Cultural Revolution (1966–76), Mao and his cohort dramatically changed the terms of relationship between the Communist Party
and minority nationalities: "Regional autonomy, toleration of national
differences, different tempos for achieving socialism, and cooperation with
traditional local leaders were . . . now violently attacked, and demands for
proceeding with immediate assimilation were again raised" (Connor
1984:422). Then, following Mao's death in 1976, the new Constitution of 1978
again promoted the development of minority languages and the preservation of minority customs, together with proclaiming the need to train more
minority cadres (Connor 1984:426). Throughout the 1980s, pronouncements
continued to emphasize that China was a united nation-state with many
nationalities (*tongyi duominzu guojia*), and at the same time Han cadres were
posted to all minority areas. In state documents, Han were described as being
"more loyal" to the state than were minority nationalities (Connor 1984:430),
which contributed to the disempowerment of minorities.

Chinese official policy is still to assimilate all nationalities eventually into
a common society, where everyone has progressed to a common level. The
rate at which, with official encouragement, minority groups are establishing schools taught in minority languages (Postiglione 1998) and colorful
minority nationalities are being promoted as tourist attractions, however,
suggests that assimilation is a long way away. Having defined minority groups

as backward and in need of training, as part of the justification for including them and their territory in the new China, it is unlikely that the Han would ever acknowledge that any minority nationality had "caught up" with the Han. As a result of citizenship, and automatic inclusion in the new order, minority nationalities are all, by definition, under state control. There are no more *sheng* peoples beyond the reach of the state. The distinction between "raw" and "cooked" barbarians has been replaced by minority nationalities either caught in different modes of production (1950s) or at different stages of development (1990s). What has endured is the certainty that the Han are the bearers of civilization and modernity, only now with socialist characteristics.

Property Rights in Rural Resources in China. Beginning in the early 1950s, with the explicit goal of increasing rural production, the central government initiated a series of changes in land tenure and the level of management. During the massive land reform of the early 1950s, agricultural land and wooded areas were wrested from landlords and distributed to small farming households. In subsequent steps toward socialist reconstruction, from 1953 to 1957 households were organized into agricultural collectives, and in 1958 into the larger communes in which teams farmed the land for communal purposes. From the 1960s to the early 1980s, communes in principle managed their own farmland and forests. In the Akha settlement Mengsong, all agricultural and forestland was collectivized, and households retained only the use of clumps of bamboo.

Prior to the 1949 revolution, there had been no Ministry of Forestry or Forestry Department. Pronouncements on land use in the early 1950s specified that areas in China's northeast and southwest, with large stretches of forest, would be designated as state forests. Most other wooded areas, amounting to about two-thirds of all forestland, were allocated to households for subsistence purposes (*China forestry yearbook* 1987; Zou Hengfang, pers. comm. 1994). The newly formed Ministry of Forestry managed state forests as a source of raw materials and treated timber as a free good, since the thinking then was that no human labor was invested in producing trees (Harkness 1998:913).

State-allocated property rights in rural resources changed dramatically in 1982 when the collective period ended.[8] To stimulate agricultural production, agricultural land from communes was contracted to households in the household responsibility system. In upland areas, households received areas for shifting cultivation as well as wet-rice fields. In a major reconfiguration of rule, the household became the basic unit of production in what came to be called a socialist market economy. In a reconfiguration of citizenship, farmers who had earlier been laborers for the state now became entrepreneurs for the household.

The national forest policy of the early 1980s, *linye sanding*, can roughly be translated as the "three clarifications of forestry." The State Council, citing the loss of forest cover and quality resulting from frequent changes in tenure and management over the previous thirty years, specified three necessary provisions: clarification of boundaries among state forests, collective (village) forests, and nature reserves; allocation of freehold forestland to rural households; and identification of the responsibilities, rights, and benefits of farmers and collectives (Cao and Zhang n.d.:3).

In Yunnan Province, the policy called *liangshan daohu*, or "two kinds of forests to the household," was raised first in 1980, at the same time that the three clarifications policy was proclaimed nationally. The idea of *liangshan daohu* was that forested land would be allocated to households in two fashions: (1) each household would be given freehold forestland to supply fuel wood, fencing, and other household needs; and (2) households could contract with the village collective to protect or reforest areas that were supposed to be covered with trees. Together with the household responsibility system for agricultural land, *liangshan daohu* formed the basis for overall rural land-use policy in Yunnan (Zuo 1997:3), including Akha areas. For rural farmers in Yunnan, property rights in land and trees were set, and farmers officially became managers of agricultural land and forests.

State Claims on Rural Resources in China. In China, the state placed priority on the collection of grain. Since policy makers envisioned grain, rather than timber, as the resource to fund economic development, they were less concerned about claiming forests as state goods. Accordingly, from the early 1950s until the 1980s, China's major procurement in rural areas was grain. This emphasis meant that, even during collectivization, villagers in upland areas were not only allowed but were even encouraged to plant swiddens, since the various ministries involved with rural production saw shifting cultivation as a grain-producing system. Only with the advent of the United Nations' Food and Agriculture Organization (FAO) teams and projects, beginning in 1977, did Chinese foresters begin to denounce shifting cultivation as a practice destructive of forests.[9] These claims resonated with historical constructions of shifting cultivation as a primitive land use employed by people who had not yet learned to cultivate wet rice. With international pressure to disparage shifting cultivation as environmentally destructive, policies began to support annual cultivation of cash crops. Throughout the 1980s and 1990s, the areas of land that had earlier been allocated to households for shifting cultivation were gradually terraced or planted in cash crops, and shifting cultivation was being brought to an end. Shifting cultivators, including Akha, were enclosed within the nation, and their land uses became targets for transformation into landscapes of productivity and rule.

Policies for agriculture and forestry, which overlapped for shifting cultivators, directed production to state goals while also declaring most forests to be subsistence resources. Policies and regulations for land use also became an instrument for "developing" rural farmers, especially hill minorities. Flowing from historical efforts to offer culture to barbarians, these policies have been a means to civilize and control minorities in the remote hills, as well as to marshal their production to state purposes.

At the same time, since identical policies were applied to both upland and lowland areas, unintended consequences often disadvantaged villagers in higher-elevation forests. Some policies, such as the wasteland auction policy discussed in chapter 4, impoverished forest-dependent villagers, many of whom were ethnic minorities. When these villagers attempted to avoid or maneuver within state regulations, their actions were often called "backward" or "ignorant," in conformance with the stereotype of upland minority nationalities. Uniform policies have, in effect, both included upland farmers in the national fold and also contributed to their marginalization. But these uniform policies have also kept rural people, forests, and land together, whether the farmers were minority nationality or Han.

Thailand: Marginalization through Exclusion

From Forest People to Hill Tribes: "Not Thai." In the early part of the twentieth century, the royal family of Siam gave considerable attention to citizenship. From 1893 to 1903, Chulalongkorn's son, Vajiravudh, learned while at school in England the importance of nationalism and the national pride of citizens (Renard 1993:35; Wyatt 1984:224). Once he became king in 1910, he imported these notions, devising the phrase *chat Thai* for "Thai race." The translation as "race" derived from the French colonial emphasis at that time on Lao and Khmer peoples as races that belonged to French Indochina. Vajiravudh's meaning may be better translated as "nation" or even "ethnic group" (Keyes 1995:144; 1997:208). According to the king, "a true Thai was loyal to *chat* (Thai race), *sasana* (religion), and *mahakasat* (king), a slogan

Is adopting christianty/buddhism an attempt to join mainstream?

actually adapted from the British slogan of 'God and Country'" (Renard 1993:35).

The king's definition of nationalism and of a Thai race or nation had profound implications for the evolution of citizenship in Siam and later Thailand. Those embraced as citizens of Siam tended to include urban people and lowland wet-rice farmers. The creation of a Thai race obscured the origins of lowland people, who were products of intermarriage among Tai, ethnic minority, and immigrant groups, many of whom had been brought in on slave raids (Wyatt 1984:1). Left out of the Thai race were people in the forest, even those who had been there for generations. They were excluded seemingly because they spoke a different language, had their own religion, and may never have heard of the king. In practice, they were equally excluded because they lived in uncivilized space (forested mountains) and because their land use, shifting cultivation, was lacking in civilized order. They did not belong to the landscape of productivity and rule.

On a visit to Chiang Mai in 1906, Vajiravudh noted that the people there (who were Tai, and previously known as *muang*) needed to be tamed through education, implying an important shift (Renard 1993:36). By this time only Bangkok Thais were considered fully civilized, and true civilization flowed from the West rather than from India, as had been the case in the past. Officials from Bangkok sent to the north further remarked on the many ethnic groups who had moved in from Burma in recent decades. Following the new national idiom, the officials saw these ethnic groups as "aliens," in place of the older *kha* terminology. The split was now between those who were Thai, and those who were aliens, or "not Thai" (Renard 1993:37). The Nationality Act of 1913 specified that citizenship derived from having a Thai father and must be inherited (Renard 1993:38).

While tributary or patron-client relationships between rulers in the north and various hill groups had been a phenomenon of the northern states before their incorporation into Siam, the new government administration, based increasingly on Western notions of a bureaucratic nation-state, replaced princes and entrenched elites with Bangkok appointees loyal to the king (Wyatt 1984:227; Bunnag 1977). As steps toward modernity, Kings Chulalongkorn and Vajiravudh, delineated boundaries around Siam and sought to identify the people within its borders (Pinkaew 1997:8). Previously, hill people had lived as *khon pa* (wild people) in wild, amorphous border regions where they belonged. Within the newly defined boundaries the *chao khao* (hill tribes), as identified by the Siam Society in 1920, now lived within the territory of Siam and under the jurisdiction of its government (Pinkaew

1997:10). In spite of this enclosure, though, the north was still conceptually a wild space.

The term *chao khao*, or hill tribes, was first used officially in 1959 with the appointment of the Central Hill Tribe Committee, and shortly thereafter the Tribal Research Center of Chiang Mai (Pinkaew 1997:11). Up to 1958 there had been a Royal Opium Monopoly, intended as a source government income from the sale of opium. Pressure from the U.S. government and United Nations (UN) agencies resulted in the establishment of the Tribal Research Center and the end of the Royal Opium Monopoly. International groups sought to stop opium growing and the production of drugs, a concern that emerged at the same time as worry about communist insurrections in Laos and Vietnam. Staff in the U.S. Drug Enforcement Agency, as well as in the Central Intelligence Agency and the UN Drug Control Program, thought hill groups who produced opium were prey to pressure from communist insurgents spilling into the north and northeast of Thailand from Laos (Wakin 1992; Tapp 1989). Thus the problems of drug eradication and of national security became linked with the hill tribes at an early date (Tapp 1989; Wakin 1992; Pinkaew 1997:27). As a result of FAO advisors to Thailand in the 1940s and 1950s denouncing shifting cultivation as inefficient and destructive to forests, hill groups who practiced shifting cultivation were castigated on this account as well (Pinkaew 1997:31).

From the inception of the Central Hill Tribe Committee in 1959, the projects associated with highland villagers had four goals: (1) to prevent degradation of forests and rivers by ending shifting cultivation; (2) to eradicate opium production; (3) to promote community development so that hill tribes could contribute to national economic development; and (4) to engage hill tribes in national security by making them loyal to the nation (Tapp 1989:31). Hill tribes were both criticized and included in state plans, since their landscapes were sources of threat to Thailand. Each of the problems associated with hill tribes in 1959—opium production, deforestation, and lack of loyalty to Thailand—came to the fore at different times in the following thirty years, from the mid-1960s to the mid-1990s, with national security related in some way to each one in turn.

In the 1960s, when the Royal Forestry Department (RFD) granted logging concessions, on a rotational basis, covering more than 50 percent of Thailand's land area (Pragtong and Thomas 1990:172), highland peoples were called "squatters," since they had no formal property rights to land and trees. Their presence in the forest was criminalized, no matter how long they had lived there. In the late 1960s and 1970s, the threat of the Laotian communist movement spreading into Thailand was linked to highland groups because they lived along the border and because, it was argued, they were "not Thai." In the 1970s and 1980s, when under pressure from the U.S. Drug Enforcement Agency and the UN Drug Program opium eradication became a national campaign, opium production was framed as a hill tribe problem, since several of the hill groups, including Akha, grew opium. And in the 1980s and 1990s, as national attention focused on forest loss and environmental degradation, again the highland peoples caught the brunt of the blame, since many used shifting cultivation, a practice linked in the national imagination with forest destruction (Pinkaew 2001:32). In its approaches to hill tribes in relation to communist infiltration, opium cultivation, and environmental degradation, the Thai state produced a series of definitions of marginal peoples that justified particular forms of state rule. Each step reinforced the marginal position of both the space of northern Thailand and the forest-dwelling people within it.

National security has been tied to each of these problems—communist insurrection, opium production, and environmental degradation. While the threat of communism from Laos may have been a legitimate problem,[10] the government used it to justify controlling highland villagers and excluding them from citizenship, whether there was any evidence of communist activities or not (Tapp 1989). Opium production, in its turn, was presented as a link in the international drug trade, and as such a threat to Thai society. As for environmental degradation, during the 1980s and 1990s, as environmentalism became popular in the press, among urban middle-class Thais, and in the government, the possibility of further loss or degradation of forests came to be seen as a threat to a national treasure (Hirsch 1987). Thailand's forests belonged to the Thai people. They were treasures inherited from the primordial past to be preserved for future generations. Encompassing arguments from international environmentalism, the Thai version targeted hill tribes as the most serious threat to the nation's remaining forests. As each problem in the north emerged as a national issue, its connection with highland peoples implied that hill tribe lack of loyalty to the Thai nation caused the problem and that the problem itself gave further evidence of hill tribe deficiency in nationalism.

The transition from hill groups as uncivilized *kha* to backward hill tribes was gradual, evolving over a forty-year period from King Vajiravudh's reign to the early 1960s, by which time the understanding of *chao khao* as squatters on Thai land was firmly entrenched. The change was from wild people, with a place of their own in the upland forests, to intruders on national territory, who presented a number of threats to the Thai nation-state. Previously, wild people were considered somewhat dangerous and powerful, but only if lowland people entered their realm, also conceived of as a perilous place. *Kha* were not a threat to lowland society. Hill tribes, by contrast, have been seen as illegal intruders on state turf, and their being "not Thai" has become threatening to national well-being and national security. Once benignly uncivilized out on the fringes of things, hill people have become an actively hostile presence in the north of Thailand.

State claims on forests for national purposes justified the exclusion of hill tribes from citizenship and property rights. These exclusions gave shape to state rule in the north of Thailand. The meaning of "hill tribes" in fact developed in concert with changes in the understanding of what forests were, how they were to be used, and who owned them.

Property Rights and State Claims on Rural Resources in Northern Thailand. During King Chulalongkorn's reign, following the delineation of national boundaries around Siam, the government claimed forests as state property. Such line drawing and claims followed patterns that had evolved in Europe and in British India, which at that time included Burma (Vandergeest 1995:161). In 1896, the Royal Forestry Department (RFD) was formed under a British conservator, mainly to secure the production, harvesting, and taxation of teak. In 1899, all "unoccupied" territory in Siam was defined as forest and allocated to the RFD (Vandergeest 1995:161).

Over several decades, the RFD tried to establish some control of forest use and occupancy, with limited success. Beginning early in the century, swidden cultivators were supposed to communicate their occupancy of land to the government, by which means they would establish their right to use, but not sell, the land. Few people did this, probably because they did not know of the requirement (Chusak 1996:5).

Until the 1960s, the main current of forest policy was protection of reserved species, based on a concern to protect commodities rather than to claim territory. The Forest Conservation Law of 1913 referred to products rather than land, dividing trees into reserved and unreserved species. The law was not enforced in areas where there was no trade in reserved species. The 1949 Forest Act attempted to curtail household use of forest products and later, in 1960, harvesting forest products for household use was prohibited (Hafner 1990:80).

A second stream of policies addressed land, or territory. The 1938 Protection and Reservation of Forests Act allowed for the protection of forestland. Surveying and marking the designated land, however, was not completed until 1985. As an example of this slow process, in 1949, at the recommendation of an FAO report, the government decided to set aside seventy thousand square kilometers in the northeast of Thailand as reserved forest. Only 12.5 percent of this area had been marked by 1957, and 64 percent by 1980. Even in established areas, few were marked in ways that rural people would recognize (Hafner 1990:81).

An overview of forest policies and their implementation up to 1960 shows a singular lack of territoriality (Vandergeest and Peluso 1995), in other words a lack of claiming land and controlling land use as a manifestation of state rule. Even the 1949 FAO recommendations to designate areas of forest reserve were carried out slowly. The RFD approach to the north up to that point echoed the mode of rule for Siam, when claiming wild, mountainous territory was not a state objective.

The 1960s brought Thailand's drive toward economic development along Western lines, which included exploitation of forests as a means to finance industrialization (Boserup 1963:207–15). In the late 1960s, when the RFD began to allocate logging concessions to timber companies, the forestry department took advantage of the exclusionary policies enacted sixty years previously, that is, those designating forests as state property. People were to be excluded, if not from living in forests, at least from using them. The distribution of logging concessions marked the initiation of territoriality in the north on a large scale, but did not represent direct state action to control the territory because logging-company staff, rather than RFD officials, usually communicated and implemented these claims to forests.

Beginning in 1971, the Royal Project began to promote cash crops as a substitute for opium in highland people's fields. Following the expulsion of the "drug lord" Khun Sa from one region of the north in 1982, the initiative to eradicate opium expanded greatly in the 1980s, with numerous international crop substitution projects in the north to implement state suppression of opium cultivation. While these projects varied in approach, and evolved over time, their target was hill tribes and their ultimate goal was opium eradication. Thus, development projects in the north reflected the original directives for hill tribes—stop shifting cultivation, stop opium production, and end the destruction of forests. The north was understood to be different from the rest of Thailand, and the focus on opium there reinforced that difference. The opium-substitution projects, meanwhile, responding to drug eradication campaigns from the United States and the UN, instituted territoriality in the north with a persistence and attention to local detail that Thai government agents had not shown in the past. Partly in response to increasing drug production in Thailand, international agencies were pushing the Thai government to claim control of the north and prevent its usurpation by drug lords. The highland development projects also encouraged plantation of cash crops on much-reduced land areas, in a bid to end shifting cultivation and return the forest to the Thai state.

In 1980, the RFD realized that forest cover in Thailand had dropped to 30 percent from an estimate of more than 50 percent in the 1950s (Anan 1996:2). As a result of logging (both legal and illegal), the movement of large numbers of lowland farmers into hilly areas,[11] and the flight of ethnic minorities from unrest in Burma, the forest seemed to be disappearing. In 1985 a national forest policy specified that 40 percent of national territory should be forest reserve, of which 15 percent would be conservation forest and 25 percent economic forest. An area designated as an A zone was degraded forest that was suitable for agriculture, and could be allocated to local people. The stated goal of the policy was inclusion of local communities and the private sector in forest management (Anan 1996:3; Chusak 1996:8).

The influence of Bangkok business on officials in the government has ensured that the private sector has benefited far more from the A-zone provision than have local people (Anan 1996:13). In fact, entrepreneurs seeking to open resorts, golf courses, or tea estates can gain access to areas of reserve forest even outside the A zone, for which they pay a nominal rent to the RFD. Ethnic minorities, meanwhile, have no legal avenue for renting forestland for their own use (Anan 1996:14).

Following a 1988 flood in the south that resulted in hundreds of deaths and that was blamed on deforestation, heightened public awareness of the effects of deforestation enabled the state to adopt environmentalist justifications for increases in state exclusion of local people from the forest (McKinnon 1997:118). In 1991, a new policy for forest conservation reversed the percentages set in 1985. By 1996, 25 percent of land area was to be conservation forest and 15 percent was to be economic forest. In 1993, the cabinet raised these figures to 27.5 percent for conservation forest and 16.2 percent for economic forest, an ambitious goal, since total forest cover in 1993 was estimated at 26 percent (Anan 1996:4). These policies, if implemented, would transform all remaining forest into national parks, wildlife sanctuaries, nonhunting areas, and watershed-protection forests (Chusak 1996:2). This kind of conservation legislation seems designed to push highland peoples out of the mountains altogether.

But the dynamics at play are more complex and ambiguous. Some state agencies, notably the RFD, have related to the north through territorial approaches, such as claiming land for reforestation (see Vandergeest and Peluso 1995). In a similar fashion, international agencies, such as the FAO and the UN Drug Control Program, have in many instances initiated the drive for territorialization, pushing the Thai government to control the northern territory. Other state agencies, such as the military and the police, have tended to use patronage relations with hill tribe elites, effecting control through relationships with people (Turton 1989:86; Hirsch 1989:49–50). Even in a territorial mode, state actions both claimed the north as Thai space and constructed that space as different from the rest of Thailand. That difference concerned hill tribes, but hill tribes in an ongoing dual role as both the source of all problems in the north and as buffers between Thailand and the world of drugs and violence in Burma.

CHINA VERSUS SIAM/THAILAND

There are some obvious similarities between the production of marginal peoples in imperial China and Siam, such as the distinctions in China between raw and cooked barbarians and in Siam between tame and wild Karen. The understanding in each case was that some primitive people were willing to come under state rule (cooked and tame) and some were not (raw and wild). In the case of China, however, there were further discriminations among barbarians, such as between those who had writing systems and those who did not, and between those who cultivated wet rice and those who managed upland swiddens. From an early era, but gaining momentum during the Qing dynasty (1644–1911), the Chinese court was much more interested than their Siamese counterparts in devising an elaborate taxonomy of barbarians to scrutinize the current and future objects of state rule. In most cases, Siamese elites referred to civilized and uncivilized peoples, without the implication that uncivilized *kha* ought to become civilized. In either case, however, the Chinese taxonomies, as well as the simpler Siamese formulation of *muang* versus *kha*, served to distinguish all those primitive people from "us," the civilized realm. The taxonomies and distinctions also justified particular forms of state rule.

What is perhaps more interesting is how civilized and uncivilized people have been mapped onto civilized and uncivilized spaces. For the Chinese, there are few references to wild or uncivilized spaces that Chinese culture and rule could not penetrate. The usual expression is "not yet" rather than "could not," leaving open the possibility of future conquest. Barbarian frontiers could become part of the Chinese realm, and indeed partially cooked barbarians functioned as buffers against potentially hostile forces in Burma. The view from the Siamese court, however, was that wild spaces were best left alone, unless the king mounted a military raid to capture slaves in the hills. For Siam, the wild space tended to be associated with mountains to the north, a region that was permanently wild.

There is also a clear difference, at least in central discourse, between civilized and uncivilized land use. Chinese scholar-bureaucrats thought hunter-gatherers were the most primitive, occupying high elevations removed from contact with superior Chinese culture. Administrators saw shifting cultivation as a primitive land use mainly because they deemed it unproductive. Barbarians who used it had not yet learned from the Chinese the use of irrigation for wet rice, thought to be a more productive system. Again, the notion was "not yet" rather than that barbarians could not improve. For court officials in Siam, people who practiced shifting cultivation out on some remote mountain were bereft of the king's moral influence to bring them into civilized order. Shifting cultivation was a marker of primitiveness and of lack of connection to society.

The twentieth-century intensification of rule in China involved a curious reversal of roles for China and Thailand, as rural citizens, including minority nationalities, became laborers producing wet rice and other grains to fund state development of industry. Property rights in rural areas, in spite of multiple changes in the level of management, have consistently been intended to allow rural people a subsistence livelihood. That included household use of trees and forestland, keeping people, land, and trees together. Former frontier spaces, such as the border in the southwest, came under direct state administration, with property rights and land-use directives serving as key means for bringing frontier people and territory under state control.

In Thailand, the imposition of citizenship produced both citizens and noncitizens within newly defined state borders. The new categories overlay former distinctions between *muang* and *kha*. Lowland Buddhists were cast as the Thai race, in spite of their hybrid history of intermarriage among immigrants, captured slaves, and early inhabitants who were not Tai. *Kha* had previously lived in wild space, but once enclosed within the nation-state, the north remained, in lowland imagination, a different, separate, wild space. Property rights were designed differently, with the north almost all under RFD jurisdiction, while lowlands were, at least potentially, allocated to households and corporations as alienable private property.

Designation of a different kind of space was reinforced by successive policies toward hill tribes, related to national security, opium, and environmental conservation. At the same time, forest and environmental policies have claimed more and more land in the north for government uses. Hill tribes, meanwhile, have been used both as the designated culprit for any problems in the north and as a buffer against Burma. While vilified in the public arena, highland villagers have been tapped as a private or even covert avenue for accessing certain products and people in Burma.

In both China and Thailand, state projects have been laid out from the center in relation to control of people and territory, extraction of products, and legitimation of rule. These state projects created borders-as-margins, with marginal peoples employing primitive land uses. The projects formalized property rights for marginal peoples, strongly shaping resource access and pulling land uses in the direction of simplified, lowland landscapes. An examination of borders-as-lines, which connect peoples and nation-states, shows how the production of borders complicates resource access and land management for the people along these borders.

3

THE PRODUCTION OF BORDERS

Sites for the Accumulation

and Distribution of Resources

Remarkably, while asserting Siam's sovereignty over Chiang
Saen, Chulalongkorn . . . did not claim that it belonged to Siam
exclusively. He suggested that Chiangmai should allow the Shan to
settle there if Burma and Kengtung allowed Chiang Saen to submit
to both sides (Burma/Kengtung versus Siam/Chiangmai).

THONGCHAI WINICHAKUL, *Siam Mapped*

Although Mengding and Gengma had paid tribute to both
China and Burma in the past, Qing officials considered
the two Tai areas to be imperial territory.

C. PATTERSON GIERSCH, *Qing China's Reluctant Subjects*

FORMAL THEORIES ABOUT POWER IN PREMODERN SOUTHEAST ASIAN
kingdoms have presented the view from the center, assuming that all power
emanates from the king (Tambiah 1976:108; Lucien Hanks 1962). While these
theories have acknowledged small principalities on the fringes of kingdoms,
the power of these small entities has been described as weak. In explaining
how power and politics work, theorists have focused on the king, his
entourage, and his appointees; tiny principalities distant from the king have
been considered unimportant.

During the nineteenth century, the state of Sipsongpanna (renamed
Xishuangbanna by the Chinese in the 1950s), the Shan States of Burma, and
the Lanna States north of Siam (later part of Thailand) were all small Tai
border polities participating in some form of what scholars have called galac-

tic polities. In this conceptual understanding, the king's power radiates from a center and diminishes with distance from the monarch, like the light of a candle (Steinberg 1987:60; Tambiah 1976:123). The capital city of the kingdom, such as Bangkok in Siam, is the center, where the king resides. Circling the capital are provinces under princes or governors appointed by the king. Beyond the provinces, at a greater distance from the king, are "independent 'tributary' polities" over whom the king holds "indirect overlordship" (Tambiah 1976:112–13). The image is not of a bureaucracy with descending ranks; rather, each succeeding ring outside the capital replicates tributary relations with smaller entities. Not only princes, but also independent tributary polities, might be surrounded by chiefs paying them tribute. Sipsongpanna, the Shan States, and the Lanna States would qualify as independent tributary polities.

To keep hold of the center, the king needs to accumulate resources and distribute them to those dependent on him. His power rests on this exchange of people and goods. The king could enhance his wealth and influence by increasing the available labor of serfs and slaves (Steinberg 1987:64; Reid 1988:122; Leach 1960:59). Kings would lead armies to raid other polities, including mountain peripheries, to bring back captives. The king could then allocate serfs and slaves to nobles, a gesture that both distributed resources and kept that labor power on tap. When needed, the king could demand corvée labor and troops from among the captives he had acquired and allocated (Kemp 1992; Reid 1988:132; Wyatt 1984:71). The impulse to increase his arena of influence also pushes the king to claim new tributary states, often demanding submission from small states and chiefdoms that are already paying tribute to other overlords (Thongchai 1994:81–88). In practice, power relations are highly mutable and contingent, with overlapping claims on tributary states, and clients on the fringes proclaiming loyalty to multiple overlords.

In this hierarchical system, if the king is at the top, with the greatest resources, the one on the bottom is in the forest, "an uncouth hunter, deserted by his wife and children," a person no one would depend on (Lucien Hanks 1962:250). In this depiction, the hunter in the forest is at the remotest edge of the galactic polity, but is still configured in relation to it. In another formulation, again gazing from the center, "the tribal people wandering in the mountain forests [are] subjects of no power" (Thongchai 1994:73). Here the tribal people are envisaged as outside the limits of the galactic polity, and also beyond the king's reach.

Another set of people linked in central imaginations with peripheral forests has been Buddhist monks, who renounce the world to live as forest recluses. Certain monks, through spiritual prowess and endurance, take on some of the wildness of woods and beasts in an alternate form of power: "the monk not only subdues the tiger by the nonviolent power of his Dhamma and metta, he also demonstrates thereby that he has incorporated, subordinated, and encompassed within him the powers of the wild beast" (Tambiah 1984:89). Through discipline, the monk is able to protect villagers and others from the tiger. Through his action and compassion, the monk gives "civilized" people both protection from and access to the power of the "uncivilized" and "wild."

These portrayals represent views of power from the capital.[1] The first construction, concerning a king's influence, is simple, with clear locations for powerful/powerless or civilized/wild. In the second construction, concerning Buddhist monks, the wild is seen as imbued with an alternate kind of power. In the first case, in both theoretical and sacred terms, the king holds the greatest power, and those at the greatest distance from the king, in the forest, have no power and are outside the hierarchy of protection. Additionally, princes and nobles, such as Tai rulers in the valleys, accumulate power; those on the periphery, such as hill people who are not Tai, are powerless.

A review of nineteenth-century relations between peripheral Tai principalities and hill peoples complicates this portrayal of power and tribute relations considerably. During that time the princes in the Lanna States related to hill peoples in a variety of ways, many of which involved collecting tribute or taxes. In 1855, the prince in Chiang Mai (the strongest principality among the Lanna States) signed a treaty with a Lua community stipulating that taxes be paid in silver in place of tribute in ironwares (Renard 1980:143). Accounts of the Shan States in Burma portray Tai princes who extracted tribute and corvée labor from both lowland and upland farmers (Hill 1998:47; Leach 1960:59; 1954). Clearly these hill communities were accustomed to participating in tributary relationships.

The Lanna States themselves meanwhile paid tribute to several overlords at the same time, a form of power relations scholars have called "multiple sovereignty" (Thongchai 1994:96). Indeed there were numerous small *muang* (governed area) between Lanna and the kingdoms in Burma that paid tribute to many overlords.[2] In the view from the center, small powers paid tribute to larger ones to receive protection from a benevolent king or overlord. The view from the periphery was different. Since the overlord could demand labor, troops, and money at will, small entities sometimes paid tribute to more than one overlord, to be able to play one lord against another (Thongchai 1994:83). In some cases, small principalities or chiefdoms were forced to become tributaries of kingdoms, rather than having sought out protection voluntarily. In such cases, small princes or chiefs would seek ways to protect themselves from rapacious "protectors" with a mafia-like style of extracting tribute. Small principalities could also use tribute to ward off an attack. When Qing soldiers attacked Sipsongpanna in the early eighteenth century, the Tai principalities of Chiang Mai and Kengtung[3] quickly sent gifts to the Qing court to prevent an invasion (Giersch 1998:92).

SMALL BORDER POLITIES AND THE CONSTITUTION OF BORDERS

Before the twentieth century, small princes and chiefs in the interstices between major kingdoms both paid tribute to larger kingdoms and tried to keep them at bay. Like kings, princes accumulated resources and controlled their distribution among clients. Princes collected grain and other products as well as corvée labor from people under their rule. In addition to sending tribute to kings, princes in border reaches maintained ritual and kin links in many directions, sending tribute to various larger and smaller entities to secure alliance. The source of their influence, in fact, derived from relationships in multiple directions, through paying tribute, maintaining alliances, and connecting with kin through blood or marriage. These networks of patronage and allegiance in fact constituted the border frontiers between larger kingdoms and empires.

Among small border polities, the authority to rule derived from the ability to gather and control access to resources. In the small Tai polities, the lord or chief accumulated resources in the form of clients as well as wealth. His influence was located in relationships of submission, protection, and extraction. Control over clients brought control over labor, taxes, and tribute. As in larger Southeast Asian kingdoms, political clout was manifested in control over people and their labor rather than in control over territory.

Relations with other small principalities and chiefdoms also involved expressions of submission or exchange, but the meaning of those rituals was often ambivalent or multivalent. Relative strength among small principalities, like the might of kingdoms, could shift quickly, or be differently interpreted by different actors.

The case of Sipsongpanna varies somewhat from other Tai polities, since Sipsongpanna related to China, an empire that operated differently than a Southeast Asian kingdom. Sipsongpanna had been a small principality of

Tai people since 1183, with a *caw phaendin* (overlord), the same title as the prince in Chiang Mai. The lord of Sipsongpanna became enfoeffed the emperor of China beginning in the thirteenth century, following Kublai Khan's conquest of Yunnan (Hill 1998:67). As was customary, the lord of Sipsongpanna paid tribute to the emperor and received gifts of greater value in return. The emperor also legitimated each successive lord (Hill 1998:67). Under the Ming dynasty (1368–1644), the emperor of China appointed the lord of Sipsongpanna as a pacification officer (*tusi*). Along the southwest border of the empire, the governor in Kunming appointed local rulers or chiefs, often non-Han people, to keep order in regions adjacent to areas administered by Han (Giersch 1998:57; Hill 1998:21). The *tusi* and their territories became a buffer (*fanli*) along the southwestern edges of the empire (Giersch 1998:72). The position of pacification officer in Sipsongpanna was inherited from the *caw phaendin* and lasted until after 1949 (Giersch 1998:45; Hill 1998:78).

Yunnan was incorporated into China during the Yuan dynasty (1279–1368). Since Sipsongpanna, a small principality in the south of Yunnan, was both a tributary of China as well as a site of pacification under a *tusi*, it was in a client relationship to China, much in the same way that Lanna States paid tribute to Bangkok. In the eighteenth and nineteenth centuries, however, both Sipsongpanna and the Lanna States were also paying tribute to the kingdom of Burma.

Beginning in the sixteenth century, the Burmese king appointed the lord in Sipsongpanna as a *saw-bwa* (prince) the same title as princes in the Shan States (Giersch 1998:50). In the nineteenth century, the king in Burma further recognized the lord of Sipsongpanna as a *dhammaraja*, a "provider of political and moral order" as a Buddhist ruler (Hill 1998:77). During the nineteenth and early twentieth centuries, Sipsongpanna's relations with Burma were more significant than those with China, since the Burmese kingdom, like Sipsongpanna, was a Buddhist realm (Hill 1998:77).[4]

religion
codifying
identity &
therefore
national
loyalty

Borders and Relative Territoriality

In the conceptual galactic polity, the king's merit and resources reside in the people he claims as clients, including both nobles and the serfs and slaves allocated to them. The system is often described as embodying wealth in people rather than in land or territory (see Feeny 1989). In Siam certainly the king's wealth was measured by the labor at his command, and nobles were ranked by the number of clients allocated to them by the king (Wyatt

1984:73; Vandergeest and Peluso 1995:393). To say that the system was not territorial is true in that power was not measured in territory conquered or areas of land under the sway of the king. But control over labor allowed nobles and the king to use the land to produce rice. The king and the lords gained access to the land's productivity through control over labor.[5] While wealth was measured in labor power, the survival of the kingdom also rested on the wet-rice fields worked by that labor.

Tribute relations in imperial China, which certainly bear a family resemblance to the tributary aspects of galactic polities, were conceptually based on an understanding, expounded by the court, that the emperor of China was the ruler of "all under heaven," meaning everyone everywhere. Other kingdoms in what is now East Asia, as well as kingdoms in Southeast Asia, paid tribute to the emperor of China and received gifts of greater value in return. Siam was one of the kingdoms paying tribute to China, whether to show respect or to keep China pacified. Thais today refer to the tribute Siam used to pay to China as a "profit-making enterprise," since the Chinese emperor sent more valuable gifts in return that people in the Siamese court could sell (Thongchai 1994:87). Even though the records of exchanges of gifts are detailed, the meaning of those exchanges was multivalent and shifting. As the power of kings and lords waxed and waned, and as relations among kings became closer or more distant, the meaning of the same gifts would change accordingly.

Chinese imperial rule, however, did show elements of territoriality, or interest in control over territory, not fully present in Southeast Asian galactic polities. Territoriality, according to Robert Sack, "is a powerful geographic strategy to control people and things by controlling area" (1986:5). States exert territoriality by delimiting and classifying spaces and the kinds of activities that are allowed in them. In Sack's view, there are degrees and scales of territoriality. For modern nation-states, territoriality is a technology of power that enables state agencies to define, bound, and control space through anonymous and therefore naturalized means, such as fences, signs, and regulations. The controller of behavior becomes impersonal—"the state," as distinct from local officials.

For officials in late imperial China, the imposition of control was not through signs, fences, and regulations, but rather through the measurement of agricultural plots and the collection of taxes. Magnus Fiskesjö (1999:154) argues that rule in imperial China was effected through categorizing and identifying people, such as various barbarian groups, as well as defining the purpose of these various peoples in relation to state rule. In Yunnan during times of imperial rule and to some extent continuing up to 1997, control over territory and people went hand in hand. Classification of land areas and peoples were related, with lowland Han farmers linked materially and symbolically to wet-rice fields, while barbarian peoples were imagined as either hunter-gatherers or as shifting cultivators, in either case lacking in the efficiency and cultural achievement of lowland Han farmers. Additionally, actual control of peoples and their land uses was often negotiated in face-to-face contacts. Policies might be impersonal, deriving from some distant imperial source. Regional officials or local heads, however, carried out actual implementation, thereby strengthening their own position as controllers of access to land and its uses.

The appointment of *tusi* in frontier areas instituted, in principle, control of local people and territory as a means to keep the border safe. Chinese imperial officers did not delineate clear territorial boundaries, but rather put in place forts and tributary chiefs, indicating that "the frontier of China is here," actions with as much symbolic as political value. Neither the occasional territorial ambitions of imperial China, nor the expansions of galactic polities, reflected an aspiration for legal, territorial entities with precisely delimited borders such as evolved in the West.

Boundaries under Tributary and Territorial States

Southeast Asian kingdoms had flexible boundaries depending on the influence of the center (Tambiah 1976:123). Although the court thought sites distant from the king, or even distant from the prince, were unimportant, frontier areas were "zones of mutual interest" (Leach 1960:50) among regional kingdoms. Kings could agree explicitly to arrangements of multiple sovereignty, as King Chulalongkorn advised the prince in Chiang Mai to do as late as the 1880s concerning the northern town of Chiang Saen. He recommended that "Chiang Mai should allow the Shan [from Burma] to settle there if Burma and Kengtung allowed Chiang Saen to submit to both sides" (Thongchai 1994:98). Rather than worrying about boundaries, the "political sphere could be mapped only by power relationships, not by territorial integrity" (79).

By contrast, the Qing court in Beijing did not condone multiple sovereignty. If Sipsongpanna paid tribute to China, it was part of the empire (Giersch 1998:238). Consonant with Chinese imperial expressions of territoriality, rulers in Beijing were interested in control of an area as well as the submission of people. Imperial officials in Yunnan found, as noted above, that the lord in Sipsongpanna paid tribute to Burma as well as to the emperor in Beijing (Giersch 1998:72; Hill 1998). Extending imperial control over the territory of Sipsongpanna meant negotiating with the overlord and his subordinates. As agreed, Sipsongpanna would pay tribute to the Chinese emperor and would serve as a buffer zone on the southwestern flanks of the empire, but Sipsongpanna continued to pay tribute to Burma until 1885 (Giersch 1998:50). Sipsongpanna played an ambiguous dual role as it constituted the border, a "zone of mutual interest" for both China and Burma.

MODERN BORDERS: NEW SMALL BORDER POLITIES

The imposition of national boundaries by the modernizing states of China and Thailand bisected political relations among small border principalities and chiefdoms, although the international borders by no means severed strong tributary and kinship relations. The demarcated borders, of course, represented the limits of the nation-states, new entities that intended to extend sovereignty to their borders. Ideologically, the nation-state is a territorial entity occupied by citizens loyal to the nation. Nationalism, citizenship, and boundaries are linked together in the territorialized nation and its sovereignty, represented by Thongchai (1994) as the "geo-body."

How political relations based on tribute and submission or power relations of multiple sovereignty evolved into a mapped configuration of distinct nation-states constitutes a fair share of the political history of China, Burma, and Thailand over the past century. World maps now show a set of separate political entities distinguished by boundaries that have become familiar, both to citizens of these nations and to scholars of Asia. Although the territorial nation-state was expected to displace and replace the small tributary states in the interstices between larger kingdoms, small border polities, in some instances, have persisted or reappeared. In fact, the processes of state building in these border regions, together with international efforts to combat the drug trade and communism, have reworked and reinforced certain small border chiefs and their patronage relations, ensuring their salience into the late twentieth century.

Looking at how imperial China and the kingdom of Siam envisaged boundaries helps explain the particular accommodations to bounded nation-states that ensued along the Chinese and Thai borders with Burma. Designating clear and permanent boundaries is similar to instituting a new system of property rights. Instead of replacing the old system, a new regime can "add possibilities of manipulation and confusion between the multiple opportunities, and conflicting constraints, of older and newer . . . regimes" (Shipton and Goheen 1992:316). Along the edges of China and Thailand, clear, unambiguous borders added to the layers of practices in power relations among border entities and between these entities and their sovereign states.

The Mountain Region under International Focus

As the two kingdoms of Siam and Burma and the Chinese empire developed gradually into nation-states, with state claims to the territory within delineated boundaries, the mountain people found themselves enmeshed within national spaces and projects in China, Burma, and Thailand. Despite new borders, people in this region still had relatives and trade relationships across this span of forested ridges. To some extent, upland people have continued to migrate, to open swiddens and to raise livestock, and to trade in valued goods throughout this region, no matter which state claimed it. However, certain forces unleashed by state building and the geopolitical conflict between capitalism and communism in this region reshaped local social relations, reconfigured land use, and gave rise to massive increases in the production of opium and heroin.

People migrating through the border region in question included not only Tai and various hill peoples, but also Han villagers escaping wars and oppression (Hill 1998:15). Another group moving through this region, beginning in the 1930s, was the Chinese Nationalist army of Chiang Kai-shek, armed soldiers who were the by-product of state-building processes. These Nationalist troops fled China following their loss to the Communists in 1949 in the war that decided the political-economic system and ideology to be adopted by the Chinese nation-state. Many of the Nationalist troops fleeing Yunnan spent ten years among the ethnic groups who were fighting the government in Burma and then escaped again into northern Thailand in 1960. A separate group of people drawn to this region by the Communist victory in China, and by potential Communist success in Laos and Vietnam, were agents of the U.S. Central Intelligence Agency (CIA), sent to shore up the anticommunist forces. Although not migrants through the region, agents were distributed through much of the Shan State and across northern Thailand. While the CIA may have seen its role as part of the international struggle between communism and democracy, its agents became involved in several dynamics: the violent struggle of numerous ethnic groups for independence from Burma, the Nationalist transition to a mercenary force, and the dependence of every political or military group in the region on opium, and later heroin, to finance its ambitions (Lintner 1994:239–71; McCoy 1972:126–45). In the aftermath of World War II, this region became an arena of political-economic turbulence in which various new groups set up small political entities, complete with rulers and local clients.

Regional Migrations: Akha, Nationalist Troops, and the CIA

There is more than one story among Akha people as to where they originated, although everyone agrees that it was in China.[6] Most Akha, however, cite their original home as the Yuanjiang area in northern Yunnan, where some people known to the Chinese as Hani still live. Many Akha tell stories of a kingdom in Yuanjiang and of a clever leader who was forced to flee by more powerful enemies. An Akha scholar in Jinghong estimates that Akha have been in Xishuangbanna for more than twenty generations and that they were the last of the Akha to leave Yuanjiang (Gao He, pers. comm. 1995).[7]

Akha villagers in various sites in Xishuangbanna say that they and their ancestors have lived in their current hamlets anywhere from 15 to 250 years. While some villagers have been forced to move by state policy in the past 30 years, other groups have migrated to seek better conditions for upland rice or to leave a site of misfortune, such as grave sickness or natural disaster. Groups usually did not move far. The Muslim Rebellion in Yunnan Province (1855–73) drove large numbers of people, including Han, Akha, and other hill peoples, into the Shan States of Burma.[8] Two members of the French Mekong Exploration Commission (1866–68), which traveled from Cambodia north to Yunnan, reported widespread devastation in rural areas of southern Yunnan, with whole villages burned by the rebels and their inhabitants gone (Garnier 1996:109; de Carne 1995:214). Ongoing turmoil in the Shan States, especially in the period since 1948, has forced many hill people, as well as Shan and Han villagers, to push onward into Thailand.

In 1937, Japanese armed forces invaded eastern China. As a result, Chiang Kai-shek retreated from Nanjing in the east to Chongqing in the southwest, where he drew substantial financial and military support from the British and the Americans. He represented for the Allies the last stand of "Free China" against both the Japanese and the Communists under Mao Zedong. Also in 1937 Chiang Kai-shek sent Nationalist soldiers to Yunnan to protect China from possible Japanese invasion from Burma. Following the end of World War II in 1945, with the Japanese gone, the Nationalists then concentrated on fighting the Communist armed forces, to whom they lost in 1949. Chiang Kai-shek and most of his army then fled to Taiwan. For the defeated Nationalists in Yunnan, the obvious escape was into Burma. Whereas once they had been part of a national army fighting to control their homeland, in Burma they gradually evolved into mercenary troops. Taiwan maintained an affiliation with them, but the soldiers also had a strong interest in establishing their own financial and political base in the fractious hills of northeast Burma.

Akha in Xianfeng hamlet in China, adjacent to the Burma border, say that two Nationalist armed companies were posted nearby in 1937. At that time Sipsongpanna was still a Tai principality. These two companies, as well as others at different sites along the border, were deployed in Sipsongpanna to protect China's southern border from Japanese invasion. In Xianfeng, Chiang Kai-shek's soldiers confiscated the locals' grain and livestock and forced Akha villagers to carry grain, bombs, and bullets for them. The Nationalist soldiers encouraged gambling and increased the cultivation of opium. From 1937 until 1950, the Nationalists also kept Akha as forced laborers to produce grain. The soldiers' role in a "national" project legitimated their demand for local labor and products.

Elsewhere in China, starting in 1945, Nationalist and Communist forces were engaged in the civil war that ended in Communist victory in 1949. Older Akha say that many of the Nationalist soldiers posted in Mengsong (the village that encompasses Xianfeng hamlet) did not want to leave, even after Chiang Kai-shek had fled to Taiwan. Soldiers had taken local "wives" and, by 1950, had children. The Nationalists also had opium trade links both in the Sipsongpanna valley and in Burma. These two companies were already operating somewhat independently, as a small border entity engaged in regional trade. As soldiers, they could effectively rule a small border enclave, extracting labor and grain by force. In 1950, however, two divisions of Communist forces converged on Mengsong to drive out the Nationalists. Villagers say that the fighting lasted a couple of hours one evening, and when they woke up the next morning, Mengsong was full of "black Han."[9] To this day, older Akha in Mengsong refer to this time as salvation from the Nationalists, whom they had hated.

The Communist troops stayed on in Mengsong, and by keeping the Nationalists out, brought in a period of calm during which villagers could again begin to farm upland rice and to "live like human beings." This history is important for two reasons. First, the Nationalist invasion of Sipsongpanna and the posting of several companies of troops there for thirteen years served to make what had been a Tai principality and tributary state into a part of China. When the Communist forces routed the Nationalists, the integration was complete. The name was changed to Xishuangbanna and the area became a Dai autonomous prefecture within Yunnan Province.[10] Second, the wretchedness of Akha life under the Nationalists ensured that villagers would welcome the Communist guerrillas as liberators from the worst direct oppression they had ever known. Nationalist virtual enslavement of Akha villagers paved the way for the Communists. When, in the early 1950s, the Communist soldiers brought stability, as well as grain rations and extra blankets, older Akha men and women said it was easy to distinguish "who was good and who was bad."

The Communist cadres eradicated opium cultivation by 1954 and posted military troops in Mengsong to keep the Nationalists and opium out. Villagers involved in the opium trade, such as moneylenders and wealthier households, lost their main source of income when opium was eliminated, and many of them fled to Burma with the departing Nationalist troops. Since the Nationalist troops had expanded opium production in Mengsong, Communist eradication of opium represented a means to break villagers' connections with the Nationalists. Ending opium cultivation also marked the beginning of a new Communist regime committed to moral probity. The posting of Communist forces in Mengsong also established a firm border, enclosing Mengsong and its inhabitants within the People's Republic of China.

Following their expulsion from China, the Nationalist soldiers settled immediately across the border in Burma. Military headquarters in Taiwan, as well as agents of the CIA, ordered the Nationalist troops to stay put and to remain ready for an invasion to retake China (Lintner 1994:101; McCoy 1972:126). The Nationalist soldiers had meanwhile arrived in an area of Burma that was highly contested on a number of axes. Newly independent in 1948, the government of Burma wanted to bring the northeast under state control. The Shan State (so-called after Burmese independence[11]) was inhabited by numerous ethnic groups, some of whom, like the Kachin and the Karen, had sided with the Allies in World War II, helping General Joseph Stillwell build the Burma Road that was to extend from Kunming across northern Burma to Assam in India (Lintner 1994). Much of the rest of Burma had initially sided with the Japanese, whose troops occupied lower Burma. Members of the Communist Party of Burma, an aboveground political group until 1948, had also sided with the Allies and had then retreated to the Shan States when they went underground. The Shan themselves had been neutral during the war and were leaning toward joining the Union of Burma, but they wanted a guarantee of their own autonomy within their own state. With the assassination of Aung San in 1947, the founder of independent Burma was gone, as well as the one person with the combined trust of the communists, the army, the Burmans, and the ethnic groups in the Shan States (Lintner 1994:xiv, xv, 71; Hall 1960).[12] The northeast plunged into a civil war that continued through the late twentieth century. The military force of Burma, representing the government in Rangoon, tried numerous times to bring the Shan State under central control. Various ethnic rebel armies, some supported by the Nationalists and Thailand, others supported by the Communist Parties of Burma and China, fought against government troops and sometimes against each other (Lintner 1994). The Nationalists, then, had withdrawn from China into a war zone, but with their military strength and connections with the drug trade it was an arena in which they were able to flourish.

In the Shan State, the Nationalists, with funding and directives from the United States and other governments, organized small polities based on the "protection" of local inhabitants and the collection of locally produced goods. As in China, the Nationalists had the backing of larger entities with strong ideological goals. Nationalist troops took over Shan principalities, sometimes by force (McCoy 1972:131; Lintner 1994:94). They extracted the opium and grain produced by local farmers, and they engaged in the opium trade that had already been running for several decades. The Nationalists linked up almost immediately with experienced Han traders who transported opium from Yunnan Province in China through Burma to the Thai border, giving the Nationalists a base of financial support (Lintner 1994:94). The Chinese soldiers set up headquarters in Mong Hsat, where the CIA began to drop arms shipments (95, 99). The Thai government was also staunchly anticommunist, and by 1953, the Thai state and the CIA were both sending military supplies to Mong Hsat. In return, the Nationalists sent mule caravans of opium from Burma into Thailand. Nationalist generals in Burma expanded the area planted in poppies and introduced an opium tax, formalizing their authority as heads of small polities (116–17). Opium had in fact become the currency of the mountain region. As it passed through Thailand, the sale of opium was also an income source for some Thai politicians and members of the police (McCoy 1972:127; Lintner 1994:116, 184). These trade links in Thailand ensured that certain highly placed Thais had an ongoing interest in drug production and political chaos in the Shan State.

The Burmese government, meanwhile, wanted the Nationalists out of

Burma, since the Burmese authorities saw the Nationalists as an independent army impeding integration of the Shan State into the new nation. Initially the Burmese army was not strong enough to force the Nationalists out. The government of Burma had maintained ties with the new Chinese government, and following years of negotiation, in 1960 established a slightly revised boundary between China and Burma. During the meetings to celebrate the agreement, the Burmese government secretly agreed that the Chinese People's Liberation Army (PLA) could enter Burma to chase out the Nationalists (Lintner 1994:165).

In 1961, three PLA divisions, some twenty thousand troops, moved into Burma from Xishuangbanna to oust the Nationalists. In the ensuing battles the Nationalists lost control of northeastern Burma (Lintner 1994:165). While many Nationalist soldiers were evacuated to Taiwan in Taiwanese and U.S. helicopters, and a few hundred troops remained in Burma, some six thousand soldiers escaped across the border into Thailand (Bo 1987:101).

One Nationalist general and his troops settled in Mae Salong in Thailand, close to the Burma border. Thirty soldiers moved to the Akha hamlet of Akhapu, where they lived for several years. While the Thai government had supported the Nationalists in Burma as a bulwark against communism, Thai leaders were less enthusiastic about armed troops from another country settled on Thai soil (Lintner 1994; Bo 1987:101–2). In the event, the Nationalist soldiers were allowed to stay, but only in the northern uplands, to serve as border guardians. Like hill tribes, and unlike other Chinese historically in Siam, they could not become citizens of Thailand. Former Nationalist soldiers continued their involvement in the drug trade from Burma to Thailand, often in collaboration with the Thai police (Lintner 1994:184; McCoy 1972:127). The former soldiers took on a role both protecting the border and enabling illegal drugs to cross it, serving to maintain the border and to transgress it.

Once they left China, Nationalist troops were no longer a legitimate national army, but rather the armed remnants of a failed attempt to take over China. While they continued to receive military support from Taiwan, where the rest of the Nationalist government and army had fled, the Nationalist troops in Burma were distant from their ostensible superiors and largely independent. Nationalist officers extracted opium and grain from local clients, much as lords had done in the past, but without the gloss of voluntary tribute. If there had been no international support, these soldiers escaped from China would have been bit players in the Shan State drama. Nationalist operations, however, were bolstered by the CIA and the governments of Taiwan and Thailand and lauded (quietly, since this was a secret operation) as being on the front lines in the international battle between democracy and communism. The legitimation for the Nationalists in the Shan State arose from their defending an ideology and economic system that the United States, Taiwan, and Thailand perceived to be the side of the angels in the Cold War. The Nationalists, operating like thugs in extracting labor, grain, and opium from local farmers, and expanding the opium trade, had meanwhile taken on an important twentieth-century role as "defenders of freedom." The coercive nature of their rule catalyzed the operation of small border polities in the Shan State, where every group was armed and every group of whatever political stripe came to depend on opium to support their activities. Their modality of rule, however, followed long practice in the region of extracting products from local people in return for protection.

4

SMALL BORDER CHIEFS
AND RESOURCE CONTROL,
1910 TO 1997

I'm off to collect taxes!
AKHEU, in military garb, as he waved his rifle
from his truck (Mengsong, China)

I could move to Burma and become Khun Sa II.
LAWJAW (Akhapu, Thailand)

THE NARRATIVES BELOW TRACE THE HISTORY OF VILLAGE HEADS IN
Mengsong and Akhapu from the early twentieth century through 1997, when
my field research ended. Many of these village heads and other influential
ethnic minority persons on the China and Thailand borders made use of
the events and processes coalescing in their locales to position themselves
as regionally important people and controllers of local resource access.

The most detailed stories concern Akheu and Lawjaw, the most recent
village heads in Mengsong and Akhapu settlement respectively.[1] The
accounts reveal the similarities in their operating modes as well as the
marked differences in context between China and Thailand. Both men were
born into a leading clan in a village an hour's walk from the Burma border. Both also took advantage of policy changes, development opportunities, and the appearance of new kinds of actors in the regional and local
milieus to turn themselves into patrons with resources at their command
and favors to dispense. And both also drew on the reworked patronage relations that emerged in Burma in the 1950s and 1960s and spilled across the
border. New opportunities allowed these two men to enhance their con-

trol over local resource access and to increase their own coffers, much as princes had done in the past. Through multiple connections on both sides of the border and shrewd maneuvering among available opportunities, both village heads managed to constitute the border as well as to enable transgressions across it.

SMALL BORDER CHIEFS AND THE CONTROL *I skipped* OF RESOURCE ACCESS IN CHINA

Akheu, the current administrative village head, rented me a room when I moved to Mengsong. This was one among four available small rooms, each with a wooden bed and a small table, where government officials and tea traders stayed during their visits. He later moved me to his daughter's room while she was at boarding school in Damenglong. The daughter's room was a floor above the others, with a bank of windows overlooking the Mengsong plain. The daughter had an elaborate sound system for karaoke which I used to listen to music tapes. I was the first foreigner allowed to stay in Mengsong to do field research. Akheu could claim me as a favorable and (perhaps) highly ranked client, one who occasionally returned with tribute in foreign liquor. He had mediated this chance for villagers to tell their stories.

Village Heads in Mengsong under a Small Border Principality, circa 1910 to 1950

Based on the genealogies of the two clans who arrived first, the earliest Akha settled in Mengsong about 250 years ago. Over the centuries these clans had intermarried and their descendants were still dominant in the leadership of the area. Older villagers knew that Akha used to pay head taxes and owe corvée labor to the Tai principality in Jinghong, which ruled Sipsongpanna (later called Xishuangbanna) from 1183 until 1949. Villagers said that the Tai had a military force and their own tax collectors, who came up for taxes three times a year. Households had to pay one, two, or three coins each time. The value of the coins is not specified, but reference to them shows that taxation per head was consistent and regular. None of the older informants thought the taxes had been exorbitant. Akha in Mengsong also owed corvée labor, which amounted to opening and repairing a road from the valley of Sipsongpanna through the mountains to the Shan States, with which the Tai polity was closely linked. This road had been a major route in the drug trade.

Early in the twentieth century, Tai officials from Jinghong started appointing the local headman in Mengsong, a process linked to Han promotion of the tea trade in Sipsongpanna (see Hill 1998). Older villagers think that Sadyeu, the Akha head in Mengsong from circa 1910 until his death in 1930, was the first to be called by a Tai title and to wear the red hat anointing him with the lowest rank in Tai administration. The Tai selected Sadyeu because he could speak their language—a multilingual local figure. Since the 1949 revolution, Chinese schools in Yunnan have taught that Akha and other hill groups were slaves of the Tai until Liberation, as the Communist revolution is called in Chinese. This narrative conforms to the 1950s Marxist (or Stalinist) classification of the Tai principality as at a slave mode of production. When current Akha villagers talked about the era under the Tai lord, they said that the exactions were not very heavy—moderate taxes and labor once a year. Perhaps this characterization of Tai/Akha relations benefited from comparison with the Nationalists, whose relations with Akha in Mengsong were clearly far more exploitative. Before the arrival of the Nationalists in 1937, Mengsong Akha were clients of a small border lord in the Tai principality of Sipsongpanna. To gain use of their swidden lands, however, which were all in an area at a lower elevation than their villages, Akha in Mengsong had to offer liquor each year to the head of the Bulang village near the fields.[2] The swiddens were in the Bulang bailiwick, but a bottle of homemade alcohol ensured continued Akha access to this land. This example of tribute shows that to consider Sipsongpanna as the sole recipient of tribute and taxes is too simple—access to resources might have involved multiple scales of gifts and reciprocal relationships.

Akha in Mengsong related many stories about their own leaders, among whom the most strict and feared was Sadyeu. Sadyeu would not let anyone who smoked opium live in Mengsong, not even his own brother. Sadyeu insisted that everyone work hard, and he prohibited other kinds of Akha from moving into Mengsong, thereby limiting access to local land.[3] Accounts told in the 1990s indicate that many local people planted opium in the 1920s and that it grew very well. Villagers smiled a little as they demonstrated with their fingers how big the poppies used to be. These stories suggest that Sadyeu encouraged trade in opium, while trying to prohibit consumption. The opium trade linked these mountain farmers in networks extending into Burma and mainland China.

Sadyeu died suddenly in 1930. In his place the Tai in Damenglong appointed Reisa, an Akha who then headed Mengsong from 1930 to 1957, through the Nationalist period, the Communist revolution, and up to the collective period.[4] In the 1930s, Reisa allowed Uqie Akha from Burma and elsewhere in Sipsongpanna to move into Mengsong, an area until then restricted to Udo Akha. Uqie joined other hamlets in Mengsong and also established the hamlet now called Dongfanghong.[5] These newly arrived Akha were traders and moneylenders, heavily involved in the opium trade.

In 1937 Nationalists troops arrived in Mengsong. In patterns reminiscent of the forced labor imposed by government forces on hill groups in Burma today, the Nationalist soldiers organized all villagers aged fourteen and older into teams to carry grain, bombs, and bullets for them in rotating shifts. Those shouldering loads took them from Mansan, at about 1,000 meters in elevation on the China side, over the ridge at 1,600 meters and down to a village in Burma. Some of the Akha men were forced to open trenches along the ridge with Burma, to protect China in case Japanese troops arrived from the south. World War II and the presence of Chinese troops established the national border between China and Burma more firmly than Tai or Akha practices had in the past. Nationalist soldiers also extracted grain and opium from Mengsong villagers, in patterns that would be replicated in the Burmese Shan State following Nationalist flight from China in 1950. Some Akha were opium traders, working closely with the Nationalists in cross-border trade. The increasing trade in opium led to enrichment for these villagers. Other villagers fell into debt trying to buy opium, and when they could not repay, they suffered serious losses. Growing disparities in income as well as the trade with the Shan States disappeared with the arrival of the Communist regime in 1950.

Village Heads during the Post-Revolution and Collective Periods, 1950 to 1982

Following the revolution and Communist takeover of Mengsong, the policy during the 1950s was for Chinese cadres to work with traditional leaders in minority nationality communities in instituting the new regime. Thus Reisa was head of Mengsong up to 1957, and in Xianfeng hamlet, my research site within Mengsong, the hamlet head also continued until 1957. The socialist approach to controlling land use moved forward in stages. Villagers resumed their former patterns of cultivation, now paying taxes to the Chinese instead of to the Tai. Major changes in the management of land and units of administration began in 1957, as collectives, and then communes, were organized in Xishuangbanna. At this point, the socialist state appointed new people to serve as Mengsong and hamlet heads, based on their revolutionary zeal. Akha and other villagers were now included in the Chinese state under the same legal system and form of administration as other villagers throughout China. Links across the border were no longer relevant.

During the collective period (1958–82), the heads of Mengsong and of its hamlets had to be approved by higher levels of administration. While a Tai, based on national state policy for an autonomous area, would have headed the government office in Damenglong, that person was to represent the Communist Party rather than the former principality of Sipsongpanna. As such, appointed heads in Mengsong now had to be Communist Party members and, during the Cultural Revolution (1966–76), villagers had to attend nightly meetings where they were called upon to criticize each other according to revolutionary criteria. For example, the clans that customarily held leadership positions in the past were removed from power and castigated as "counterrevolutionary" elements. In at least one case, a household accused of being "rich peasants" had to exchange houses with a poor household. The rich household also had work points docked for several years.[6] Others who were criticized during this time included households who had moved to Burma for a while and then returned, men who had more than one wife, and anyone who smoked opium. Those who had gone to Burma were suspected of being in league with the Nationalists and were therefore traitors to the revolution and the new Chinese nation-state. Cross-border connections had become dangerous.

Particularly during the early days of the Cultural Revolution, party cadres watched everyone's behavior closely. The hamlet head at the time, a man who was still alive during my stay, was once jailed for three days because children had been caught eating fruit they had picked. No one was supposed to eat anything other than what was prepared in a communal kitchen, and the hamlet head was blamed for all deviation. On the other hand, even though many policies and pronouncements came from above and simply had to be implemented, the hamlet head also sometimes broke the rules. A woman confided that the hamlet head had bought a red cloth for her to wrap her father's body for burial according to Akha custom. This was also during the early Cultural Revolution, when any such "superstitious" practice could have gotten both the village head and the woman in trouble.

Another episode from this era reflects direct confrontation between a hamlet head and cadres from outside. Chinese cadres told Akha villagers in the late 1960s that they would have to build Han-style brick apartment buildings on the ground, instead of their "primitive" wood and thatch houses built on stilts. The hamlet head, with the concurrence of all villagers at that time, simply refused. He pointed out that they kept animals under their houses and used materials from the nearby forest for construction. Building with bricks made no sense. The Chinese cadres finally had to defer, but said villagers should build smaller houses than before, since all labor was needed to produce grain for national goals.

During the collective period, the role of village and hamlet heads was largely to organize labor to carry out commands from above (*shangmian*), usually from the commune level in Damenglong. [7] Akha heads were not involved in local resource control or cross-border activities. The issue of grain production was a point of conflict among villagers in Mengsong. During the late 1960s, and again in the late 1970s, national policies emphasized grain production and local self-sufficiency in grain. State procurement quotas rose at the same time, however, putting local villages in a squeeze (Xu 1990). The amount of grain available locally was chronically too little. The Xianfeng accountant in the 1970s was able to encourage and prod people to open new wet-rice fields in the valley near the Burma border. When this accountant died during my stay, Xianfeng villagers truly mourned his passing, saying that their survival through the 1970s had depended, in no small measure, on his forcefulness in getting the wet-rice fields going. As of the late 1990s, this accountant represented the model socialist leader, working hard for everyone's benefit—increasing available resources and distributing them equitably.

Village Heads during Economic Reforms, 1982 to 1997

During the period of economic reforms, communes were broken apart. The township government, previously the commune, reconfigured groups of hamlets into administrative villages under heads elected by villagers from a slate of candidates drawn up by the township. Since this reorganization there have been two administrative village heads in Mengsong. The first was described as a selfless leader, a person of true socialist values, who procured state funding and organized the labor to install running-water systems for all hamlets in Mengsong. The second, a former People's Liberation Army (PLA) member, became a small border chief and patron of local resources.

The PLA had been a steady presence in Mengsong since 1950. Initially troops were posted on the border to keep the Nationalist soldiers from returning. During the 1950s, since the Nationalists were just across the border in Burma, the military post in Mengsong remained fairly important to the Chinese government. The people's militia person[8] for Xianfeng in the late 1950s took part in the Chinese invasion into Burma in 1960. He pointed out that once the Nationalists were gone, Akha could go back and forth across the border safely. Before that, traveling across the border meant stepping into a war zone between the Communist forces and the Nationalists.

The military post established in 1950 remained in Mengsong, however, to prevent both the Nationalists' return and local villagers' resumption of growing and trading opium. In 1972, a rebel army hostile to China was based right across the border in Burma. During the Cultural Revolution, the former people's militia person for Xianfeng said that villagers were no longer allowed to leave China for Burma. Local people were arrested during that time, both for trying to escape to Burma and for resisting other political instructions. His job as head of security was to watch over them. Villagers said that in the late 1970s, once the Cultural Revolution was over, the government of China made a formal appeal to those who had fled, telling them it was safe to return. One man in Xianfeng came back in 1978, following fifteen years in Burma, including a stint in one of the ethnic rebel armies.

The Shan State in Burma was still unsettled in the 1990s and the location of rebel armies kept shifting. There were villages immediately across the border where people grew opium. The military post in Mengsong was still in place. The squadron of soldiers was relatively small, but the post patrolled comings and goings across the border.

From the beginning, the Communist guerrillas in Yunnan, who later became part of the PLA, had recruited minority nationality members. This was an important component of including all residents in building the new China. Older Akha in Mengsong reported that when the Communist guerrillas first arrived in 1950, there were Akha among the soldiers. "We had breakfast with them, and they could talk with us" local people said. Since the early days of the People's Republic, Akha have been able to join the army, an important arm of the central state. For Akha, joining the army has become one pathway to advancement in Yunnan and also within Mengsong itself.[9]

The head of the administrative village of Mengsong while I lived there, Akheu, had joined the PLA in 1974 as a path for social and political advancement. From 1974 to 1978, he was posted as a communications officer in Burma, just across the border from Mengsong. In 1978, he returned to Mengsong as the security officer for the Mengsong production brigade, the level of administration that later became the administrative village. This man spoke fluent standard Mandarin (a rarity for anyone without a high school education), as well as Yunnanese Mandarin and Akha—a multilingual border head. In an emergency measure, Akheu was appointed village head by leaders in the Damenglong township in 1993, when the former administrative village head died suddenly. Township officials at this point included Tai, Han, and some Akha. A number of Akheu's relatives had headed Mengsong in the past. Leading clans tend to stay leading clans, in spite of the aberration of the Cultural Revolution, when they were vilified.[10]

Beginning in 1982 with the opening of economic reforms, and gathering steam since then, national policies implemented in Yunnan and Xishuangbanna have encouraged local people to plant cash crops, wet rice, economic trees (fruit trees), and to market their produce. The administrative village head participated in this transition with particular flair, since his many contacts included business people in Burma and in the Damenglong valley. In addition, since Mengsong was right on the border, and the site of a military post, Xishuangbanna invested more development money in Mengsong than in districts in the Damenglong valley only twenty kilometers away. Akheu was in the right place to take advantage of his contacts and the development projects coming his way.

Although Akheu came from a leading clan, that qualification alone would not have assured his appointment to his present position. His enlistment in the military, and his position in Burma, enabled him to make contacts with village heads, government officials, business people, and the Burmese military. His subsequent appointment as security officer for Mengsong widened his contacts on the China side among state officials and entrepreneurs (sometimes the same people) at the township, county, and prefecture levels. Before becoming administrative village head, Akheu had cultivated a wide network of people from whom he could ask favors. As an important local-level administrator, he was then able to gather and distribute resources to an array of people within and beyond Mengsong. Consonant with the mode of operation of a small border chief, he gathered connections that increased his ability to accumulate and distribute resources, making himself into a regional patron. His practices also fell within the Chinese practice of developing *guanxi* (connections), the means to getting things done in China.

By the time of my research, Akheu's military experience in Burma allowed him to argue with Chinese leaders that he was "in the know" and particularly well qualified to defend the border. He exuded the aura of someone who could handle things in multiple languages and multiple contexts. These were qualities needed for an important post along the border, since most Han officials spoke only Chinese. Akheu was using his ethnicity and his cross-border experience to set himself up as the guardian of the border. When he provided township and county officials with information from

Burma, or wild game that was illegal to hunt on the China side, he also served as an informal conduit for goods across that border.

In another form of resource control, Akheu found ways to use his formal government position, together with his informal network of connections on both sides of the border, to control local people's access to resources. In a context where personal relationships represented channels of access to influence and information, as well as to material goods, "resources" included not only land, trees, water, and capital, but also access to state agents and business people, in this case in both China and Burma.

Early in the period of economic reforms, state cadres had allocated commune land to households and hamlets for contracts of up to fifty years.[11] For villagers, these property rights seemed relatively set, even though villagers traded pieces of land among themselves and manipulated land-use regulations. As reforms deepened and markets expanded, however, more and more natural resources were becoming commodities. What became commodities and who benefited were sites of serious conflict in Mengsong.

Three ventures in particular illustrate Akheu's attempts to control the commodification process and local people's access to newly valued resources. They also illustrate ways in which people in Xianfeng hamlet have contested Akheu's attempts to insert himself as the local patron controlling the distribution of resources. These stories depict a relationship between state agents and villagers that is distinctly different from the form of state surveillance during the Cultural Revolution. The stories represent conflicts over resource access, appropriate Akha development, and villagers' relationship with the state.

Whose Tin Is This? In 1985 the Geology Office of Xishuangbanna sent a geological survey team to Mengsong to assess the availability and quality of tin there. The team found abundant tin in two places, one of them in a section of Xianfeng's wet-rice fields. In the paddies and extending up into the small streams feeding into these fields, the survey team found tin right on or near the surface.[12] The team started mining, and shortly thereafter hired twenty young men from Xianfeng to mine the tin for them at 10 yuan per day (about US$2 per day at that time). The young men were excited, thinking their status had been changed from peasants to workers, a considerable jump in the social order in China. Villagers also thought that the geological survey team was mining the tin to serve some national purpose for China.

Within a couple of months, however, villagers discovered that the members of the geological survey team were simply selling the tin for their own income. Villagers were furious and enlisted the help of Akheu, the security officer, to oust the survey team. At this point Akheu, in return for his help, claimed the tin as a resource belonging to the whole administrative village. He declared that anyone within the eleven-hamlet area of Mengsong could mine the tin. In a second step, Akheu and two of his colleagues formed a company at the administrative village level to receive the tin. While anyone could mine the tin, everyone had to sell their tin to his company for 12 yuan per kilo. To say "company" conjures up a private enterprise, but in China at that time a company had to belong to a government unit, in this case the administrative village. Additionally, since the administrative village head had stronger ties with government officials than hamlet heads did, Akheu could force villagers to comply with his company's demands. Akheu and his friends ran the company for their own benefit, but a certain percentage of the profit from selling the tin in Jinghong was to be invested back into Mengsong. Shuosan, the administrative village accountant, said that the company ran for four years, and the figures never came out right. Akheu and his cronies allegedly managed to skim off 100,000 yuan (about US$20,000) that should have gone to Mengsong.

Villagers in Xianfeng were particularly upset about the tin arrangement, since the mining was destroying their wet-rice fields and Akheu and his company were getting the profit.[13] Akheu's company folded in 1992 as he moved on to more lucrative enterprises.[14] At that point, Xianfeng villagers claimed the tin for themselves, mined on their own, and sold the tin to companies in Jinghong. In 1994, Xianfeng leaders signed a contract with the police administration in Jinghong, another business venture involving a unit of government.[15] In return for a share of the profits, the police administration would invest the funds to buy pumps as the mining dug deeper into the fields.

Akheu canceled the contract between Xianfeng and the police administration to prevent Xianfeng villagers from garnering the profit themselves. He was able to do this based on his connection with government officials and his claim to represent the whole administrative village of Mengsong. In response, villagers pooled funds to buy or rent their own pumps and continued to mine as fast as they could. At this point, villagers did not have approval from any level of government to mine tin in their wet-rice fields, but they argued that if they did not mine someone else would. Their fields would be ruined in any case, and villagers wanted the income. In 1997, tin was the single largest source of household income in Xianfeng.[16]

The nature of the conflict over the tin raises several points. In his role as security officer, Akheu claimed the tin as a resource belonging to Mengsong rather than to any individual hamlet. Xianfeng villagers considered this to be using the "official" imprimatur to justify what amounted to personal gain. They also suspected that the security officer's connections in the Damenglong township were involved in the business deal and had agreed to back him up. They thought that Akheu's cross-border connections and occasional delivery of illicit goods strengthened his position with township officials. Because villagers perceived Akheu's handling of the tin as corrupt, the head of Xianfeng took this case to the township, county, and prefecture governments. He also complained, in part, to protect himself. He was aware that mining in the wet-rice fields violated land-use regulations. He wanted administrators above him to understand the Xianfeng viewpoint on the tin conflict, and why villagers continued to mine.

This incident also illustrates villagers' experience of the transition to a socialist market economy. Villagers at first thought the geology team mined tin for national purposes, an instance of a planned economy. They soon realized the geologists were making money. Adjusting to the new possibility, villagers wanted to mine tin themselves. The security officer, Akheu, claimed the tin as belonging to the lowest level of state administration, the administrative village. But again, "state agents," in the form of Akheu and his friends, got involved in tin to make money. Xianfeng villagers argued that the land where the tin was discovered, and therefore the tin, was theirs, and if someone was to make money, it should be them. The lines between public/private and state/personal had become fuzzy, shifting, and contested in new ways, as it became possible to market more and more locally produced goods. Akheu, as security officer and later as administrative village head, redefined the role of Mengsong government to include profit making. Villagers meanwhile reconfigured themselves as entrepreneurs determined to claim the newly valued tin as belonging to them.

Villagers argued that the land in Xianfeng and the tin were theirs. This claim was based both on the length of their experience in the area (250 years), in what amounts to a customary claim, as well as on legal ownership of their land. The wet-rice fields had been allocated to them by the state in 1982–83. At that point, the state was the owner of all land and the government distributed it to various levels of administration for management. In 1987, collectives (hamlet administration) in China became the legal owners of the land where they were located (Zuo 1997:3). By the late 1990s, villagers' sense was that they had historical as well as legal rights to the tin. They also saw the tin mining as an instance of development, or as the marketing of a local resource that increased the income of almost every household. The local expression of a socialist market economy had accommodated the administrative village head's exploitation, as well as villagers' desire to have more cash.

The tin story shows how Akheu claimed a new resource and controlled local access to it. He managed to do this by inserting himself as the patron collecting the resource and benefiting from its sale. He backed up these actions with his many government connections, undergirded by his aura as border protector for the state.

The Wasteland Auction. In the early 1990s, to speed up the pace of reforestation, the Yunnan Forestry Department implemented the wasteland auction policy, allowing villages to auction areas of village wasteland, either to local residents or to outsiders, for contracts up to ninety-nine years.[17] Buyers were to maintain the purchased plot in trees and prevent soil erosion. The policy allowed for the privatization of lands previously allocated to collectives. In the past, degraded uplands had been allocated free to hamlets for collective use. The uses were multiple and overlapping, with unclear boundaries between degraded lands and other pieces of forest. Now individuals could effectively buy measured parcels of wasteland for planting trees—a single use. The boundaries, owners, and users were all clarified in an intensification of state territorialization. The auctions actually changed formal property rights, opening up a new means for claiming land, and a new site of conflict.

When I visited Mengsong in the spring of 1996, numerous villagers, including Shuosan, the Mengsong accountant, were angry about the wasteland auction that had occurred in the watershed above the Mengsong reservoir. At their urging I hiked up to take a look and came back with dramatic photographs of a large denuded slope leading down to the reservoir (fig. 8).

A former hamlet head in Guanming, one of the hamlets in Mengsong, had privately gone to the administrative village head and to the forestry station in Damenglong to buy 2,900 *mu* (about 193 hectares) of land under the wasteland auction policy. The land in question had brushy ground cover, but few trees. The administrative village head signed the papers, and the township forestry station accepted them, since the papers stipulated that the buyer had the agreement of all villagers in the affected area. Once it came out that the former hamlet head and Akheu, the head of Mengsong, had operated in secret, the forestry station still claimed that the deal was already done. Once again, villagers sensed that township-level administrators were in Akheu's pocket as a result of his role in border protection and his gifts to them from across the border.

FIG. 8. The wasteland auction in Mengsong

There was a storm of protest. Villagers had several reasons to complain about this action, not least that it was done without their knowledge. Villagers from all the hamlets in Mengsong contributed labor to construct the reservoir from 1970 to 1979. The reservoir allowed a large plain in the middle of the hamlets to be used for wet rice. Water from the reservoir flowed through a generator that provided electricity for all the hamlets daily from 6:30 to 8:30 in the morning and from 6:00 P.M. to midnight. Additionally, several hamlets had running-water systems that were hooked up to the reservoir. The reservoir was a communal resource for many services, as well as an embodiment of collective labor—an achievement that, from the villagers' perspective, now represented positive socialist values, the pooling of labor to take care of everyone.

Economic development in China, as articulated in state policies, had two strands: one concerned with poverty alleviation and the extension of benefits to poor villagers, and the other encouraging household production for the market on an individualistic, competitive basis. The auction of land in the reservoir's watershed resulted in a local conflict that pitted these two strands against each other.[18]

Villagers worried that the wasteland auction was enabling one person to claim a lot of land and to enrich himself. They saw this as an instance of development in which resources would be accumulated in a few people's hands—the opposite of their understanding of poverty alleviation. They also pointed out those land uses that would now be excluded—herding livestock, collecting fuelwood, picking mushrooms—multiple and overlapping uses enjoyed by many in Mengsong in the past. In their place, one man would plant fruit trees for personal gain, a greatly simplified landscape.

On the bare slopes, the former hamlet head intended to plant corn for two years, followed by walnut, pear, and peach trees. Proceeds from the sales of these products would be his. His argument to the forestry station was that he would plant economic trees in this former wasteland of brushy stuff, turning useless land into an economic resource. His logic was couched in the terms of development, where resources are to be used efficiently to create wealth.

The wasteland auction policy was implemented to encourage reforestation and soil conservation, but was articulated in the terms of economic efficiency so as to attract entrepreneurs. The former hamlet head claimed that he was reforesting. According to villagers, the forests above the reservoir had been allowed to regenerate since 1970, when work on the reservoir began. In some places regrowth had been brushy, but it was sufficient to prevent erosion and to regulate water flow into the reservoir. Villagers claimed that the denuded slopes were causing erosion that now funneled silt into the reservoir instead. In their view, the local wasteland auction was causing, not preventing, serious erosion.

Shuosan and several of the hamlet heads in Mengsong had approached township, county, and prefecture administrators to express their strong disapproval of this wasteland auction. As I left in early March 1997, the issue was to come before the People's Congress in Jinghong for discussion. Villagers' protests contributed to the eventual demise of the wasteland auction policy, but the former hamlet head still owns the land.

Many villagers believed that Akheu should never have agreed to the auction and suggested that he must be benefiting personally, although they could not pinpoint how. The reservoir was Mengsong property, created by their long years of labor. It had become emblematic of socialist values that villagers were now nostalgic for, as well as representing the strand of development emphasizing poverty alleviation. Villagers expressed grave concern over the strand of development supporting individual gain, since they perceived this as a predatory aspect of development, an opportunity for those in power to profit at others' expense. The reservoir provided numerous benefits to all the hamlets there, and villagers thought it should be protected. On this issue, the head of Xianfeng indicated that he had told administrators at several levels that he thought the administrative village head should be removed from office. "How can it be legal to destroy our watershed?" he asked.

When Akha villagers in Xianfeng told this story, "Akha values" and "socialist values" had merged for them. They presented themselves as always having taken care of everyone in the hamlet, often through projects that required communal labor, such as building roads and ditches. While other stories suggest that this had not always been the case, in this instance villagers had mobilized around notions of community that were at odds with Akheu's plans. Villagers described their own "true Akha" values in contrast to the "socialist market" or "individualistic" values of Akheu and the former hamlet head, although of course these two were also Akha. While the former hamlet head appealed to the strand of development favoring individual competition, he and Akheu had clearly violated the intended terms of the wasteland auction policy, under which all villagers were supposed to agree to the sale. The stories told by different actors appealed to differing audiences, as property rights were contested through narratives about community, morality, and a desired future.

In this case, wasteland auctions made it possible for an individual to buy land owned and managed by a village collective. Land itself became commodified in a dramatic new way, one that the former village head exploited with Akheu's assistance. Akheu had also controlled how state territorialization of forestland played out in Mengsong. Although Akheu may not have benefited directly from this transaction, the wasteland auction enhanced his role as a patron controlling access to new resources. He got away with this ostensibly illegal action in part because wasteland auctions were seen as protecting the environment. He was the man on the spot implementing government conservation policy. He also succeeded in part because of his carefully tended relations with township officials. His management of the border and offerings of illegally procured venison had done their job.

The Lodge: The lodge appeared in the spring of 1997. Akheu, the head of Mengsong, mobilized the men in his own hamlet to cut the trees needed to build a huge guesthouse. Up to that time, most visitors, including increasing numbers of tourists, stayed in the guest rooms below Akheu's main house. But there were only four rooms, and Akheu thought guests needed better accommodations. The builders used customary Akha construction methods to make a guesthouse that looked like a large Akha house (fig. 9). Then Akheu painted the outside trim red, blue, green, and orange. Local onlookers derided the outcome, saying that Akheu had created a monstrosity. Villagers also suspected that although Mengsong labor and trees went into the construction, the income from the lodge would flow into Akheu's hands.

The construction of the lodge can be put in context by comparison with another building put up at the same time. The teachers in the school in Mengsong had for several years lived in a Han-style brick building with a row of small apartments. Ten years before, the teachers in the school had all been Han sent by administrators in Jinghong. By 1997, however, all were Akha. These teachers hated the brick housing, saying it was dank and cold. In February 1997, they had the brick structure taken down and in its place built a large, Akha-style house with rooms for each of them and a common kitchen around a large central porch. They added large windows (which Akha homes normally do not have) and a set of wide stairs going up to their second-story rooms.

Other villagers liked this house, even with the added windows and room divisions. Their complaint about the lodge was that with its colorful trim, it seemed like a Han imitation of an Akha lodge. There were plenty of imitation Tai lodges in Jinghong that many villagers had seen. They knew what

FIG. 9. The lodge in Mengsong (Akheu in foreground)

a Han imitation of a minority nationality building was like. The accusation seemed to be that Akheu was catering to Han taste in unnecessary ways. The villagers objected not to change, but to the implications of the administrative village head's style. The new teachers' house seemed, for them, an assertion of Akha identity, while the new lodge seemed an assertion of Akheu's greed.

The commodity in question here was partly the lodge itself and partly the development of tourism. Akheu was mobilizing hamlet trees and labor to build a structure that would increase the flow of visitors and add to his own wealth. He was also using "Akha"-ness, as well as Mengsong's border location, to develop the area in ways that made other villagers uneasy. Farmers in Mengsong had strong feelings about ways in which development should unfold. The colorful lodge was not one of them.

Akheu had been born into a leading clan in Mengsong and learned as a child how to operate as a member of a locally influential family. In addition to this, however, Akheu had managed to take advantage of the streams of change converging on Mengsong, as any small border chief would do. He joined the PLA and made good use of his time posted in Burma to establish many connections. Within the military itself, he knew many people, and he managed to perfect his standard Mandarin. As development opportunities arose in Mengsong, Akheu took full advantage of them, such as setting up a company to profit from the local tin.

This head of Mengsong also benefited from the presence of the military post. Although originally involved in protecting China from the Nationalists and from opium, the military operation, by the time I arrived, was largely a source of business contacts for possible ventures throughout Yunnan. Soldiers were frequently involved in enterprises on the side. Akheu used this proximity to the military post and strong connections to the military to raise his own visibility and to create opportunities for economic gain, mainly for himself and his family.

For the benefit of local and regional government staff, Akheu portrayed himself as keeping local villagers in line, herding "wild" Akha in the border lands. In the epigraph at the beginning of this chapter, Akheu was striking off with his rifle to collect taxes. As I learned over time, this pose was for visiting state officials. Few villagers in Mengsong resisted paying taxes, and they were unimpressed by Akheu's rifle. Far from being wild border Akha, they were trying to insert themselves, more firmly in some ways, as good citizens of the state.

Largely because local villagers perceived Akheu's style as corrupt and self-serving, there was considerable opposition to and contestation of his leadership. In part because of his own activities, such as building an "Akha" lodge, local people expressed their mistrust of him by saying he was not true to Akha customs and interests. Villagers claimed he was "in league" with corrupt government officials in Damenglong, or with his many business partners, in activities that undermined the well-being of Mengsong. By presenting their argument in this way, villagers established themselves as a group representing true Akha values, in contrast to the administrative village head's selling out to the Han. At other moments, Xianfeng villagers construed the conflict as between socialist (selfless) and socialist market economy (selfish) values. In stating their case to township, county, and prefecture officials, however, the Xianfeng hamlet head used the language of modernity and development, arguing that the administrative village head was exploiting villagers unfairly, hindering the spread of development to all villagers and contributing to environmental degradation. Heads of individual hamlets had learned the terms needed to express their concerns effectively to wider levels of government headed by Tai and Han administrators, through long contact with these people. Villagers participated in the drive for development, but wished it would play out differently than the administrative village head's plans.

Villagers were also asserting their citizenship in China and legal property rights in resources. In contention with a predatory small border chief, they preferred to rely on the government of China as the source of membership and resource access. As we will see in chapter 6, ordinary villagers, both men and women, manipulated state regulations and used the border in numerous ways to increase their access to an array of resources. Like Akheu, they were border people, as well as citizens, an ambiguous role that they exploited in their own ways. In contention with Akheu over new resources and opportunities, however, villagers claimed their inclusion in China and allied with the state version of resource control. Hamlet heads insisted on speaking to state agents themselves, without the intervention of a patron.

The Constitution of the Border—China

In the nineteenth and early twentieth centuries, Sipsongpanna served, on the one hand, as a "zone of mutual interest" to the Chinese empire and the kingdom in Burma, and on the other hand, as an entity in itself, a governed area (*muang*) that amounted to a small principality. For the Qing, Sipsongpanna was a buffer on its fringes, but a buffer ruled by lords who were supposed to be loyal to the emperor. For the king in Burma, Sipsongpanna was a Buddhist client state, a tributary that added to the king's luster and merit. Viewed as an entity in itself, Sipsongpanna varied from a relatively strong principality to a "loose confederation of lords" (Hill 1998:76), but was a Tai Buddhist domain. Its relative independence, in fact, derived from its paying tribute to both China and Burma and to its network of connections with other Tai border principalities.

At least at some points, hill people in Sipsongpanna paid taxes and owed corvée labor to the principality's court in Jinghong. Villagers wanting to escape a rapacious patron could flee to another lord. They did not cross delineated borders to escape from oppression, but moved from one patron to another. In a region where tributary relations linked political entities, there were no idyllic sites where villages were totally autonomous, and from available evidence it seems that a savvy village head might have wanted to affiliate with a lord to avoid being attacked.

In the twentieth century, as China, Burma, and Thailand demarcated territorial boundaries, the border regions were frequent sites of conflict and even violence. In a number of instances, the border was constituted by enemy armed forces on either side. For example, the border between Sipsongpanna and Burma became not only a national but also an international site of confrontation during World War II, as Nationalist troops arrayed themselves on the China side to repulse Japanese forces from the south. Following the 1949 revolution, the Communist forces were posted on the China side to keep the Nationalists out.

Some Akha in Mengsong followed the Nationalists into Burma, either as political allies or to continue as traders in opium and other goods. Akha who settled across the border then became enemies, in the state's definition, to those Akha who remained in Mengsong. The border in some cases split families down the middle. Up to the Cultural Revolution in 1966, Akha could move across the border if they chose. From 1966 to 1976, however, the border was closed and more intensely politicized, both by national policy and by the military and security personnel who enforced the hardening of the border. Villagers caught fleeing were shot.

Since 1976, alongside the gradual opening up of markets in China has come a softening of the border, and indeed the 1990s witnessed significant Chinese business and investment in the Shan State. Chinese renminbi became the currency used well within Burma. As the state with the more robust economy, China allowed its minority nationality citizens to cross into Burma without a passport or other permission. This easing of restrictions also reflected the official position of valuing minority nationalities in China and respecting their cultural differences. Akha could visit family members across the border to join in Akha festivals, participate in agricultural labor exchange, and to engage in petty trade. Akha from Burma could also cross the border, and they frequently visited the market in Mengsong.

The administrative village head in Mengsong also crossed the border, but he visited a different set of people than ordinary villagers did. As a government official, Akheu met with government and military leaders, and he might discuss business deals or development projects with appropriate contacts in Burma. His connections in Burma had more political, economic, and even military clout than did the farmers whom most Akha went to see. In this sense, the administrative village head crossed a different kind of border and returned with a different set of connections than villagers did. Also, Akheu drove across the border in his own truck, while villagers invariably walked.[19] Over the past fifty years, while national policies determined the porosity or hardness of the border, local social relations created the meaning of the border for Akha in Mengsong, although that meaning varied with political position and with the nature of the business conducted on the other side.

SMALL BORDER CHIEFS AND THE CONTROL OF RESOURCE ACCESS IN THAILAND

When I arrived in Akhapu, Lawjaw sent for me. The village head had already received from Chiang Mai University a letter asking him to allow me to stay and to keep me from harm. He agreed and invited me to live in a separate room in his house. His was a large Thai-style concrete house with divided rooms. Conveniently enough, my room was right next to the roofed-over platform where villagers held meetings. Villagers at first thought I was an anthropologist interested in Akha rituals. I persisted in asking about their history and their land use. I went with them to their fields and asked about their use of trees. Gradually people opened up to me, this foreign woman who spoke Chinese with an Akha translator. Slowly I was able to explore the village with Lawjaw's blessing.

Akhapu is the oldest Akha village in Thailand. When first established, Akhapu had the blessing of a Shan prince in Burma, who named the village and gave the village head the title of *pusaen*, which means "leader of one hundred thousand" (Hanks and Hanks 1999:111–12).[20] There is no evidence that these early settlers owed taxes or corvée labor to the Shan prince, although it is possible that the first *pusaen* sent tribute from time to time. Owing to eminence derived from first arrival in a frontier area, heads of Akhapu continued to be influential: "Though lacking formal authority to compel . . . , the first Akha to arrive (1910) manifested considerable influence for decades" (Hanks and Hanks 2001:110).[21] For many years after its founding, Akhapu continued to be oriented toward the Shan States rather than toward the lowlands of Siam. By the 1960s, the center of gravity shifted toward Thailand.

For Akha village heads in twentieth-century Thailand, means of extending control over local resource access were similar in some ways to those in China. Village heads tended to connect up with any influential people or organizations located in or moving through the region. But there was a major difference in the nature of the important groups with whom village heads could form links. In China, these groups were all part of the state—political cadres, military troops, even local enterprises. In Thailand, by contrast, a state agent represented only one kind of important player in controlling resource use, and at times not the most important.

Another difference between the two countries was the dynamics of state involvement in appointing local leaders. In China, the state appointed administrative village and hamlet heads by 1956, making sure that the appointees were Communist Party members who would carry out state directives. In Thailand, the state appointed a hill tribe representative in the 1960s for the far northern frontier, and for the past thirty years the state's arrangement with respect to hill tribes has amounted to indirect rule. These contrasting state approaches to dealing with mountain ethnic minority people helped determine the extent to which Akha village heads could gain a toehold as small border chiefs on the fringes of China and Thailand.

The Chiang Rai hinterland, part of the former Lanna States, has a long history of being claimed by stronger entities, including princes in Chiang Mai, rulers in Burma, and courts in Laos. Even as late as the 1970s, this part of northern Thailand was claimed by Khun Sa, the drug lord from Burma, as his domain. Local heads were patrons to their village clients, and that style of operation reflected not only the array of small border entities in the Shan State, but also the history of border lords in their relationships with larger kingdoms. Through the 1980s and 1990s, state agents actually participated in the production and strengthening of small border chiefs, those who had positioned themselves to protect the border and provide access to people and goods from the other side.

The Nationalists in Thailand, 1961 to 1997

In the 1950s, Nationalist forces in Burma had configured themselves as armed chiefs in the Shan State, taking over principalities by force, collecting opium and grain from small farmers, and defending their drug operations with military might. Once they moved into northern Thailand in 1961, the Nationalists set up headquarters in Mae Salong. They extracted grain contributions from villagers in return for protection from ethnic rebel armies from Burma on their incursions into Thailand (Hanks and Hanks 2001:165). Although the Thai state forced the Nationalists to remain in the hills, without Thai citizenship, the soldiers became the *de facto* local army, and to some degree the local rulers. Researchers wanting to study hill villages in the area in 1963 had to get permission from General Duan Xiwen in Mae Salong (Hanks and Hanks 2001:xviii).

U.S. Central Intelligence Agency (CIA) agents had worked closely with the Nationalists in Burma since the early 1950s, and by the late 1950s CIA field staff in northern Thailand were linking up with village heads, organizing local militia, and generally mobilizing support in the defense against the spread of communism. In the 1960s, the Nationalists and the CIA continued to collaborate on the Thai frontier.

The Thai government tried unsuccessfully to disarm the Nationalists in 1963 (Bo 1987:121–25). Shifting gears in approach, in 1968 Thai leaders sent the Nationalists to fight against Hmong communist forces in another part of the north. In return for Nationalist soldiers' service to Thailand, their dependents were granted Thai citizenship, and the soldiers themselves were given residency permits (138). The Nationalists also became a paramilitary unit under the Thai military Supreme Command. The Thai state had an incomplete monopoly on the means of violence and, through a mechanism of inclusion, the government tried to incorporate armed rural patrons into their own circles. With state approval, the Nationalist army held greater legitimacy in the hills than did hill peoples who had lived there for decades. Nationalist forces, operating as a small border polity, helped protect the border for Thailand, while at the same time engaging in the opium trade that brought illegal goods across the border.

Village and regional actors in the area surrounding the town of Hin Taek and extending north to the Burma border made use of political, economic, and military events to extend their arena of influence. To some extent, their activities were supported or co-opted by the Thai state. Connections with a variety of patrons on both sides of the border increased these actors' ability to control local resource access. Several patrons, including former Nationalist soldiers and so-called drug lords, played a major role in shaping land use and access to local resources. The state, in its various manifestations in the hills, was only one entity among many in influencing what local resources were valuable and who controlled access to them. To assert government influence, state agents engaged rural elites to control or police their local populations on behalf of the state (Turton 1989:88). Small border chiefs, whose connections included regionally influential people and armed groups on both sides of the border, could make demands as well as concessions in their ongoing negotiations with state administrators.

The Hill Tribe Representative, 1965 to 1997

Yibaw was a young Lisu village head in 1965 when the Thai government appointed him the hill tribe representative for a fifty-four-village area surrounding Hin Taek.[22] The Thai government wanted advice on what these villages needed and where to allocate the funds for roads, agriculture, and medical care. The Hill Tribe Welfare Office selected Yibaw because his influence already extended well beyond his own village. Many hill people credit Yibaw's rise to his mastery of seven languages—Thai, Chinese, Shan, Akha, Lahu, Northern Thai, and Lisu. When I talked with him, Yibaw spoke excellent standard Mandarin, and I knew him by the Chinese name of Liu Yibo. His many languages allowed him to work widely in this multilingual frontier area of the north.

In a related move, CIA agents recruited Yibaw to organize hill villagers into anticommunist militias. In fighting communism, CIA staff in Thailand were collaborating with the Thai police and the Border Patrol Police (Lintner 1994). By 1965, CIA operatives were concerned about communists not only in China, but in Vietnam and Laos as well, fearing the possibility that a communist insurgency would spread into Thailand (Wakin 1992; Bo 1987:81). Convinced that many Hmong villagers in Thailand were supported by communists, CIA staff gave arms to (non-Hmong) village militias to prevent communists from entering village territory. In Mae Kham, where Yibaw lived in 1997, there were still more than one hundred M-16 rifles remaining from earlier CIA distribution.

CIA agents were also worried about people streaming over the border from Burma into the area north of Hin Taek. According to Yibaw, the CIA built airstrips for Pilatus Porters to land along the Burma border to monitor this influx of people. Since some CIA agents were involved in the transport and sale of drugs, the airstrips served other purposes as well (Lintner 1994:191; McCoy 1991:11, 19; 1972:138, 144). By flying in agents who distributed guns and who engaged in transporting and selling opium, the CIA contributed to the proliferation and strengthening of important small chiefs along the border. Although approved by Thai state authorities, CIA agents represented yet another military force and supplier of arms to hill groups who might defend Thailand against communist insurgents.

Yibaw built up a wide array of contacts through his long connection with CIA staff and Nationalist officers, as well as through serving as hill tribe representative for thirty years. Additionally, large amounts of money flowed through his hands to fund both militias for the CIA and development activities for the Thai government. Yibaw took his cut from every transaction, and by the late 1990s he was a wealthy man. Profiting from a patronage role was customary in Thailand at that time (Pasuk and Sungsidh 1994:9–10).

Yibaw's appointment as hill tribe representative was somewhat like the

Qing appointment of local pacification officers (*tusi*) in non-Han areas along the imperial borders. The position ensured Yibaw's loyalty to Thailand and the safety of the border by co-opting his stature as an influential highland leader. Indeed, state appointment increased his arena of contacts among state and business people and bolstered his role as a small border chief, allowing him to enhance his own wealth and his control over the dispersal of resources.

In 1984, the government posted Yibaw to Akhapu to help usher in a large, internationally funded highland development project. Both the project and Yibaw were introduced in Akhapu to make sure that Khun Sa, the "drug lord" who had been chased out of Thailand in 1982, would not return (Khun Sa is discussed below). Quite apart from the highland development project, a few Nationalist soldiers who had earlier lived in Akhapu had come back to start a tea company with financial support from Taiwan.[23] Yibaw and a handful of wealthy Akha were early investors in the tea company, profiting nicely from their earlier patronage of Nationalist soldiers fleeing Burma. The head of the tea operation, an ethnic Chinese with Nationalist sympathies and the Thai name of Tawee, has done even better.

In an attractive reception room at the main tea company, multiple photos show Tawee with various prominent people and groups, including the provincial governor's wife, the Chinese Association in Chiang Rai, and bankers from Mae Chan.[24] Perhaps most importantly, there is a picture of Tawee receiving an award for securing 4,300 votes for members of parliament. Another photo shows Tawee at a temple in Taiwan—initial funding for the tea company came from Taiwanese investors. There is even a photo of Tawee's wife pouring tea for Princess Surindthorn, the Thai king's eldest daughter. Unlike most Nationalist Chinese, Tawee had managed to get a full Thai ID card. Through all his connections, he had established the credentials, including Thai citizenship, to be accepted in Thailand as an important businessman. Through his links in Akhapu, Tawee arranged to rent exceptionally fertile forestland in the community forest and to launch a thriving and lucrative tea business. Tawee was more than a small border chief; he was a "Thai" entrepreneur.

In 1984, Phase Two of the Thai-Australia Highland Agricultural and Social Development Project got under way. The Thai-Australia Project, with World Bank funding, was one of numerous international projects in the north of Thailand to eradicate opium cultivation and to end shifting cultivation by introducing cash crops. Phase One had begun in 1980 but had skipped villages surrounding Hin Taek, including Akhapu, because Khun

Sa had controlled the area at that time. Phase Two encompassed Akhapu within its domain.

Tea seemed like an ideal crop to replace opium in a forested area at high elevation (1,000 meters). As one of the project officers, Yibaw brought agricultural extension agents to Akhapu to teach villagers how to cultivate the tea that was growing wild in their forest.[25] Yibaw extended the benefits of tea cultivation directly to villagers so that they learned to grow a suitable cash crop, but one that was much less lucrative than the tea company tea, known locally as "the boss's tea." Through his role in the highland development project, Yibaw's stature as a patron grew as he brought in not only someone to train people in tea, but also extension agents bearing plum saplings and new varieties of rice. At the same time, Yibaw introduced the Akhapu village head to the intricacies of working with the Thai state.

The Village Head in Akhapu, 1960s to 1997

Lawjaw, Akhapu's current village head, came from a clan whose members had long been village heads. That village elders in the 1960s selected Lawjaw to become head is no surprise. At issue is how this man made use of the events and processes manifested in Akhapu to enhance his position as a small border chief.[26]

When Lawjaw was sixteen, the CIA built an airstrip above Akhapu on the ridge separating Thailand from Burma. The flattened part of the ridge where planes once landed is still visible. Lawjaw used to spend time at a heroin factory just across the border in Burma, where he gambled with Nationalist soldiers and learned to speak Yunnanese Chinese. He sold pigs to the Chinese soldiers and cut fuelwood for them, and he watched when Americans came by to buy heroin.[27] He learned at an early age the value of making connections.

When Lawjaw was twenty (in about 1966), Thai government helicopters landed on the airstrip and confiscated heroin from the factory just over the border where Lawjaw had spent considerable time. After the Thai government raid, the Burmese government landed helicopters on the airstrip, sent out troops, and blew up the factory. Lawjaw learned firsthand that disputes over lucrative and illicit resources could be punctuated by violence.

Beginning in the late 1960s, when Lawjaw became head of Akhapu, he made frequent trips into Burma to see relatives, do business, and to meet more members of the Nationalist/CIA alliance. During these years he was learning the drug trade and operating as a small-scale client of the larger

Nationalist/CIA operation. In Burma he observed how the Nationalists extracted opium and other products from villagers under them and then traded the opium, or later heroin, to finance their small military domains.

Khun Sa, the "Drug Lord," 1960s to 1982

The man who became renowned as Khun Sa was born in the Shan State of Burma of a Han father and a Shan mother. As an adult in the violent and unsettled environment of the Shan State, Khun Sa gathered a group of armed men around him and enlisted them as a government militia unit. Like many heads of militia units in this part of Burma, Khun Sa became a drug merchant, but he was involved in transporting and selling on such a grand scale that he became the most famous drug lord in the Golden Triangle (Lintner 1994:188; Bo 1987:4–5). His armed forces fought with both the Nationalists and the Communist Party of Burma at different times, establishing him as a relatively independent border chief.

In 1969, the Burmese government arrested Khun Sa for high treason and imprisoned him until 1976. When he was finally released, Khun Sa headed immediately for Hin Taek, the town in Thailand just south of Akhapu (Lintner 1994:229). Yibaw, the hill tribe representative, maintained that Khun Sa had built Hin Taek, investing money in the town for more than a decade before he retreated there. Once based in Hin Taek, Khun Sa built heroin refineries and operated his drug business from there. His troops, now expanded and named the Shan United Army, protected an area reputed to be larger than the fifty-four villages in principle overseen by Yibaw. Khun Sa operated like the lord of his own principality, collecting taxes and requiring fees from people to reenter his domain (Bo 1987). According to Lintner (1994:254), Khun Sa's operations were tacitly protected by the Border Patrol Police, since his arrest in Burma had been for supporting a noncommunist leader that the Thai government favored. More significantly, General Kriengsak Chomanand, while premier of Thailand in the late 1970s, made Khun Sa a citizen of Thailand (*Bangkok Post*, December 18, 2001). The Thai state related to Khun Sa as chief of a small border polity, just as he set up his domain like a small lord, reinforcing the "otherness" of this northern space.

While not everyone in the Thai government can have been happy with this arrangement, it was not altered until 1981, when the U.S. government pressured the Thai state to eliminate drug lords within Thailand. Khun Sa was the easiest target and a Thai military force, aided by former Nationalist troops, attacked Hin Taek in 1982 and routed him within two weeks. He fled to Burma, where he reorganized his operations just across the border (Lintner 1994:262).

Villagers recalled that Khun Sa's troops protected them from the rebel armies in Burma and that Khun Sa treated them well. They sold their opium to him and if any household fell on hard times, Khun Sa sent money and help. Villagers from the poorest to the richest said that Khun Sa offered much better patronage and protection than the government of Thailand. His style of patron/client relations played well in the local understanding of what a good ruler should do. From his experience in the Shan State, Khun Sa knew how to operate as a "lord" of a border domain.

Lawjaw's many dealings with Khun Sa included buying jade in Burma to sell for Khun Sa and sharing in the cross-border livestock trade. Khun Sa wanted to make Lawjaw the armed leader of a 240–man Akha militia, but Lawjaw refused, not wanting to be involved with fighting. In 1982, when the Thai military chased Khun Sa out of Hin Taek, he hid out in Lawjaw's home for a week before slipping into Burma. When Thai authorities asked Lawjaw why he had harbored this criminal, Lawjaw replied that Khun Sa had been driven out of his home. How could he not offer hospitality? In 1997, Lawjaw was still in contact with Khun Sa, who now lived in Rangoon. When I asked about Khun Sa, Lawjaw said that Khun Sa had called him the week before to invite him to visit. Whether Khun Sa had really called Lawjaw just then or not, there was no reason to doubt that the village head and Khun Sa were close business partners.

Once Khun Sa was gone, the Thai military governed his former enclave. In a structure similar to elsewhere in Thailand, the military installed a district head and a subdistrict head. At the same time, the military administration appointed Lawjaw as an official village head, or *phuyai ban*, over three hamlets. To represent the Thai government in the village, Lawjaw was also made a Thai citizen. Yibaw took Lawjaw to the district office to get a Thai ID card and initiated him into the intricacies of working with the Thai government.

According to Lawjaw, the whole structure of administration changed to resemble the hierarchy of offices elsewhere in Thailand. Above him were the subdistrict head, the district head, and the governor of Chiang Rai Province. In Lawjaw's view, Yibaw's role diminished as these new people took their positions. Yibaw, as the hill tribe representative, had previously been in charge of everything. Beginning in 1982, he was responsible only for the area's agriculture.[28] Once Lawjaw became an official *phuyai ban*, he met government staff from the Royal Forestry Department (RFD), from the agriculture department, from the planning department, and so on. His style was to establish a convivial relationship with people in official or influential positions, who saw him as someone with the charisma that generates respect.[29]

According to Philip Hirsch (1989:52), the appointment of local leaders as *phuyai ban*, together with the many development projects and enterprises that flow from state-encouraged development, enables village leaders to benefit financially from almost every transaction going into or out of the village. In turn, village heads are pulled into the ambit of wider worlds of economic and political endeavor, and their attention to matters in the village dwindles. What Hirsch does not include in his analysis is the way a border chief like Lawjaw was able to make contacts not only with government staff at various levels, but with other critical purveyors of money and influence: Nationalist soldiers who became residents of Thailand, CIA agents, and business and personal contacts in Burma. Indeed, the village head's friendship with Khun Sa increased his bargaining position with the Thai state. In the 1960s Lawjaw had been a neophyte in the role of patron, but by the 1980s he was well versed in the workings of developing contacts, accumulating resources, and distributing them in ways that increased his influence and control.

In spite of policies in the early 1980s that look like the establishment of direct administration, however, the state was perpetuating indirect rule. Lawjaw was the only one in Akhapu to be made a Thai citizen. His role was to keep order on the border on behalf of the Thai government among peoples who were not citizens (cf. Hart et al. 1989:33; Turton 1989:84). As official village head, Lawjaw was then able to take advantage of events and processes coalescing in Akhapu to increase his control over resources and their distribution.

The advent of the tea company had created an informal land market in Akhapu. Villagers could now use their tea fields as collateral for local loans. Villagers who borrowed money from Lawjaw, but were unable to repay, would yield their tea fields to him. At the same time, wealthy villagers such as Lawjaw could now buy wet-rice fields. Over time, Lawjaw controlled more and more of the surrounding land area, either through purchase or loan defaults. By 1997, Lawjaw owned more than 100 *rai* (about 16 hectares) of wet-rice fields in Akhapu, in an area where other wealthy households might have had 10 *rai* (1.6 hectares) in wet rice. In addition to demonstrating his wealth, these fields also represented critical control of local labor: one-third of villagers share-cropped the village head's wet-rice fields.

timeline of land aquisition system?

what about working to gain land system?

Lawjaw also decided who could move into Akhapu. Households that had recently migrated to Akhapu, most from Burma, invariably knew Lawjaw in advance. He had encouraged them to come and had then sold them land for houses and small gardens. Before 1980, newcomers to Akhapu did not have to buy land. If the village head welcomed them to stay, they could just find an abandoned swidden and use it. But as a result of the informal land market, new arrivals by the mid-1980s had to buy land. By the late 1990s, there was no more land to cultivate around Akhapu. Swidden fields and wet-rice fields were all claimed and the forest understory was planted in tea. Newcomers became Lawjaw's clients, as laborers Lawjaw helped to place in jobs. By the late 1990s, both land and labor had become commodified and Lawjaw was involved in allocating both.

Through his own efforts to amass a network of contacts on both sides of the border, and to accumulate resources that he could dispense, over time Lawjaw established himself as a regionally important small border chief. In the 1990s, two state policies actually strengthened Lawjaw's hand, giving him increased control over access to jobs, land, and security.

In the 1990s, two state policies changed the nature of the village head's role in the village, his status in relation to other villagers, and his control over resource access. Under the first policy, inaugurated in Akhapu in 1990–91, the Public Welfare Department under the Ministry of Interior issued hill tribe ID cards. According to both Akhapu villagers and the Chiang Rai Committee (1994), with a hill tribe ID villagers were not allowed to work outside Chiang Rai Province without permission from the governor. Villagers first had to find a job, get a letter from the employer, and then secure the village head's signature. Then the district head and the governor had to sign. The cumbersome process involved some outlay of money for travel and getting the approvals.

The village head was part of this approval process. Lawjaw was the state representative in Akhapu with a full Thai ID. Through the state's issuance of hill tribe ID cards, the status difference between him and other villagers had been increased and hardened. He not only approved people to work outside the province, but he also served as an excellent source of contacts for villagers looking for work. There were other people from Akhapu working in Bangkok and Chiang Mai who could recruit villagers to join them, but the Lawjaw was well positioned to take advantage of this recent change in villagers' status relative to his. He could funnel work to his favored relatives and cronies, for instance, while ignoring other villagers' requests for help. In principle, hill tribe IDs could later be exchanged for full citizenship if villagers spoke Thai, had been born in Thailand, and had not been involved in the drug trade. In a sensitive border locale like Akhapu, however, Thai officials were wary of granting citizenship. If anyone qualified, officials would check with the village head to make sure Thai IDs went to the right people. In that case, Lawjaw would be the mediator of access to citizenship as well as to land and jobs.

The second policy that changed Lawjaw's relationship to villagers was the RFD reforestation project in honor of the fiftieth year of the king's reign (1996). Across the north of Thailand, the RFD was in the process of reclaiming all shifting-cultivation land for reforestation. As a result, many villagers were scurrying in various directions to find wage labor, as well as trying to share-crop Lawjaw's wet-rice fields. Poorer households were becoming more dependent on the village head, either for use of his wet-rice land or for help in getting jobs. Lawjaw actually stood to benefit from the reforestation, since other villagers were becoming more reliant on him. As most villagers were losing their shifting-cultivation lands, I discovered that Lawjaw had swidden fields in another particularly fertile area, not subject to reforestation.

In 1996, Akhapu was declared an official village, the only one in Mae Faluang District. The Public Works Department had approved Akhapu for state recognition, in contrast to other villages in which people were officially squatting on government land. One criterion for gaining official status was the absence of heroin users or drug traders. According to villagers, Lawjaw and other leaders actually expelled a few drug users so that Akhapu would qualify. Official villages received electricity and other government services, which Akhapu was in the process of getting in 1996–97. Lawjaw shared with me a highland security military report, which designated which villages were to be moved out. While this kind of plan was always subject to negotiation, both among government departments and with influential village heads like Lawjaw, it was still safe to say that Akhapu now had a greater chance of remaining in place than would a nonofficial village.

According to Lawjaw, in an official village, villagers would be able to keep their wet-rice fields, their tea fields, and any fruit trees that they have planted, but shifting cultivation would not be allowed. As elsewhere, with the reforestation policy any shifting-cultivation fields would revert to the RFD if they had not done so already. I asked Lawjaw what would happen if the government changed its policies and took away more of their land, such as the tea fields. Lawjaw replied that in that case, they could retreat across the border into Burma, and he could become Khun Sa II.

Lawjaw was the first person to tell me that reforestation was slated for all shifting-cultivation land in the region. In six other Akha villages that I visited in the surrounding area, none of the village heads realized that all of their shifting-cultivation land would be taken for reforestation. The RFD had planted trees on about half of their swidden lands, and village heads thought it might stop there. None of these other men were nearly as well connected with state officials as the Akhapu village head. Lawjaw was meanwhile able to persuade, or bribe, RFD officials to exclude his own shifting-cultivation lands from this plan, managing to negotiate how state territorialization played out in Akhapu. This arrangement probably came about in the context of negotiating how Akhapu would become an official village.

Akhapu was favored, largely because of its location on the border and its long history as an important village. Since Akhapu was the site of a CIA airstrip, government drug confiscation, and of Nationalist Chinese residence and entrepreneurial activity, various departments in the government paid close attention to it. In this milieu, the village head maneuvered himself into a central and influential role. By affiliating himself with CIA agents and Nationalist officers, he learned the ropes of operating as a patron in the drug trade. Through connection with Khun Sa, he raised his profile as a cross-border entrepreneur. As a result of these and other dealings, by the early 1980s Lawjaw was exceptionally rich by Akhapu standards. With the arrival of the tea companies, Lawjaw was able to invest in what became a lucrative business. The village head forged his role as a small border chief by his creative use of opportunities. His maneuvering enhanced his local status and control over resources, as well as his leverage for bargaining with the Thai government. Forces that included a defeated national army (the Nationalists), the intelligence agency of the United States, the drug trade and drug lords in Burma, as well as various projects of the Thai government, converged to produce Akhapu as a site of exchange, investment, and economic development. The village head contributed to this process, helping in critical ways to make Akhapu an important border juncture. He had used his knowledge of how to accumulate and distribute resources to make this a favorable location, with the benefits flowing to himself.

In contrast to the vocal, sustained complaints I heard about Akheu, the administrative village head in Mengsong, I heard very little that was negative about Lawjaw. No one complained about how much land Lawjaw owned in Akhapu or about how rich he was in comparison to them. When I asked how Lawjaw had ended up with so much wet-rice land, the response would be something like, "Oh, he is very smart and very active." Additionally, though the electrification that came with being an official village was always "two months away," and did not appear during my stay, locals credited Lawjaw with the development that was taking place in Akhapu.

Villagers were dependent on Lawjaw to an extraordinary degree, since they lacked full Thai ID cards. He was their patron, and a major one. With a hill tribe ID, villagers could not legally own land anywhere, or a house in town. Their hill tribe ID linked them to a particular village and to a particular patron. Villagers could not contact agents of the government to express their own views, unless the village head mediated the discussion.[30] In all, Lawjaw had made himself into the source for the most valuable resources for hill tribe farmers: land, security, jobs, and citizenship.

The Constitution of the Border—Thailand

Since 1910, village heads in Akhapu had derived their authority from their relationship to a *saw-bwa* in the Shan States, connecting the leaders loosely with a small border principality rather than a nation-state. There was no awareness of an international border until World War II, when Thai troops informed villagers that they lived in Thailand and that an imaginary line separated them from Burma. In the 1950s and 1960s, village heads from Akhapu and other hill villages turned to Thai government officials, the subdistrict heads, to perform the premodern ritual of submission, but the officials "treated it jocularly as a barbarian's request" (Hanks and Hanks 1999:161). Thai administrators had stopped performing this kind of ritual in the 1890s, when Bangkok reorganized the government into a modern bureaucracy.

The opening of the CIA airstrip in the late 1950s, together with the arrival of the Nationalists in the early 1960s, recast the border as a line communists might come across. By then the other side also held rebel armies that were fighting the Burmese state and that occasionally made forays into Thailand. Fighting between the rebels and the Burmese army escalated during these years, forcing hill farmers to flee to Thailand in increasing numbers. Again and again, the border was constituted by violence.

Like many borders, this one was a site for contraband trade, but in this case this meant lucrative narcotic drugs on a mammoth scale. The effects of this trade reshaped power relations in Akhapu, as the village head Lawjaw became wealthy through the sale of illicit drugs. At the same time, some villagers grew opium to sell to drug producers in Burma.[31] Once Khun Sa moved into the region, villagers sold their opium to him.

During the Khun Sa era (1976–82), the region surrounding Hin Taek was configured much like a small border principality. As Khun Sa's domain, where he collected taxes and maintained his own military, this region *was* the border, in the premodern sense of a stretch of land extending between the states of Burma and Thailand (Thongchai 1994:74–77).

Once the Thai military had ousted Khun Sa, a highland development project claimed Akhapu within its purview. The project, in fact, allowed the Thai state to extend administration to the region in the same patterns as elsewhere in Thailand. In line with what James Ferguson (1994) describes as an anti-politics machine, a development project such as this one depoliticized increased state control over a rural area. From 1982 onward, this district of Thailand, formerly Khun Sa's domain, came under a state bureaucracy that descended from the provincial governor to the district head, the subdistrict head, and to the village head. The chart of state administrators suggested that sovereignty was reaching to the village level and extending to the border of Thailand. To signify this transformation, the town name of Hin Taek was changed to Toed Thai, which means "the village upholding Thai spirit" (Lintner 1994:262). | but not even Thai people officially

By allocating citizenship and authority to Lawjaw, however, and defining all other villagers as "hill tribe," the state was in effect perpetuating indirect rule. State policies in the 1990s have actually strengthened Lawjaw's role as the controller of resource access in Akhapu, enhancing his position as a small border chief. First the Public Welfare Department issued hill tribe ID cards to villagers, in contrast to the full Thai ID card granted to the village head, creating distinctions in official identity that weakened villagers in relation to the village head. Second, the RFD reforestation project reclaimed villagers' shifting-cultivation land, forcing poorer villagers to rely more heavily on the largesse of the village head for access to land and jobs. In spite of moves to extend the state bureaucracy to the village level, and to territorialize state authority through reforestation, these state policies paradoxically increased the village head's control of important local resources, leaving him more firmly positioned to constitute the border himself.

As a sign of his regional clout, Lawjaw could also expel heroin users from the village, while at the same time continuing his own involvement in the drug trade. For Thai authorities, Lawjaw held a different position in relation to drugs than did villagers, for whom trading heroin would have been a dangerous activity. The village head and Thai official pronouncements could claim drug eradication, while Lawjaw and certain state officials continued to benefit from the narcotics industry.

Lawjaw's network of connections reached both across the border and within Thailand. He could decide how to dispense his considerable resources in multiple directions, as well as who could live in his village. From the state's perspective, hill tribe villagers continued to be "not Thai," and the land available to them was reduced, while the village head was responsible to the state to keep order in the village. Lawjaw was the one who negotiated how Akhapu land was territorialized. Lawjaw's combined connections in Burma and Thailand positioned him as a regional player, able to influence how policies were implemented in Akhapu. He used the border and his connections across it to fix other Akha in the border-as-margin, implemented through his control over resource access.

SMALL BORDER CHIEFS AND RESOURCE CONTROL IN CHINA AND THAILAND

In considering the role and spectrum of small border political entities, it is important to note their prominence in a frontier area with a history of small principalities ruled by lords whose strength derived from alliances and patronage relations in multiple directions, as well as from extraction of local goods and labor. From the 1950s onward, all small border polities in China, Thailand, and Burma relied on local villagers to provide grain and sometimes opium in return for some kind of protection. Like border lords before them, small border chiefs derived their clout by maneuvering among larger and smaller political entities, playing them against each other and negotiating for operating room. Over time, small border "chiefs" have ranged from Tai princes with an administration and a military force, to Nationalist officers who coerced services and goods from local villagers, to Khun Sa and his drug-producing domains, to Akha village heads with cross-border connections and the ability to control local resource access. In all cases, alliances across borders, as well as the role of protecting local clients, helped constitute small border chiefs as guardians of the border. Following the sharp delineation of borders around nation-states, small border chiefs in Mengsong and Akhapu presented themselves as defenders of the border for the home state while also enabling transgressions across it. In different ways in China and Thailand, state officials have benefited from either condoning or supporting small border chiefs in this role.

The Nationalist army was the catalytic agent in reworking small border political entities across the region. In China, Nationalist soldiers operated on behalf of Chiang Kai-shek, who claimed to rule a new nation-state, and were hence a manifestation of a modern political goal. In practice, however, Nationalist soldiers behaved like armed bullies in extracting labor, grain, and opium from local farmers. In Burma, international political and military support, particularly from the United States, heightened the role of the Nationalists as the front line in the regional war between democracy and communism. In addition to expropriating villagers' products and labor, the soldiers participated in the escalation of drug production and its trade. Although the Nationalists were by no means the only actors in this drama of drugs and violence, their activities increased the scale of military and narcotic operations. *not dwelled on in opinion museum ...?*

In contrast to the ongoing chaos in Burma, the Thai and Chinese governments have sought to control people and territory through clearly marking the boundaries of state jurisdiction, identifying citizens of the nation-state, and articulating legal property rights and land-use regulations, including claiming and managing areas for the state. In the Shan State of Burma, no entity, whether government, rebel army, or drug lord, was able to control people or territory consistently. But the chaos in the Shan State was pregnant with possibilities, especially for clandestine enrichment through the drug trade. The Shan State exuded a dark power, the counter face of civilized governance, but one that was compelling. State agents in both China and Thailand needed to keep an eye on activities in Burma, and at times some sought means to benefit from illicit goods, whether narcotics or endangered species of wildlife. *lots of description of Burma / Shan state as dark source*

As village heads, Akheu and Lawjaw, somewhat like forest monks who subdue and incorporate the fierceness of the tiger, were able to engage with and manage the dark forces of Burma. In so doing, they each acquired a certain charisma, as monks do, in overcoming the beast.[32] Through Akheu and Lawjaw, state administrators gained access to information and goods produced in a chaotic terrain. These two small border chiefs played a ritual role in transgressing the border, as well as a political-economic one.

In China since 1949, the state has been the major patron for access to all resources. During the collective period, the state allocated land, capital, and labor, and collected grain from rural areas to support its operations. Since 1982, with the opening up of markets under the period of economic reforms, the state in its multiple agencies, and often conflicting agendas, is still the patron for most development projects and, until recently, for new businesses as well. In rural areas, the state determined the allocation of important subsistence resources, land and forests, through policies that divided communal land to villages and households. Although the state continued to adjust land distribution, through means such as wasteland auctions, the allocation of rural resources was largely set. What the economic reforms opened up, however, was a process of commodifying crops and other rural resources, such as tin. New resources kept moving into the market and were available for the taking. The site of contention, then, was how resources became commodified and who controlled the stream of benefits. As the discussion concerning the village in China shows, state and nonstate actors were battling over this process, with villagers and the administrative village head in Mengsong pitted against each other in deciding what got sold and who got the income. This conflict was reflected in the two main strands of development, one that emphasized poverty alleviation and recalled the benefits of socialist collective action, and the other that fostered individual competition in a market economy that was becoming more and more freewheeling.

In this arena, the administrative village head sought to control how resources became commodities and to direct the flow of benefits to himself. Part of Akheu's motivation as a small border chief was to define how development played out in Mengsong. As the local official, he played a central role in this process. Akheu heightened his own visibility as a person knowledgeable about what went on in Burma. Akheu spread his influence quite widely, linking up with many state and military contacts in both China and Burma. For the Chinese state, he represented a buffer or source of information that would protect China's interests. Akheu also highlighted his ethnic minority status and fluency in multiple languages, pointing out that he was uniquely qualified to both defend and mediate across the border. As small border chief, Akheu maneuvered to claim new resources as they become commodities, both to enrich himself and to insert himself as the local patron controlling access to and distribution of newly valued resources. He sought to control communication with major state agents as the "voice" of Mengsong, a role strongly contested by local villagers.

Part of state building is the definition of citizenship, ethnic minorities, and property rights. To the extent that Akheu could subvert or modify the practices surrounding "Akha" development, access to resources, and villagers' relationship with the state, he managed to negotiate these definitions and create for himself a realm for patronage and accumulation. The point to note, however, is that state agents collaborated with Akheu in enhancing his role as a small border chief. Township and county officials relied on an "Akha chief" to handle border issues and control his local population, collecting tin and allocating wasteland auctions as he saw fit. Akheu delivered illicit goods to these officials, of course, but his border role was based on more than bribery. It depended on his many influential connections in Burma and his ability to operate in different languages and contexts. State officials in

China were complicit in enabling Akheu to become the border protector and the one who helped information and goods to come across the line.

On the Thailand side, the picture is somewhat different. Prior to World War II, the village head in Akhapu, the local patron, drew his legitimacy from a prince in the Shan States. This part of northern Thailand continued to be a frontier realm until the late 1970s, and even in the late 1990s administrators in Bangkok treated the north as a space different from the rest of Thailand.

Beginning in the 1960s, a new set of nonstate patrons appeared in the north in close succession. The arrival of both the Nationalists and of CIA agents drew Thai government interest in establishing a state presence in the hills to combat communist influence. The state appointed Yibaw hill tribe representative to operate in two senses: to dispense state benefits to local villagers and to report back on their activities. Yibaw was also protecting national security. The Thai state in effect implemented indirect rule in the north. Yibaw mediated among different hill groups, Nationalist and CIA officials, and Thai state administrators. He also accumulated resources over which he could control the dispersal, functioning as an important small border chief.

Both the Nationalists and the CIA brought guns and drug connections to the Thai hills. Local people who worked closely with these forces, often village heads, developed a connection to the drug trade and to other influential people who dealt in coercive claims to local labor and valuable resources. In the operations of Khun Sa, the means of accumulating clients and resources and of distributing the benefits looked much like those of a lord of a premodern Southeast Asian principality, but one with links to the drug cartel.

The village head in Akhapu, however, was the one who pulled together all the threads of resources and patronage. Lawjaw had ongoing links with the drug trade and contacts with Khun Sa and other business people in Burma. In Thailand, meanwhile, he was involved, as official village head, in the opium-eradication project, the tea company, and the establishment of Akhapu as an official village. Through state policies related to ID cards and reforestation, Lawjaw gained increasing control over local access to land, jobs, and security. Those were the resources that the Thai state had still not guaranteed to hill tribes and for which villagers had to seek local patrons. Lawjaw had a set of clients dependent on him, as well as connections with important actors in both Burma and Thailand. He could negotiate how policies were implemented in Akhapu and who derived the benefit. To a greater extent than Akheu, Lawjaw operated as the border patron in a realm under his control. State policies, far from reducing his influence, increased his ability to control resource access. His role as the only Thai citizen in Akhapu enabled him to help define what it meant to be hill tribe, who might become a citizen, and how access to new resources would be allocated. Important components of what are usually thought of as state building, or acts determined by the center, could more usefully be viewed as state formation, or how people internalize state definitions and regulations. The meanings of citizenship, hill tribe, and resource access and use were all arenas of negotiation between an influential small border chief and state agents who relied on him to control the border.

These Chinese and Thai border areas were sites where village heads and other small chiefs with multiple loyalties and multiple connections could accumulate control over people and resources. In their role as protectors of the border for the state, they engaged in smuggling and other illegitimate operations. Small border chiefs were well positioned to oppress and exploit local people marginalized by geography and by state policies for "backward" hill people.

In addition to international boundaries, or because of them, other kinds of borders have flourished in these mountains. During World War II, the boundary between Japanese and Allied forces was located somewhere in the hills separating Burma and China. Another shifting boundary appeared in the 1950s, with the U.S. efforts to contain communism, as the CIA and other governments supported Nationalist troops in their engagements with militias supported by Chinese Communists. In the midst of these boundaries and battles, small border chiefs maintained personal relationships of patronage and trade across political and ideological borders. The internationally supported war in the Shan State contributed to the production of small border chiefs and their exploitative practices well beyond its borders.

To analyze the operations and surprising strength of small border patrons, the classic theory of galactic polities provides little help. A theory based on a view from the center obscures the power on the periphery, in this case the location of mediators with multiple languages and multiple connections. Border realms are also not merely "zones of mutual interest" to larger kingdoms and empires, an artifact of the past, but are also sites of influential "chiefs" who have continued to mediate and indeed to constitute the border into the late twentieth century.

5

PREMODERN BORDER LANDSCAPES
UNDER BORDER PRINCIPALITIES

Akha responses to political domination have been migration or flight
and occasionally submission, although their egalitarian ideology resists
this. Under conditions of semiautonomy, they have been able to produce their own spaces in the hills, including the establishment of villages, households, fields, and other intrasocietal hierarchies, all of which
rely on the carrying out of Akha ancestral practices.

DEBORAH TOOKER, *"Putting the Mandala in its Place"*

THE GREAT HIMALAYAN RANGE STRETCHES FROM WEST TO EAST ACROSS
central Asia, massively dividing China from Pakistan, India, and Nepal. At
its eastern edge, the Himalaya loses elevation and bends southward, forming steep north-south ridges through much of Yunnan Province, northeastern Burma, and northern Thailand. Major rivers originating in Tibet—
the Yangtze, the Mekong, and the Salween—descend rapidly through these
mountains in Yunnan, cutting deep valleys along their paths. Indeed, at one
point in northwestern Yunnan, these three parallel rivers are separated by
only 75 kilometers in a narrow mountain band, before they fan out to the
East China, South China, and Andaman seas.

The rough terrain created by these north-south ridges has for millennia
been home to numerous peoples, mentioned in documents from as early
as the Han dynasty (206 BCE–220 CE) in China (Armijo-Hussein 1996:104).
As people slowly migrated in search of fertile forest sites or to escape violence, they were channeled by the ridges south into Burma and later into
what is now northern Thailand. The area is sometimes referred to as part

of mountainous mainland Southeast Asia, designating a geographic unit that extends across contiguous parts of China, Burma, Thailand, Laos, and Vietnam. While the low valleys in this region are mainly tropical, the higher slopes and ridges are subtropical due to their elevation. People who call themselves Akha generally live at 1,000 meters and above, although state building and economic development have pushed some Akha villages to lower sites, particularly in China and Thailand. Until recent decades, Akha were not aware that they inhabited China, Burma, or Thailand.

Although considered by the center to be remote, villagers' livelihoods have been, for them, at the center of an active and meaningful world that reaches temporally back for fifty-five to sixty-five generations, to the first Akha, and spatially and socially into the markets and politics of surrounding valleys and beyond. Until the 1950s, those politics concerned small border polities rather than nation-states.

Until very recently, Akha in the Chinese and Thai border hamlets of Xianfeng and Akhapu have used, and to some extent continue to use, shifting cultivation to produce grain and vegetables, in concert with other land uses. By its nature, shifting cultivation entails fairly rapid changes in the landscape as forests are cleared for fields, fields are cultivated for one or two years, and then allowed to regenerate into forests.

Villagers' experience of shifting cultivation has contributed to their knowledge of the plasticity of the landscape. To produce their livelihoods, over time Akha farmers open plots across their land area and then allow them to regenerate into trees, sometimes with enrichment plantings of perennials (Xu et al. 1995:80). Fields at different elevations may have separate rice varieties as well as distinct combinations of vegetables intercropped with the grain. Depending on household labor, changes in weather, and infestations of pests, Akha farmers can open fields of varying size in different micro sites. While aware of the length of fallow time needed to restore fertility to cultivated fields, Akha can also vary the length of fallows depending on the natural fertility of the site and on changing production demands. This successive use of various sites for somewhat different purposes enables Akha to envision the landscape as an extensive setting with multiple possible trajectories for future use. In addition to cultivating upland rice in swiddens, Akha in Xianfeng and Akhapu also manage wet-rice fields, raise large numbers of livestock, hunt wild game, and collect myriad kinds of wild fruits, vegetables, and herbs in surrounding fields and forests. Like shifting cultivators elsewhere, Akha base their livelihoods on a composite of activities

make note of where we've observed this (each)

that allow them to shift labor allocation as required by subsistence needs and taxation. If one field or one crop fails, households almost always have other sources for grain and vegetables.

What is the knowledge form, or conceptual understanding of the landscape, that underlies risk-averse, composite land-use practices with long time horizons? In addition to an intimate knowledge of microsites across the landscape (spatial knowledge), Akha have an understanding of the plasticity of land cover over time (temporal knowledge). These two aspects, spatial and temporal, enable villagers to adapt quickly to changes as well as to strategize into the distant future. The notion of landscape plasticity is not an Akha term, but derives from my own extended experience in Xianfeng and Akhapu, as well as from visits to almost thirty different Akha villages in China, Burma, and Thailand.

Strategies for cultivation involve the ability to imagine how the current landscape could be otherwise or how parts of it could be allocated to new uses for a while, knowing that use could revert in the future. In Akha imagination and planning, not only can forests become swidden fields and fields then regenerate into forests, but fields can become pastures, and pastures can become forests again at a later date. In Akha experience, even wet-rice fields, usually deemed a permanent landscape feature, can change into pastures or even forests once again, given enough time.

This knowledge of future potential is based on memory of land uses and of regeneration pathways in the past. In general, villagers remember how various sites were used, and by whom, over the past several decades. This richness of experience and memory is reflected in stories embedded in the landscape, stories that come to light when walking around the village area with Akha. Certain sites evoke narratives of wealthier times or of cruelty and conflict over past access and use. The past is also a source of visions of how things could be revived or reworked in new contexts. This might mean planting crops used in the past or claiming sites previously used by members of one's household. Involving memory as well as imagination, landscape plasticity stretches backward as well as forward in time, as previous uses and events are recaptured and reworked in current contexts.

This understanding of the plastic quality of the landscape is underscored by Akha connection to their ancestors. The ancestors oversee Akha land use, particularly in opening new swidden fields, planting seeds, and harvesting upland rice. The ancestors protect fertility and sanction customary rules of access and use. The immediate ancestors taught current villagers how to man-

ask about stories "embedded
ask about in the landscape"
ancestor role

age upland forests and fields by rotating their use and by attending to signs of regeneration. They also taught villagers to protect certain areas of forest. Up to 1950 in China and up to the present in Thailand, the oversight of the ancestors has been the major source of legitimation for Akha mountain livelihoods. Akha connection to their ancestors has shaped access to land, land use, and productivity. The knowledge of plastic landscapes, together with sanctions from the ancestors, produces a long-term view of landscape mutability and potential.

What is role of elders now? connection to ancestors?

The years 1930 to 1949 in Xianfeng and 1930 to 1972 in Akhapu were periods when villagers' strategies for land use and livelihoods were not yet much influenced by government policies and regulations from China and Thailand. Both villages were located in a mountain region in which upland peoples usually submitted to a lowland patron, in many cases a Shan (or Tai) prince or lord. In principle, hill farmers exchanged grain and corvée labor with the lord in return for his protection against outside predators. In practice, these patronage relations varied considerably, with gradations of coercion involved in the extraction of grain and services, as well as a spectrum of patrons from local armed chiefs through princes with a court and an army. In some instances, villagers voluntarily sought the protection of patrons, while at other times patrons forced their "protection" (and extraction) on villagers. The small polities in question constituted the frontiers or border realms between larger political entities. Patrons' demands for products and labor were periodic or occasional; for the most part Akha villagers carried out their activities under the purview of the most intimate of patrons, their own ancestors.

The history of landscapes in Xianfeng and Akhapu begins with largely subsistence land uses and the role of the Akha ancestors in shaping access and productivity. Villagers' livelihoods centered on shifting cultivation as the heart of land-use practice. Akha farmers also engaged in many other land uses. In each site, within the mosaic of different land uses, growing certain crops for trade contributed to the patterns of landscapes and daily work but did not transform agricultural production. In most cases, cash crops and other mountain products from Xianfeng made their way to sites throughout China, while those from Akhapu were traded to various places in Burma and northern Thailand. In other words, the trade was not simply barter or local exchange. In the twentieth century, as small border patrons began to demand larger quantities of specific products from Akha farmers, these shifts in production and trade also brought about changes in resource access and the meaning of certain land uses.

I skipped

BORDER LANDSCAPES IN SIPSONGPANNA, 1930S TO 1950

The valley that once held the Tai principality of Sipsongpanna (now Xishuangbanna, under the Chinese) extends from east to west in the very south of Yunnan Province. The valley climate is tropical, unlike the rest of Yunnan, but is similar to other lowland areas of Southeast Asia. The ridges south of the valley, like most of the mountains in Yunnan, are composed of basalt, granites and gneisses, and sandstones (Li and Walker 1986:367; Richardson 1966:33; Chinese Academy of Geological Sciences 1976). In Yunnan as a whole, the surface rocks are predominantly limestone. The acidic soils in the hills of southern Yunnan developed on various formations (Richardson 1966:33). Where there are forests the soils tend to be high in organic matter (Li and Walker 1986:379). The limestone rocks near the surface at higher elevations weather into soils that can produce high-quality opium (F. Grunfeld 1982).

Xishuangbanna is characterized by a monsoon climate, with 85 to 90 percent of the rainfall borne by southwesterly and southeasterly winds between May and October. During the dry Yunnan winters the weather in Xishuangbanna remains relatively humid, with morning fog at higher altitudes. At elevations of 1,200 to 1,400 meters the mean annual temperature is 15 degrees Celsius in winter and 22 degrees Celsius in summer, with annual precipitation of about 1,800 millimeters (Xu et al. 1995:74). The valley in Xishuangbanna is about 600 meters above sea level, while the ridges reach as high as 2,000 meters (Yin 2001:79). The Mekong River flows north-south through Xishuangbanna as it heads toward Southeast Asia and forms the boundary between Burma and Laos. All of the rivers and streams in Xishuangbanna eventually join the Mekong, making the valley and its surrounding hills a great watershed of this major river (see fig. 2 in the introduction).

There are three major forest types in Xishuangbanna: tropical evergreen forest, found at low elevations in hot, humid pockets; tropical semievergreen monsoon forest, found below 1,000 meters in areas with cool temperatures and morning fog in the winter; and subtropical monsoon evergreen broad-leaved forest, ranging from 1,100 to 1,500 meters (Li and Walker 1986:371). This last forest type surrounds the hamlets in Mengsong. It requires a constant relative humidity of more than 80 percent, ensured during the dry winter by the morning fog. Many of the villagers' swidden fields, especially before 1949, were opened at lower elevations of 800 to 1,000 meters, within the tropical semievergreen monsoon forest. The soils under this forest tend to be more fertile than those at higher altitudes, with moist clayey or loamy soils sought after by farmers practicing shifting cultivation (Santisuk 1988:12).

Older villagers tell many stories about the abundant wildlife that used to roam in these forests, including tigers, leopards, bears, wild oxen, deer, wolves, monkeys, and wild boar. In the time of their grandfathers, hunters used to catch sight of wild elephants from time to time. In the 1930s, there were also many kinds of small animals, such as bamboo rats and pangolins, and a huge variety of birds, including peacocks and silver pheasants.[1] Because of the prevalence of dangerous animals, people never walked alone very far from the village, and men always carried handmade rifles. Men hunted all these animals, whether with rifles or a wide array of bamboo spring traps and pits. When hunters returned with a kill, according to older men, they customarily gave the right foreleg to the hamlet head; all other villagers shared the trunk and left foreleg; and the hunters kept the two hind legs for themselves. These customs came from the ancestors, who were thought to protect the community's well-being.

In the early decades of the twentieth century, the forest extended everywhere, and space for houses and trails had to be hacked from the abundant woods. Akha used simple tools—knives of various kinds and axes—to cut the trees for swiddens and houses. At that time their houses required trees only for posts and beams. Roofs were made of thatch from *Imperata cylindrica*, and walls and floors were constructed from various species of bamboo. The houses were small compared with those today, but they were usually raised on stilts so that livestock and fuelwood could be kept underneath.

When discussing past customary practices and land uses with me, older villagers undoubtedly presented a somewhat idealized picture. Like any conceptualizations, these accounts left out variations, such as those caused by bad weather, invading armies, predatory princes, or major localized conflicts. These descriptions are nonetheless based on dozens of extended conversations in each research site and form the basis for my understanding of landscape plasticity.

In the early twentieth century, there were strict customary rules for use of the forest, as well as scaled punishments for transgressions. Around each hamlet in Mengsong, of which there were then five, was an area of protected forest where people could not cut anything. The ancestors taught that this forest protected the hamlet from evil spirits. Although the size of protected forest would vary from hamlet to hamlet, generally villagers kept it large enough that it took about an hour to walk from their houses through the forest to their cultivated swidden fields. Part of this forest was designated as a burial site. Customary rules forbade villagers from cutting or removing anything from the cemetery forest, and indeed people entered the cemetery only to bury people and clean the graves. Covering the hills above the hamlets were watershed forests where villagers were also forbidden to cut.[2]

For Mengsong as a whole, there was a large separate area of protected forest called Sanpabawa. This site of particularly moist primary forest produced abundant rattan. To protect the rattan, Mengsong Akha elders prohibited cutting anything in the Sanpabawa, except once a year at a specified time. Then each hamlet could send a couple of people to cut rattan for all households in the hamlet. Villagers used the rattan in making headgear, knife handles, and the edges of baskets, but in those days did not sell rattan.[3]

In addition to enduring rules for protecting areas of forest, farmers also had flexible customary arrangements for access and use of shifting-cultivation fields. Access depended on residence in a hamlet in Mengsong, and residence itself depended on membership in certain clans. In the 1930s, villagers cut swiddens at about 1,000 meters in an extensive area with fertile soils.[4] The site was large enough that farmers could fallow used fields for at least thirteen to fifteen years, but often longer. Older farmers say that they opened swiddens wherever they wanted, large enough to meet household needs for grain. Farmers had to visit the fields almost daily, since wild animals often ate their crops. Once a field regenerated to forest, anyone from the hamlet could open that site for the next planting. Villagers grew up knowing not only how to open and prepare fields for upland rice, but also the patterns of successive regeneration from the first year of grasses to the twentieth or thirtieth year, or longer, when forests reached 25–30 meters in height. In other words, villagers lived with swiddens in various stages of regrowth, in a landscape tapestry that changed rather dramatically from one year to the next.

Older villagers say that aside from opening fields to plant upland rice, they were not allowed to clear any area of forest. Swiddens were almost always opened in secondary forest, since Akha had lived in a hamlet in Mengsong and used the same area for shifting cultivation for almost two hundred years. Villagers believed that their ancestors would punish them with serious illness or death for opening new areas of primary forest.[5] While villagers could cut individual trees for housing and fuelwood, except in prohibited areas, there was strong local sanction against actually clearing primary forest. Akha elders fined villagers who cut a few trees in prohibited areas by making them provide homemade liquor for everyone in the hamlet. For more serious breaches, a villager would have to slaughter a pig to be shared with the whole hamlet. These punishments suggest that people did not always follow the rules. In the 1930s, though, farmers would have had no reason to clear primary forests, a job entailing enormous labor. There was no commercial logging then.

Older villagers recount that there used to be twelve festivals or rituals each year related to the agricultural calendar. Among them were rituals devoted to opening new swiddens, planting rice, taking care of insect pests, harvesting rice, and showing gratitude for the forest that made their lives possible. All of these rituals were linked to the Akha ancestors, for whom an ancestor basket was set up in a prescribed place in each house. At one of the major festivals, ancestors for the past seven generations would return. The ancestors were believed to help ensure an abundant harvest, protect villagers from malevolent spirits, and to punish transgressions of rituals or rules. To the extent that rules were followed, Akha villagers' connection with their ancestors shaped their access to land, land use, and harvest, as well as their deep feeling of connection to the surrounding woods. Each year, three stalks of grain from each field were put on the ancestor basket. These offerings, together with three small branches that stayed on the ancestor basket, represented the ancestors in each house. The ancestor basket, then, embraced the ancestors, the potential for future productivity of the land, and the rules governing land use for both upland rice and forests. While punishment for cutting trees in the wrong place would be meted out by village heads, the ancestors were also believed to be keeping account and could bring bad fortune to those who broke the rules.

Xianfeng hamlet is nestled at the southwestern end of a plain on the ridge top around which Mengsong is sited.[6] Like the four other hamlets in the early 1930s, Xianfeng sits at some 1,600 meters in elevation. At that time a handful of households from the hamlet had wet-rice fields in the plain, but otherwise people relied on upland rice as the staple grain. From the ridge on the southern side of this plain, villagers could look down on the river marking the border with the Shan States. They could also survey the extensive forests and scattered villages in Burma, which they frequently visited to see friends and relatives. At that time their most active trade networks extended south into the hills of the Shan States as well as into Sipsongpanna. This was a premodern border landscape, comprised of complex, flexible land uses and strong trade and kin relationships across the border.

Participation in Trade

By the late nineteenth century, Akha in Mengsong planted two main cash crops, tea and opium. Each deserves an excursion into regional political-economic history to understand why Akha planted as much of these two crops as they did, and the conflicts that emerged, particularly over opium.

Tea had been grown in the forest understory and was traded in this region for centuries before opium appeared. There are documents from the Tang dynasty (618–907 CE) mentioning trade in Pu'er tea, a famous and coveted variety from Sipsongpanna (Hill 1998:73). Beginning in the late nineteenth century, Han tea merchants came to an arrangement with the Sipsongpanna *tusi*, the Tai lord in Jinghong, which allowed them to control the trade in this famous tea. The tea merchants collected tea grown in Tai, Jinuo, and Akha villages and sold it to destinations as distant as Hong Kong, Tonkin, Siam, Burma, and Tibet, as well as elsewhere in China (Hill 1998).

The Tai lord in Jinghong supported the tea trade, since it brought in taxes not only from the merchants, but also from villages that, as a result of selling tea, were now able to remit taxes in cash (Hill 1998; 85). By the early twentieth century, the town of Menghai in western Sipsongpanna had become a major tea-trading depot run by Chinese merchants.[7] Tai villagers sold tea to the village head, who in turn sold it to the Chinese merchants in Menghai. In hilly areas surrounding Menghai, including Mengsong, "upland village headmen were given lower ranks within the Tai political system" (80). Once a year, the tea merchants association decided on the price of tea and informed village headmen, including those in mountainous areas. Headmen paid a slightly lower price in buying tea from villagers, so that the headman made a profit each year when he sold tea to the merchants (81).

The head of Mengsong early in the twentieth century was a man called Sadyeu. With the advent of tea merchants, Sadyeu was brought into Tai government administration and Tai officials began appearing in Mengsong to collect taxes. As the first head of Mengsong to hold a Tai title and to wear the accompanying red hat, Sadyeu was also connected to a tea network that extended throughout China and beyond. His encouragement of tea planting served to enrich himself and to strengthen his influence over what crops were planted and valued. Since he was benefiting from the tea trade, Sadyeu enthusiastically planted whole hillsides full of tea and encouraged other villagers to follow suit. Tea planted in the forest understory was allowed to grow into large bushes with abundant, glossy leaves that villagers picked frequently. It is unlikely that the fairly sparsely planted tea had a major effect on forest condition, although it may have affected some understory plants. Tea bushes were productive for many decades and would be replaced one by one as they grew old.

For as long as older villagers could remember, but probably beginning some time during the second half of the nineteenth century, Akha planted opium in gaps in the forest on limestone-derived soils. As noted earlier, sites with limestone soils were ideal for opium, as was the high elevation in Mengsong. Until 1937, villagers sold their opium to horse caravans that came up the horse trail from the Sipsongpanna valley. The caravan traders also bought their tea and sold villagers salt, silk thread, and beads. Informants today say that the traders were Tai and that they sold the opium both in Burma and to what is called in Mengsong "the interior of China." Understanding the opium market requires a short diversion into a broader history that links not only Mengsong, but China itself with British colonial enterprise.

The opium poppy was introduced to China by Arabs in the eighth century, although for many centuries it was used mainly for medicine (Spence 1975; Cameron 1931). In the eighteenth century when Westerners arrived with the habit of smoking tobacco, Chinese also took up tobacco, and both Westerners and Chinese began to mix tobacco and opium to smoke (Cameron 1931:136). In 1773, the British East India Company took over the Indian opium trade from the Portuguese. The British had tried numerous trade goods in trying to open markets with China, but discovered that the only product they could push on the Chinese was opium. For many decades British traders smuggled opium into China in defiance of a 1729 central government edict banning the drug (Cameron 1931; Baumler 1998:8).

By the 1840s, opium had become a major trade good in China, as well as a form of currency. Many merchants and trading houses were involved in the circulation of opium, which was used by then throughout China by people of all classes. While not everyone used the drug, everyone knew someone or had a family member who smoked opium (Baumler 1998:2). Government officials at numerous levels were alarmed at the prevalence of opium use and its ill effects on the Chinese workforce. The imperial commissioner in Canton in 1839, Lin Zexu, ensured his lasting fame by burning the supply of opium brought in on British ships. Lin's action also precipitated the Opium War, which ended in 1842 with a stunning Chinese defeat (Cameron 1931:137). British traders continued to smuggle opium into China until 1858, when the Treaty of Tientsin legalized the trade, at least tacitly (Cameron 1931; Baumler 1998:4). Following the treaty, both the central and local governments began to derive income from taxes on opium (Baumler 1998:4).

From 1858 on, domestic production of opium increased. Although from time to time officials in the central government tried to suppress opium, their hands were tied by the realization that if domestic production decreased, imported opium would rush in to take its place (Cameron 1931: 137). By the late nineteenth century, domestically grown opium outstripped the imported drug. Opium was grown in all parts of China, but the ecosystems of southwestern China were particularly well suited to poppies, especially the highlands of Sichuan, Guizhou, and Yunnan. Also, mountain areas were remote from the reach of government suppression policies, and mountain villagers continued to plant poppies year after year. The opium produced in Yunnan was reputed to be the best, probably because the morphine content was the highest (Baumler 1998:9).

By the 1920s and 1930s, the nature of opium as a lightweight, high-value product, and its use as both a trade good and currency, resulted in a curious political-economic effect: "All of the major warlords got significant revenue from opium, and opium made it possible for the rulers of otherwise poor provinces like Yunnan to be important actors in the national scene" (Baumler 1998:10). Once Chiang Kai-shek had deployed his troops in various parts of China to fight against the Japanese from 1937 to 1945 and against the Communist troops from 1945 to 1949, those Nationalist divisions in areas far from cities were able to support their endeavors through extraction and sale of locally produced opium (Baumler 1998:11).

Following the Japanese invasion in 1937, the Nationalist government was unable to prevent rampant inflation. The market for opium took off as the drug replaced currency almost completely, especially in the southwest. Demand for opium, both for use as money and for soldiers to smoke, drove opium production to unprecedented highs that lasted until the Nationalists were driven out of China in 1949 (Baumler 1998:12).

By the 1930s in Mengsong,, farmers had been growing opium for decades to sell to Tai horse-caravan traders.[8] For some time Akha had paid taxes to the Tai in coins, which they earned from opium (their main source of income) and from tea. During the 1930s, the head of Mengsong, Reisa, allowed Uqie Akha to move in both from Burma and from Menghai, a town in the Sipsongpanna valley. Many Uqie Akha were traders who plied their wares along trade networks that extended from Kunming in China to Kentung in Burma. Many among them dealt in opium, so that their arrival in Mengsong brought money from the drug trade into the community. While Mengsong Akha were undoubtedly involved in trade and labor exchange with kin in the Shan States before this time, now they were producing for markets on either side of their border ridge. Uqie Akha planted much more opium than had been grown in Mengsong before. Stories older villagers tell indicate that more local people began to smoke opium as well, since from this era until the early 1950s members of many families went into debt to buy opium and then lost household wet-rice fields when they could not repay.

When two Nationalist army companies, numbers 8 and 9, took over Mengsong in 1937, production relations changed radically. Nationalist soldiers enlisted Akha farmers as forced laborers to produce grain and vegetables for them, a practice that seriously limited Akha choices about how to spend their labor. The soldiers also confiscated and slaughtered all Mengsong livestock, removing an important part of the composite landscape. The troops further increased local production of opium, which they sold to support themselves. Nationalist soldiers also introduced gambling to Mengsong, staging games of dice that lasted for five days at a stretch. Some villagers lost the family fortune, or all their wet-rice fields, in an unfortunate toss of the dice. Many older men and women recount stories of grandfathers and uncles who gambled away the household wet-rice fields or who lost them to Uqie Akha moneylenders when they could not repay their debt. To this day, Dongfanghong, the hamlet where moneylenders once lived, has more wet-rice land per person than any other village in Mengsong, a holdover from transactions in the 1930s and 1940s.[9] During this time, Xianfeng wet-rice fields amounting to some 300 *mu* (about 20 hectares) in the Mengsong plain were lost through gambling or unpaid debts. The incursion of Nationalist army companies reduced landscape plasticity both through requisition of Akha labor and through villagers' loss of land through debts and sale.

In 1942, Mengsong Akha fled into hiding in the nearby forest. They hid in the densest forest in the protected watershed where they hoped they would not be found. Although opening small swidden fields in primary forest broke their own rules, villagers at that time skirted the ancestors in a bid to stay alive. Plastic landscapes allow such malleability for survival. As of 1996 there were still traces of the small huts they built then, and of deep holes dug to hide their grain. For three years villagers could only occasionally open small fields for grain, since they feared the Nationalist troops would see their fires. Many villagers starved during this time, as they tried to survive on small animals they could catch and on fruits, banana flowers, bamboo shoots, and tree roots and bark gathered in the forest. In 1945, they returned to their hamlets, even though the Nationalists were still in control there. They resumed carrying grain and arms for the soldiers and planting crops for them to eat.

In 1996, I asked seven Xianfeng villagers to make a map of land use in Mengsong circa 1945. Figure 10 shows the border with Burma,[10] the road from the Sipsongpanna valley (still a horse trail), the six hamlets at that time, the river, and the Sanpabawa.[11] The makers of the map noted that any unmarked areas were all primary forest. Since most of the map is blank, dense forest surrounded their hamlets, fields, and trails in the mid-1940s. Within the forest, the map also shows upland rice fields planted while the villagers were in hiding. The trail for carrying grain and arms for the Nationalists is partially filled in, indicating the direction toward Mansan in China and the route across the border to the Shan States. Markers indicate where Nationalist army companies 8 and 9 were stationed, as well as an airstrip villagers opened for small Nationalist planes to land. Fields planted in opium and tea are indicated, and wet rice fields lost in gambling are circled. Also of note are areas of *Imperata* (*maocao* in Chinese), which villagers used in making roofs. These may also represent sites where opium was planted in the past. Villagers keep these land uses in their memories as the landscape of oppression and hunger. These are also landscapes with links to both China and Burma.

While Akha believed that their ancestors continued to watch over the fertility and use of their forests and swiddens, the ancestors offered little protection when Akha became involved in opium and extortionist production relations with Tai and Akha traders, and later with Nationalist soldiers. It seems that the ancestors protected subsistence livelihoods, but had little sway in relationships of trade.

There was no premodern time when Akha in Mengsong were untouched by commodity markets that extended into Burma and the interior of China. The production of opium linked people on ridges on the Burma/China border to the politics and trade sparked by British colonial ambitions. In Mengsong itself, Sadyeu tried to rework the meaning and function of opium into a trade good that would enrich local Akha without addicting them, and he managed to keep Uqie Akha and the drug trade outside the local community. His successor, Reisa, invited in Uqie Akha, their wealth and money-lending, and the local production, sale, and use of opium. This change in community in the 1930s commodified land, such that Uqie Akha could buy wet-rice fields when they moved in and villagers could use wet-rice fields as collateral for loans. Access to land had previously involved kinship, residence in Mengsong, and labor. Beginning in the 1930s, access to land could also be bought.

During this period, the locus of patronage and extraction shifted from

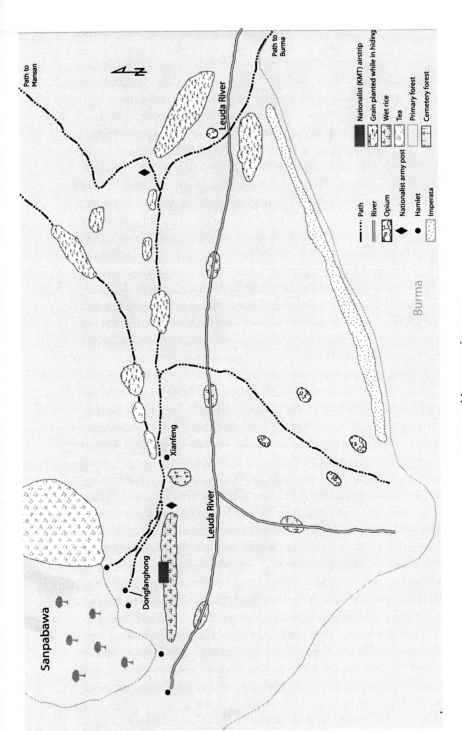

FIG. 10. Mengsong circa 1945

Legend:

- ∙∙∙∙∙ Path
- ═══ River
- Opium
- ◆ Nationalist army post
- ● Hamlet
- Imperata

- ▇ Nationalist (KMT) airstrip
- Grain planted while in hiding
- Wet rice
- Tea
- Primary forest
- Cemetery forest

Path to Mansan

Path to Burma

Leuda River

Burma

Xianfeng

Dongfanghong

Sanpabawa

Leuda River

the lord of Sipsongpanna to the Nationalist troops based in Mengsong. The former was a small border ruler; the latter were part of a national army engaged in a state-building crusade. The local manifestation of state building, however, looked like local bullies setting up their own small border polity based on forced labor and on an opium trade reaching into China and Burma.

BORDER LANDSCAPES IN NORTHERN THAILAND, 1930S TO 1973

The hills in what is now northern Thailand are extensions of the north-south ridges descending through China and Burma. Like the mountains in the Shan State, these hills are characterized by calcareous-shaley sediments. The whole of northern Thailand is striated by north-south bands of Triassic granites and punctuated by outcrops of Carboniferous and Permian limestones (Santisuk 1988:12).

The Mekong River forms the international boundary between northern Thailand and Laos along a stretch of Thailand's eastern border. All of the smaller streams and rivers in the north feed into the Mekong, making Chiang Rai Province a great watershed of the river, just as Xishuangbanna serves as a Mekong watershed farther north.

Forest types in northern Thailand, at elevations below 1,000 meters, range from seasonal rain forest (moist), through mixed deciduous forest (intermediate), to deciduous dipterocarp forest (dry). Montane vegetation, defined as above 1,000 meters, is divided into lower montane (1,000 to 1,800 meters) and upper montane (above 1,800 meters). In the lower montane altitudes, where Akhapu is situated, the forest types vary from moist, lower-montane rain forest, to drier, lower-montane oak forest, to driest, lower-montane pine-oak forest (Santisuk 1988:24). The forests surrounding Akhapu are primarily lower-montane oak forest. While there are no forest taxonomies linking the forests of Xishuangbanna and northern Thailand, my forest data (see appendixes 1 and 2) show that they are quite similar.

The whole of northeast Thailand is characterized by a monsoon climate. Although in some geography texts the year is described as divided into a hot, dry season and a rainy season, in reality three seasons can be distinguished: the rainy season; the northeast monsoon; and the hot, dry season (Santisuk 1988). The rainy season lasts from May to September, with winds from the southwest. July through September brings the heaviest rains of the year and an overall relative humidity of about 80 percent. From October to February comes the northeast monsoon, bringing cool, dry air from the north. During December and January there can even be frost at higher elevations, and morning fog from November through March. Mean temperature at 1,000 meters during this season is 17 degrees Celsius. The hot, dry season then lasts from late February through April, when the relative humidity drops to about 60 percent (Santisuk 1988:13–14). Mean temperature at 1,000 meters is 25 degrees Celsius during these months. Annual precipitation at the altitude of Akhapu is about 1,700 millimeters. Compared with Xishuangbanna, this area of Thailand is slightly warmer and drier, but generally the climate and geography of the two areas are much the same.

The soils of northern Thailand are derived from many parent materials and are weakly to strongly acidic. These soils tend to be shallow and stony, with a loamy surface and a clayey subsurface. Farmers using shifting cultivation tend to choose areas with more fertile and moist clayey or loamy soils, such as are found with lower-montane rain forest or seasonal rain forest (Santisuk 1988:12). As in China, soils derived from limestone are ideal for producing opium (Santisuk 1988).

Documents record people living in the mountains of the north in the sixteenth century (Renard 1980:143–44), but in all likelihood there have been forest dwellers for much longer. As discussed in chapters 1 and 2, people in the forest were regarded by elites in Siam as on the fringes of the known, civilized world. They were unimportant and inhabited a wild, dangerous land where no one would want to go. Beginning in the mid-1850s, the Muslim Rebellion in Yunnan caused many hill peoples to flee to Burma. In many cases, villages and households spent a number of generations in Burma before some of them ventured farther south. In Burma, hill groups such as Akha allied themselves with Shan princes in the valleys, to whom they owed grain and corvée labor. Even after moving to Akhapu, the village head continued to be affiliated with a Shan prince.

The current village head's two elder brothers say their children are the fourth generation in Akhapu. Their ancestors, while still in Burma, had heard that around what is now Akhapu there were wild oxen and elephants, indicators of abundant wildlife. Learning that the soils were also good, about sixty households moved here in about 1910. Other households continued to join the village, until it reached more than one hundred households in the 1940s. At that point more than half the households split off and moved to other sites in the north of Thailand.

There were still wild oxen when the two brothers (now in their late sixties) were young, as well as tigers, wild boar, porcupines, many kinds of birds, and eight kinds of monkeys. One old man watched a tiger walk under his house when he was young. The brothers hunted all of these animals with crossbows and, more recently, with rifles they bought from Wa hunters.[12] Men would hunt in groups of four or more, since many of the animals they sought were dangerous.

When the sixty households first arrived in the area, the *zoema* (customary administrative head) chose the village site in the saddle of a ridge at about 1,000 meters. He designated areas of watershed forest, a cemetery forest, and a forest encircling the site where people built houses to protect the village from malevolent spirits.[13] He also selected a wooded spot where villagers would honor the Owner of the Land. In these areas villagers were not allowed to cut trees. Aside from these protected forests relatively close to the village, primary forest then extended in all directions, since other inhabitants were few. The immediate surrounding forests, extending to the watershed forest on the local peak at 1,300 meters, included lower-montane oak forest and evergreen oak forest very similar to the forest around Mengsong in China.

Akha in Akhapu held twelve annual rituals or festivals, almost identical to those carried out in Mengsong before the Communist revolution in 1949. These rituals punctuated the agricultural calendar, marking the opening of swidden fields, the construction of new village gates, the honoring of ancestors from seven generations, the completion of the harvest, and gratitude to the Owner of the Land, among other annual events. As in China, these rituals linked fertility and agricultural labor with villagers' ancestors, ensuring the ancestors' blessings in return for carrying out customary practices and rules. As in Mengsong before Communist rule, in Akhapu each household had an ancestor basket, with three grain stalks and three small branches representing the ancestors in each house. The offerings made to these ancestors were virtually the same as those described to me in Xianfeng.

Villagers today say that they used to open swiddens "anywhere," or "wherever they wanted." This changed in the early 1970s, when a large number of Loimi Akha, as well as a group of ethnic Chinese villagers, joined them in the settlement of Akhapu. In 1997, I asked a group of older villagers to draw a map of land use in the 1960s, before the arrival of other hamlets. Figure 11 shows extensive areas of shifting cultivation along slopes above the Plek River to the west of the village. Villagers could apparently open fields anywhere in this customary area for shifting cultivation. These sites ranged in altitude from 700 to 1,000 meters, in all likelihood originally transitional forests between mixed deciduous and lower-montane oak forests. Beyond the protected forest surrounding the village, areas north, east, and south of the village were still primary forest where villagers cut

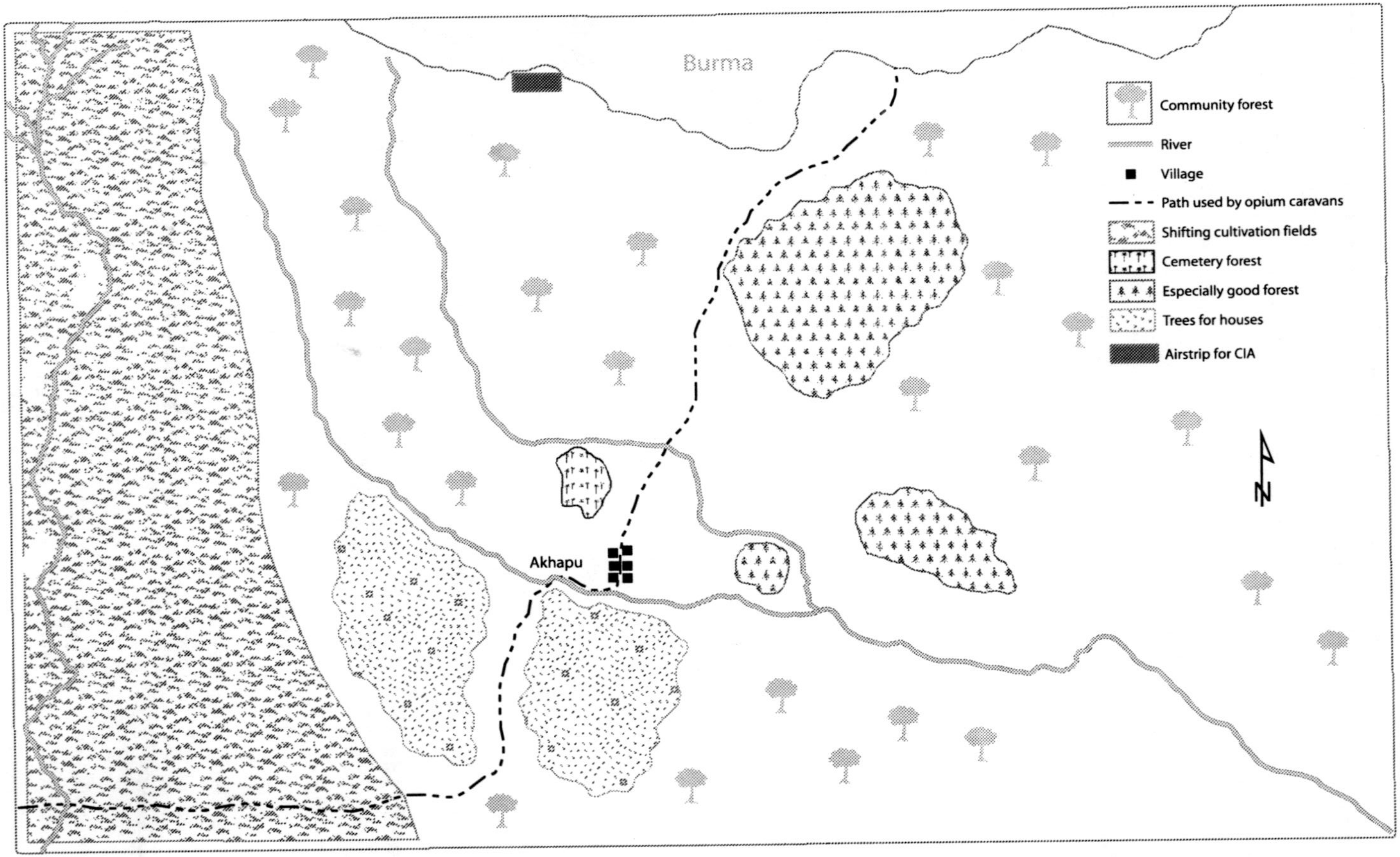

Legend:

- Community forest
- River
- Village
- Path used by opium caravans
- Shifting cultivation fields
- Cemetery forest
- Especially good forest
- Trees for houses
- Airstrip for CIA

Burma

Akhapu

FIG. 11. Akhapu in the 1960s

individual trees for housing and fuelwood. Akha farmers also kept large numbers of cattle, water buffalo, and horses that grazed in the forest but were kept out of swiddens. Like their counterparts in China, these Akha maintained a composite of land uses within which they could manipulate the deployment of labor.

From the 1940s to the early 1970s, most households opened new swiddens every year and then left the field fallow for thirteen to fifteen years. Sometimes Akha farmers opened fields in secondary forest and sometimes in primary forest, as there was no prohibition against cutting primary forest as there was in China. If cutting in primary forest, they used large knives weighing a kilo to cut huge trees and large bamboo. When possible, men preferred to open secondary forest since it was easier work. There would be more weeds in swiddens cut in secondary forest, however, which women had to manage. Cutting in secondary forest meant less work for men but more work for women. In either case, villagers waited until trees were 25 to 30 centimeters in diameter before cutting again, when villagers claimed that soil fertility would be the same as before. The use of shifting cultivation produced a rotational landscape with multiple future possibilities, similar to the landscape in China.

One older man estimated that, when he was young (in the 1940s), his household planted about 20 rai (about 3 hectares) of grain to feed nine people. They planted half upland rice and half corn, with sesame intercropped with the upland rice. An older woman said her household planted about 16 rai of grain, again for a nine-person household. Farmers had to visit their fields frequently, because wild boar and other wild animals ate their grain. On the edges of swiddens, farmers planted pumpkins, winter melon, sorrel, radishes, sweet potatoes, spinach, cabbages, hot peppers, cantaloupe, coriander, green onions, green garlic, ginger, anise, bananas, sugar cane, and peanuts. Where they had piled weeds from their swiddens they planted cassava. Their swiddens delivered a diverse and often abundant harvest.

Like their counterparts in China, Akha in Akhapu depended on an understanding of the landscape that was extensive both spatially and temporally. Renewing soil fertility involved knowledge of regeneration patterns as well as soil types. As in China in another sense, farmers used risk-averse strategies in producing a wide variety of products in their swiddens, as well as raising livestock, hunting wild game, and collecting a multitude of wild fruits and vegetables. Villagers' cultivation patterns and long-term use of the landscape relied on an intimate knowledge of microsites and an understanding of the plasticity of land cover over time.

ask about understanding of soil / fertility / etc

Participation in Trade

When Akha settled Akhapu, there was tea in the forest understory. The tea was probably planted by the few Lahu farmers who had lived where the Chinese village is now, but who departed when Akha began to settle there. For decades, Akha picked tea for their own use, but did not sell tea until the 1980s.

Akhapu lacked the proper limestone-derived soils and climate for growing poppies. Those villagers who planted poppies, apparently a minority in Akhapu, did so mainly on the other side of the ridge in Burma. In any case, villagers would have sold their opium to traders in Burma, or later to Nationalist soldiers, since their strongest ties were with patrons and traders along the border and in the Shan State. Up to 1957, opium produced elsewhere in the hills was sold to the Thai government opium monopoly, which enabled the government to earn revenue from the opium trade. It is unlikely that villagers in Akhapu had connections with agents of the Thai government until the 1950s and 1960s. Situated right on the Burma border, accessible from Chiang Rai only by several days' ride on horse trails, Akhapu was remote for Thai government administrators, who saw the village as part of the border frontier.

In addition to opium cultivation in the hills of Thailand, opium had been arriving from China for many decades. In the 1920s and 1930s, as opium production in China approached its peak, Han traders who for a long time had plied their trade between Yunnan and the principalities north of Siam, began to carry opium as well as cotton, tea, and other goods from China to mainland Southeast Asia.

In the 1950s and 1960s, increasing numbers of horse caravans brought opium from the Shan State in Burma south through Thailand, partly in payment for Thailand's contribution to the anticommunist forces in Burma. Some of the caravan members were customary traders from families who had worked these routes for centuries. Others were newly enlisted by Khun Sa and other drug lords as the production of opium and heroin rapidly expanded. Owing to the value of their cargo, the drug lords provided much heavier armaments for the guards than had the Yunnanese traders in the past (Lintner 1994:189).

In 1960, thirty Nationalist soldiers fleeing Burma settled in Akhapu for eight years. As a result of their presence, as well as its border location, Akhapu began to serve as a rest stop for caravan traders. At that time, villagers were linked to Burma and its various armed patrons much more closely than to

ask older villagers about opium

any agents of the Thai state. Each caravan made two or three round-trips each year, and the traders and their guards lodged with villagers and bought grain, chickens, and pigs from them, for which they paid in Burmese (Indian) rupees. With this cash villagers bought salt and metal products in Mae Chan on their annual visit to town.

This trade represents some commodification of local resources, since villagers were not used to being paid for grain. These transactions did not dramatically change local cultivation practices, however. During those years (1961–68), many households produced more grain than they could eat each year, since the soils were still very fertile and areas for expansion were still extensive (Hanks and Hanks 2001:98). Households stored grain against the possibility of poor harvests in the future or they sold it to Chinese traders. Villagers remember this as a time of abundant production, when providing grain for the caravans was not a problem. This was a landscape of fertility and abundance.

Asa, sixty-nine at the time of our interview, recalled that he used to go to a Shan village about a day's walk into Burma. Asa was one among a handful of villagers who engaged in trading in livestock. He went two to three times a year to buy pigs, water buffalo, or cattle. Asa sold pigs to the opium caravan traders. He sold the cattle to the Nationalist soldiers living in Akhapu. He sold the water buffalo to Thais who came up to Akhapu from Mae Chan. For these livestock, Asa was paid in either Indian rupees or Thai baht, depending on what he needed at the time. His trade route reached into the Shan State, a small border polity, crossing multiple languages and an international border. Asa stopped making these trips to Burma when a state agent appeared to collect customs on livestock coming in from Burma. For him, this was the first appearance of an agent of the Thai state trying to control trade in local resources.

In the memory of older people in Akhapu, the 1960s represented a peak time, before the fall from grace. The soils were productive, vegetables tasted better than they do today, livestock and grain were abundant, and the forest was intact and full of wildlife. Asa exemplified this sense of abundant times past when he said that for his visits to Shan villages in Burma he would wear all his Akha finery. He had a beautiful embroidered coat, then, and wore silver around his neck and wrists, as well as silver rings on every finger except the first digit of each hand. When he visited other villages, he donned an Akha hat and shoes of calf leather, which he removed when he entered someone's home. But in 1997, Asa considered himself poor. He had sold all his livestock except for a pig or two around the house. He had lost his shifting-cultivation land to reforestation and had little wet-rice land. He rarely ate meat, and his household had to deploy its labor in various directions to earn enough to buy grain.

For Asa, as for other older Akha, the era under small border patrons, whether princes or more recent incarnations of border lords, was a time of plenty. It was also a time when an Akha trader enjoyed a certain prestige among Shan neighbors. The period he described as one of poverty was the late 1990s, when Akha livelihoods and land uses that depended on landscape plasticity had rapidly been overridden by the landscapes of development and a modernizing Thai state: landscapes of productivity and rule. For farmers in Akhapu, this was a landscape of deprivation.

PREMODERN BORDER LANDSCAPES IN CHINA AND THAILAND

Customary Akha land use, carried out largely under the oversight of the Akha ancestors, was informed by a temporal and spatial knowledge of landscape plasticity, both in Xianfeng and in Akhapu. The twelve annual rituals set the rhythm for acknowledging the links among agriculture, the forests, and the Akha who had gone before. Nurturing the present generation of villagers was inseparable from attending to Akha in the past. Rituals also paid tribute to the next world, where current Akha would go in the future. These annual rituals were temporal markers of spatial cultivation practices. Akha made use of spaces at different elevations and with various soil and microclimatic conditions. Land uses included producing subsistence and cash crops; gathering wild fruits, vegetables, and medicinal herbs from the forest; raising various kinds of livestock; and hunting wild game. Together, these activities generated products for household consumption, ritual use, exchange, and sale. Akha farmers, both men and women, engaged in several of these activities, devising strategies for long- and short-term purposes. Those purposes, meanwhile, might involve serving different masters, whether the regional lord, the trader, the household, or the ancestors. Villagers used all this spatial and temporal diversity in planning for the future and in responding to various demands.

For Akha in Xianfeng, trade in tea and opium connected villagers with buyers in Sipsongpanna, Burma, and in the interior of China. China was a country they had heard of, but one more distant from their lives than either Sipsongpanna or the Shan States. Akha were more familiar with Tai, Shan, and Akha traders and the small border polities with whom these itinerants were linked. For Akhapu in Thailand, trade in livestock was also with Shan and Akha communities in the Shan States. Villagers in Akhapu had come from that area and shared a common history of patronage and trade. In Akhapu by the 1940s villagers knew about Thailand, but they were more closely connected to traders and relatives in Burma.

For cultivating upland rice, the Akha ancestors gave meaning to the whole annual cycle. The ancestors were also intimately involved in the regeneration and protection of forests. Prohibition against cutting trees extended to the abundant forest around the hamlet, watershed forests, and to the cemetery forest (where recent ancestors were buried). All these practices came under the umbrella of ancestral care. The meaning and practice of cultivating cash crops, meanwhile, derived mainly from trade with and obligations to small border polities, including relations with princes and border chiefs. In earlier centuries and in the beginning of the twentieth century, these practices would not have been in conflict with the ancestors, although land in cash crops would not have come under ancestral protection. Overall, however, introducing cash crops added a new dimension and complexity to livelihoods, with new meanings, social connections, and cash incomes. These added to possible livelihood strategies, but did not supplant the ancestors as the most important patrons.

The arrival of the Uqie Akha in Mengsong (China) brought changes, expanding the cultivation of opium and commodifying wet-rice fields. As more Akha began to smoke opium, they also began to offer their wet-rice fields as collateral for loans to buy opium paste, and later lost their fields if they could not repay. In this way, the opium trade threatened livelihoods. At the same time, however, households were opening shifting-cultivation fields with sanction from their ancestors. The two kinds of production, for markets and for subsistence, operated at the same time.

In Akhapu (Thailand), even up to 1972 land was not yet commodified. The sale of products (livestock and grain) was accommodated within the array of customary land uses under the ancestral purview. Though opium was being transported through Akhapu rather than being produced there, Akha in Thailand were equally well enmeshed in the world of patrons and traders in the Shan State and in the spectrum of small border polities that relied on the opium trade. But in Akhapu's case, villagers' livelihoods were enhanced rather than threatened by the drug trade.

6

LANDSCAPE PLASTICITY
VERSUS LANDSCAPES OF
PRODUCTIVITY AND RULE

Akha Livelihoods under Nation-States

Seuzon, a woman of sixty-six in 1997, married into Xianfeng (China) in 1949 when she was twenty years old. In 1960 her husband decided to take a second wife. Seuzon objected and moved back to Guanming, her natal hamlet in Mengsong, taking along her small son. When her son grew up he wanted to move to Chala, yet another hamlet in Mengsong. Seuzon did not want to move again, but she also did not want to lose her son as she had lost her husband (they were separated, not divorced). So she and her son moved to Chala in 1980 and back to Xianfeng in 1982. Unfortunately for Seuzon, the government allocation of land to households took place before their return to Xianfeng. Seuzon holds officially allocated land in Chala, but not in Xianfeng where she now lives.

While still in Guanming, Seuzon's son married a capable woman who helped increase the family's holdings of pigs, water buffalo, and cattle. Then, five years ago (in 1992), someone from Guanming killed the wife. That person had stolen a pig from an Akha hamlet in nearby Burma. At a meeting of the Guanming collective, attended by Burmese pig owners and Seuzon's daughter-in-law, it was decided that the pig be returned to Burma. After a time, when no one returned the pig, Seuzon's daughter-in-law took the pig back to its owners across the border. Shortly after that, at a festival in Guanming, the thief took the daughter-in-law into the forest and killed her. For this crime he was arrested and killed by the police.

These days Seuzon plants her husband's younger brother's wet-rice fields, since he has more than he can use. This is an informal arrangement in place since 1982. Her son, meanwhile, has opened some wet-rice terraces across the border in Burma. This arrangement is also informal. Another brother-in-law gave Seuzon a lot of tea land, which a grandson helps to pick. A second grandson works in tin and manganese mining. Through cobbling together these various sources of grain and income, her household is now doing fairly well.

At eighty-two years old in 1997, Mini is the oldest woman in Akhapu (Thailand). She was born in nearby Burma and married at twenty in Namo, a village in the Shan States of Burma. Then Burmese army troops came to Namo and took everything they had. The whole village escaped to the mountains, where they lived in hiding for three or four years. They planted a little upland rice wherever they lived, but did not dare hunt or keep dogs, for fear the barking would give away their hiding places. The villagers ate many kinds of bamboo shoots and wild vegetables, but could not keep pigs or chickens. Sometimes when they had prepared a meal they heard soldiers coming and fled. When they returned to their huts, they found their food, clothes, and other belongings gone.

They heard that there was a place called Akhapu that was safe, so they moved there some forty years ago. In the 1960s there were a lot of Chinese traders in horse caravans that came through Akhapu from Burma. During their stays, Mini's family sold them chickens, pigs, and grain. At that time her household had cattle and water buffalo, which they allowed to graze in the mountains until ready for sale. The family opened swiddens for upland rice and for many years reaped harvests that were more than they could eat. They were able to plant for a year or two and then leave the land fallow for ten or more years.

These days the household plants a small swidden for two to three years and fallows it for only a year or two. Mini says that the soil fertility is low because of overuse and the harvest is not enough for their needs. They lost land earlier to the Loimi Akha and more recently to government refor- estation. One grandson works in the town of Chiang Rai in a gas station, and a granddaughter cooks there in a small eatery. Because of their hill tribe ID cards, these jobs are insecure. Mini comments on the marked decline in grain and security in recent years.

THESE TWO LIFE STORIES SPAN PREMODERN AND MODERN LANDSCAPES in Xianfeng and Akhapu. Both narratives show how Akha have wended their way across the border and back again, weaving together flexible land uses that traverse the Burma border and transgress notions of settled agricul- ture. Increasingly, though, these are landscapes curtailed by property rights and land-use directives from the state. In China, the policies implicated include 1980s land allocation to households, which was part of the house- hold responsibility system. In Thailand, the transforming policies involve reforestation for the king on all shifting-cultivation lands in the north. The trajectories of change in each locale bear exploration. How was an older woman in Xianfeng who missed out on land allocation able to put together a reasonable livelihood by the 1990s, while an older woman in Akhapu who escaped from Burma into a seemingly safe haven instead found her family's security being eaten away over time?

During the period when Xianfeng and Akhapu came firmly within the physical and mental boundaries of modernizing nation-states (1950 onward in China; 1973 onward in Thailand), Chinese and Thai policy makers were shaping modern rural landscapes of agricultural production to serve national purposes. Official visions in each case entailed landscapes in which farmers produced increasing amounts of valued crops based on annual plans. State visions also came to include forests, with their increasing national value, as resources to be both protected and carefully used. The meaning and purpose of forests, like agricultural productivity, came to be defined by the state. In both Xianfeng and Akhapu, state agents began to govern these peripheral areas, including them in the border-as-margin of the nation-state.

Although the landscape of productivity and rule for upland sites differed in China and Thailand, in both cases that landscape comprised state-allocated property rights and land-use regulations; intensified production of wet rice and cash crops on smaller land areas; and a clear and legible landscape in which property lines and productivity were evident to state planners. These landscapes would "look" governed and productive to agents of the state. Plastic landscapes, by contrast, as managed by Akha farmers, were characterized by flexibility of access and use, under rules learned from their ancestors. The time frames for plastic landscapes were both mutable and long-term, producing a complex mosaic of uses with multiple future possibilities.

In both settings over time, Akha farmers incorporated some aspects of state landscapes into their practices and plans. To some extent, plastic landscapes and state landscapes began to shape each other. Villagers increasingly produced wet rice on set plots of land and adhered to new temporal arrangements for markets and wage labor. Both time and space became regularized in new ways. At the same time, however, practices of access and land use continued to be more complicated and flexible than what state agents envisioned.

Chinese planners successively used two different modes of rule in rural areas. From 1950 to 1982, state policies exerted control through making labor legible. Rural farmers were organized into teams to produce grain for the state, and Akha, in the same manner as lowland farmers throughout China, became grain producers in a national project. Beginning in 1982, state policies shifted emphasis from control over labor to control over land. Land and forests were allocated to the local level under state-defined property-rights regimes and land-use regulations. The unit of decision making became the household. In upland areas, policies began to separate agricultural land from forests, to make the lands and their uses more "legible" and manageable for state planners. In spite of these set and regulated land uses, however, Akha began to refashion complex, flexible landscapes that flowed across property lines, state rules, and the boundary separating China from Burma. Even as Akha welcomed the allocation of household land, they started to fashion plastic landscapes in new ways.

In Thailand, meanwhile, state policies for the north sought to harness the region as a landscape of extensive forests, whether as state assets to be exploited or more recently as national treasures to be protected. This vision represented a change in Thai government understanding and practice in relation to space in northern Thailand. The region recently ruled by Khun Sa, with tacit support from the Thai government, was now to be claimed by Bangkok in a territorializing bid to control Thai space up to the border. In response to the threatening conflict in Burma, the Thai government set out to reduce the land area available to ethnic, "non-Thai" upland farmers. The new landscape vision separated the forest from all those categorized as "hill tribes," whose use of shifting cultivation and forestland was to be seriously curtailed. As a manifestation of this vision in Akhapu, an international highland development project to substitute cash crops for opium introduced the landscape of intensified agricultural production on greatly reduced land areas. More recently, the Royal Forestry Department (RFD) reclaimed all shifting-cultivation lands in the north for reforestation. In Akhapu, this move in effect constituted an enclosure, pushing local people off the land and into the lowest ranks of wage labor. Through claims on forests and shifting-cultivation lands, the state pushed Akha farmers out of state forestland and away from the realm of plastic landscapes altogether.

XIANFENG, 1950–97: AKHA UNDER A SOCIALIST REGIME

For local people, the Communist forces that took over Mengsong in 1950 represented liberation from the Nationalists.[1] They also represented the beginning of state definition and control of local agricultural production. In stark contrast to the Nationalist soldiers, the Communists paid for what-

ever food villagers provided. Over the first few months, the Communist soldiers gave villagers large knives and hoes for farming. The troops also brought
in the security necessary for villagers to resume opening swiddens in their
lower-elevation lands. In 1950, the twenty-five households in the hamlet of
Xianfeng opened fields at 1,000 meters, where they planted upland rice, corn,
sesame, cucumbers, cabbages, spinach, pumpkins, winter melons, cantaloupe, ginger, and green beans, as well as other vegetables and spices. The
government also gave out free comforters, clothes, and grain to the poorest households. Due to deaths from starvation in the 1940s, some households lacked the labor to produce enough grain for self-sustenance. In discussing the early 1950s, older villagers note that land was available, but the
critical variable for self-sufficiency was enough adult hands to help with farming (cf. Selden 1993:139–40). Since there were no landlords in Mengsong,
there was no land reform in this area. For the first few years after Communist
control, farmers resumed cultivation patterns from the past.

The Communist troops stationed in Mengsong stopped local opium cultivation by 1954. In anticipation of Communist rearrangements of wealth
among householders, many of the Dongfanghong traders fled to Burma in
the early 1950s. Some had strong ties with the escaping Nationalist troops
or were heavily involved in the opium trade. Some simply had considerable
wealth from trading in tea and other goods. Either way, they feared that
Communist troops would confiscate their capital and thought that Burma
might prove more welcoming to their lifestyle. They escaped to the world
of small border polities. Those villagers remaining in Mengsong were all
relatively poor.

Up to 1957, following the national policy that Communist cadres should
work with traditional leaders and accommodate minority nationality customs, the hamlet heads and the head of Mengsong from before the revolution continued in place. Additionally, villagers held their twelve annual festivals, although on a less elaborate scale than before, since they lacked animals
to sacrifice to their ancestors. National policies specified that there should
be a transitional period with gradual implementation of socialist rule.

In the late 1950s, policies brought about more dramatic changes, organizing rural production through control over labor. The socialist mode of governance sought to make labor legible. In addition to producing grain for the
state, villagers were organized to build a road, a school, and a reservoir—the
accoutrements of a modern society. Governance also meant collecting grain
for the state to build an industrialized economy and transforming Akha into
modern socialists.

Beginning in 1957, cadres from Damenglong, the nearest town, organized villagers in Xianfeng into mutual-aid teams of seven to eight households to carry out planting and harvesting rice. The following year, 1958, marked the real beginning of the collective period, as Mao Zedong's Great Leap Forward began. Hamlets in Mengsong became production teams within the Mengsong production brigade. The brigade, in turn, was one of several in the Damenglong commune. From 1958 until the dissolution of communes in 1982, Xianfeng hamlet became a production team under the Mengsong production brigade. Land in Mengsong was collectivized, as was tea, most bamboo, and all livestock. State production quotas were delivered to the production team, whose leaders organized the work to meet those quotas.

Since the state focus was on labor rather than land, production teams could temporarily trade shifting-cultivation land back and forth during the collective period, depending on which community needed the land. These kinds of flexible arrangements were made at the production-team level, as teams devised strategies to meet state grain quotas, not to claim land.

In 1958, at the beginning of the Great Leap, cadres from the Damenglong commune told villagers that they had to take down the ancestor baskets in each home, burn the three branches and grain stalks, and never hold these rituals again. Believing in and worshipping ancestors was superstitious, according to the new ideology, which instead promoted reliance on science and rationality in managing people's lives and in organizing agricultural production. In place of annual rituals and festivals that linked the Akha ancestors, the forest, and the production of upland rice, villagers were now to rely on ideological instruction and commands from a government administration that stretched beyond Damenglong to the county, the prefecture of Xishuangbanna, the province of Yunnan, and ultimately to Communist Party leaders in Beijing.

Work Points and Grain: Keys to the Legibility of Labor

Before the arrival of the Communists, Akha trade in tea and opium had linked them with the political economy in Sipsongpanna (Xishuangbanna under the Communists), as well with trade networks extending into Burma and China. Under the socialist regime, local farmers were not to be concerned with trade, nor with relations across the border. Local household strategies for labor allocation were overridden by state plans for local production. Additionally, the product extracted was not "extra" like tea or opium, something that could come and go without disrupting the pattern

of cultivation. The product was grain: central to both state and local livelihoods and structures of meaning. The state was claiming the main product protected by and offered to the ancestors. As collectivization proceeded, policies changed the meaning of rice through practices of labor and
payment for work. In spite of policies promising to preserve ethnic minority cultures, plans that reorganized labor and altered the role and meaning
of rice cut to the heart of Akha ritual practice.

Collectivization in Mengsong mobilized local participation in the nation-
wide Great Leap Forward, Mao Zedong's political movement to advance
China into the ranks of industrialized economies within a short period of
time. In Mengsong, the predominant change was that the production-team
head, a local Akha, now organized villagers into work teams to carry out
projects. The production brigade (Mengsong) initially allocated land and
livestock to each production team (former hamlet). Among the now thirty-
five households in Xianfeng, some villagers were assigned to upland rice,
some to herding livestock, some to producing vegetables, and others to cooking and other activities as needed. During the Great Leap, all villagers ate
together in one big room.

Beginning in 1958, each person earned work points for labor. The frame-
work was basically to each according to his or her labor, within a maximum
possible number of 8 points per day. Villagers working in upland rice and
in cooking earned 8 points per day, since these tasks were regarded as hard
physical labor. Those working in vegetables, which were planted in plots
close to the village, were often women with small children. These women
earned 7 points per day. Those assigned to herding, who were often men
past the peak of their physical vigor, earned 6 points per day. Villagers
thought that the points were allocated fairly and equally to men and women,
since women could work in upland rice. Women who were nursing babies
or who had small children, however, often earned less than adults able to
go out to distant fields every day. Children seven to nine years old could
earn 2 points, while those ten to fifteen years old earned 4 points per day.
Children in school half the day could earn 2 points for half a day's work.
Teenagers sixteen years and older could earn the full 8 points. If people
failed to do the work assigned one day, their work points would be docked,
so that they might receive 7 instead of 8 points each day for three to four
days. If people repeatedly did not do the work they were told to do, their
work points would be docked for "a long time." State control over labor
and its rewards was detailed and thorough. The allocation and redemption
of work points made labor legible to an extraordinary degree.

In the early days of collectivization, before any villagers were literate in Chinese, the hamlet accountant gave people slats of bamboo with various numbers of holes drilled in them, based on the number of work points earned. At the end of every month, each person turned in bamboo slats to the accountant. At the end of the year, each person got the annual allotment of grain based on his or her total accumulated work points. In addition, each household received a small amount of cash, between 30 and 45 yuan, also based on total work points. With this money, a household could buy salt, oil, and so on. If the household had sold tea for cash during the year, the amount of the sale would be deducted from their annual cash allotment. If a household had borrowed grain from the collective, that amount would be deducted from their annual grain allotment. At the end of the year, collective (production team) pigs were killed and everyone got some, unless a household was in debt to the collective. The locus of collection and distribution was clearly the production team.

Early in the Great Leap, one-third of Xianfeng households fled to Burma, fearing that they would starve under the new system. They fled to kin and familiar social relations in the Shan State. Later, most of these households returned, but their fears about having sufficient grain were justified: from 1958 until 1982, when land was allocated to households, there were many years when grain harvested in October ran out in March or April. Some stretches were worse than others, and the reasons for the grain deficiency were multiple.

The pattern of insufficient grain was common in many parts of China (cf. Oi 1989). In Jean Oi's study, the primary reason for insufficient grain was the severity of state grain procurement from the rural sector to fund industrial development.[2] While the policy proscribed the procurement of "excess" grain, Oi demonstrates that state requirements often ate into supplies needed for basic sustenance. In Xianfeng, however, villagers did not blame government procurement as the main source of their grain deficit, although there were certainly times (in the late 1960s and early 1970s) when state emphasis on increasing grain production (taking grain as the key link), plus regional self-sufficiency in grain, forced villagers to open new areas of forest (see Xu 1990).

Villagers cite other reasons for the difficulty in producing enough to eat. During the Cultural Revolution (1966–76), people found it hard to work during the day, since they had to attend political meetings and criticism/self-criticism sessions every night until midnight. Additionally, whether they worked hard or not, people earned 8 work points every day for being out in the field. Some village leaders today say there were people (always in families other than their own) who did not like the discipline of working for work points. Some people working in upland rice planted very slowly, taking three months to finish. By the time planting was done, the early rice was already high. That there should have been "everyday forms of resistance" to such a stringent and unproductive labor system is unsurprising (see Scott 1985). But the former village head notes that, especially during the Cultural Revolution, 70 percent of hamlet labor was devoted to tasks other than grain—to building the road from the Xishuangbanna valley to Mengsong, building the reservoir and power station, herding livestock, and even, in some cases, going from commune to commune to beg for grain. Too few people were assigned to upland rice. Although the upland-rice teams opened swiddens on a huge scale, larger than anyone had ever seen, the area opened per person was only 1–2 *mu* (0.06–0.13 hectare), too little to produce enough grain. The emphasis was on building a modern China, but not necessarily on feeding it.

Just before the Cultural Revolution, there was a three-year hiatus when Mao Zedong was out of power in Beijing. During the so-called Liu Shaoqi period (1962–64), when Liu was briefly able to push through new policies, villagers were allowed to withdraw from the collective and to produce grain on their own if they chose. In Xianfeng, the former hamlet head withdrew. To illustrate the difference between collective grain and household grain, he points out that in the collective, each person could earn 50 to 60 *luo* of grain per year with work points (1 *luo* equals about 25 kilos, and 1 *luo* equals 3 *mu*). His household left the cooperative for two years. In 1963, his household produced 130 *luo* per person. In 1964, they produced 150 *luo* per person. They had enough grain for two years, outside of what they contributed to grain procurement. In 1965, however, the policy was rescinded. His household returned to the collective and, as he says, "to poverty." In his view, Akha farmers knew much more about production in upland areas than did cadres from lowland offices.

Villagers remember 1967–72 as the leanest years. To combat the deficits, they agreed in a meeting in the late 1960s to open new wet-rice fields. In their lower shifting-cultivation fields, below 1,000 meters, they worked in teams to cut terraces for several hectares of wet rice. In spite of this effort to increase the local availability of grain, there was still not enough grain to last through the year on a consistent basis until 1979, when households were allowed to open their own swiddens again.

During the mid-1970s, as the Cultural Revolution began to wind down, national policy makers decided to stimulate grain production by revising how work points were determined. By 1974, political meetings in the evenings were fewer, so that those who wanted to work hard could do so. Under the revised system, points were allocated more according to the amount of work accomplished, rather than the kind of work done. For example, instead of allocating the same number of points to all those who worked in upland rice, people were rewarded based on the area planted each day or the number of steps performed. Villagers could earn anywhere from 30 to 100 or more points per day for their efforts. There were still chronic shortages in grain, since, as before, some villagers worked little but they continued to eat. As national policies in the late 1970s emphasized further increases in grain production, state grain procurement also managed to take a huge bite out of the harvest (see Xu 1990).

State priority on grain production and procurement during the collective period thus shaped much of the relationship between state and villager, defining citizens as laborers for the state and hard work as that which earned 8 points (and later potentially more than 100). Indeed the state's primary claim on all of rural China was the collection of grain to feed urban populations and to fund industrialization. Additionally, all work in Xianfeng was directed toward earning enough grain at year's end to last through the following year. Grain was the payment for all work. While previously grain had been the heart of ritual life as well as the source of sustenance, it became a product whose use and value were determined by the state, both as extracted quota and currency. The production of grain was legitimated by state needs rather than by the protection and sanctions of the ancestors.

The organization of labor was to some degree turning Xianfeng farmers into socialist people, and the collectivized system changed villagers' relationship with one another. Villagers depended on everyone's work for survival in a more direct way than they had in the past. Certain conflicts in the hamlet during my research, although not centered on events in the collective period, were inflected by memories of those (in other households) who loafed all year and still ate the collective grain.

Forests during the Collective Period

Elsewhere in China, even in Xishuangbanna, the Great Leap drive to produce steel in each locality resulted in the construction of crude blast furnaces and the destruction of huge areas of forest to fuel them.[3] In Mengsong, there were no backyard blast furnaces. Early in the Cultural Revolution, though, the state announced that forests were an inefficient land use. Trees were either to be exploited or moved out of the way for the production of both grain and economic crops, such as fruit trees. In 1967, the commune appointed a local Akha in Xianfeng, Yah Teh, to serve as the people's militia person. The commune gave Yah Teh a gun and enjoined him to enforce new policies. Following new state directives, he told villagers that the primary forest that stretched from the village out to the closest shifting-cultivation fields was an inefficient use of this land. This site was to be cleared and planted in pear, apple, and walnut trees. Yah Teh was ordering villagers to disobey the most serious injunction from their ancestors, not to clear sites of primary forest. Additionally, this particular forest included the woods around the village that protected them from evil spirits. For his role in this event, the ancestors punished Yah Teh severely.

According to villagers, this particular forest held the largest trees, many from canopy species found only here and in the Sanpabawa, the Mengsong forest protected for some two hundred years. Although farmers acknowledged that Yah Teh was following orders from above, they still blamed him for the loss of this forest. When recounting this event, in the next breath several informants told me that one day when Yah Teh was opening a swidden in primary forest, he developed stomach pains. It turned out that he had stomach cancer, a disease that later killed him. Villagers saw a cause and effect relationship between clearing primary forest and Yah Teh's death. For Xianfeng Akha, the ancestors did not disappear when the ancestor baskets were burned and, in this instance, the ancestors were in direct conflict with a state directive.

After this initial dramatic clearing of primary forest, however, other customary rules held less force. Although villagers continued for the most part to protect an area of forest around the hamlet, some people began to collect dead trees there, a practice that had been forbidden before. There were also occasional cases of people actually cutting trees in this forest. It was as if the ancestors were right: with the loss of some forest encircling the hamlet, villagers were less protected from evil.

During the collective period there were no state policies for forest protection to substitute for the ancestors' rules. State maps of Xishuangbanna from this era show forested areas as wasteland, a designation reflecting their value at the time.[4] According to older people who lived through both the collective period and the ensuing period of economic reforms, the forests

around Mengsong were in better condition in 1997 than they had been during the collective era.

During collectivization, the practice of shifting cultivation also began in
wooded sites, joining forests and agricultural fields together in Akha experience. Cleared swiddens ordinarily moved successively from grain production through different stages of forest regeneration. While villagers used
products from all these stages, government policies drove the system toward
greater production of grain and shorter periods of fallow. Although total
area of forest cover stayed about the same in Mengsong from the early 1960s
to the mid-1980s, much of that cover shifted from primary to secondary
forest (Xu 1990). Older villagers thought that by the late 1970s, even some
of that secondary forest had become fairly scraggly.[5]

Aside from opium production, the various forms of land use during the
collective period stayed the same as before the 1949 revolution: villagers
opened swiddens as well as wet-rice fields; they herded livestock; they cultivated tea for local use. While the ecological plasticity of the landscape
remained largely in place, as swiddens regenerated slowly into forests, villagers' choice about where to put their energy was heavily constrained by
government directives. The plasticity of land cover continued, but the flexibility of labor allocation was seriously limited. This was not landscape plasticity, but rather the control of rural labor for the socialist state.

The Period of Economic Reforms: Landscape
Plasticity within Landscapes of Productivity and Rule

Beginning in 1982, national policies brought the collective period to an end.
To stimulate agricultural production, land that had been managed by communes was distributed to hamlets and households. In 1982–83, the household responsibility system was implemented in Mengsong as it had been
for agricultural land all across China. Since this initial allocation nation-
wide resulted in immediate increases in grain output and was deemed a success, a second wave of land distribution was carried out for forestland. In
1984, some areas were designated as state forests and nature reserves and
kept under state ownership and management. Other wooded sites that had
been managed by communes, often somewhat degraded forests, were allocated to hamlets and households. The stated purpose for distributing forests
in this way was to increase both the protection and productivity of wooded
areas. Teams from the United Nations' Food and Agriculture Organization
(FAO) and other international organizations convinced Ministry of Forestry

officials that trees had economic as well as ecological value that needed to be protected. This point of view, held all along by some Chinese foresters, was now allowed to drive policy formulation.

The breaking apart of communes and allocation of land to hamlets and households represented a profound policy change in China, shifting focus from labor to land as the significant factor of production. This represented a new landscape vision, one based on increased agricultural productivity and economic development with the household as the unit of production. In China, five-year plans laid out the march into the future, with each plan divided into annual production goals. Allocating property rights to households not only encouraged households to produce more, but also enabled state planners to view the map of property allocations, add up the area of wet-rice and upland-rice fields, and make annual predictions of grain production. Mapped and quantified production figures made land use legible and allowed state planners to control agricultural production, or at least that was the driving desire. The state's need to plan and predict, both for agriculture and economic development more broadly, served as the legitimating rationale for focusing the production landscape at the household level. In this landscape vision, farmers were to become entrepreneurs. Additionally, this vision separated agricultural from forest land, both on the ground and under separate ministries. This division represented a major step in creating clearer, simpler landscapes in the uplands for the benefit of lowland planners.

In the reform period, state grain procurement continued, but with the state now paying households for the grain at a set low price. Once villagers fulfilled their procurement quotas, they could sell any additional grain at the higher market price. Over time, the state allowed more and more agricultural goods to be sold in open markets, leading to the commodification of many agricultural and nontimber forest products. In response to state encouragement, farmers sold more and more products to generate cash income, but timber remained a subsistence good. Two-thirds of forests across China had been allocated to hamlets and households, but households were not allowed to sell trees.

In Mengsong, the allocation of wet-rice fields took place in 1982. At that time teams of villagers in each hamlet worked with delegates from Damenglong, the headquarters of the former commune, to measure and distribute terraced fields. Each household was to receive 1.2 *mu* (0.08 hectare) per household member. The teams generally gave to each household fields of two different qualities, one that required fertilizer and one that did not. Most villagers thought that distribution of wet-rice fields was fair. The hamlet head from that time said dividing the wet-rice fields was relatively straightforward and easy. Like the allocation of all other kinds of land in Mengsong, both agricultural and forest, these distributions were secure for fifty years.

In dividing the wet-rice fields, the team discovered that some terraced fields opened during the collective period were actually in Burma. Xianfeng officials negotiated the continued use of these fields, since Xianfeng controlled the water for these fields and for agricultural lands in the neighboring Akha hamlet in Burma.

The allocation of shifting-cultivation land occurred in quite a different way. Beginning in 1979, before the dissolution of communes, households had been allowed to open their own swiddens on days off. Although they continued to work collective wet-rice fields during the week, on Sundays they could tend their own fields of upland rice. According to the Xianfeng hamlet head during that period, it was very difficult to get people to do collective work once households had their own fields.

In 1982–83, when shifting-cultivation lands were formally distributed to households, three teams divided the land in Xianfeng hamlet. The teams headed off in different directions, and made decisions with each team using somewhat different criteria, although in principle each household was to get 9 mu (0.6 hectare) of land per household member. In cases where households had already opened swiddens, those fields were often simply allocated to that household. This default decision meant that those households with the labor to open swiddens in 1979 now managed to get permanent use of the best land. At this same time, livestock, tea fields, and bamboo were also distributed equitably to households.

The former hamlet head remarked that villagers in general welcomed set property rights. In his own judgment, though, the ability to exchange lands during the collective period had resulted in more equitable harvests for everyone. Once a hamlet or household's land was set, it became hard to change. If a hamlet got only a little of something, it stayed little.

Based on the forest policy directives in 1984, forestland was allocated to hamlets and households in the same manner that agricultural land had been. In 1984 the forestry station in Damenglong sent a forester, Mr. Chen Yongsan, to help Mengsong define and distribute its forestland. A local team made up of one person from each hamlet and one from the administrative village worked with Chen to decide what pieces of forest belonged to whom. The Sanpabawa, which had continued to be protected by local people during the collective period, was designated as state forest, since it was the best-quality forest in Mengsong. Then each household was given freehold forestland (*ziliushan*), 4 or 5 *mu* of land (about 0.3 hectare) where they could cut trees for fuelwood, poles, fences, and other subsistence needs. In the next step, each hamlet was given an area of collective forest (*jitilin*) based on the population in the hamlet. Xianfeng got 500 *mu* of forestland (about 33 hectares) to be used for house construction. As of 1996, there was still considerable grumbling about the division of freehold forestland to households. As the administrative village head conceded, even 5 *mu* was not really enough to provide a household with enough fuelwood for the whole year. From the start, households looked to fuelwood sources outside state allocations. In this instance, state allocations pushed farmers to transgress property lines.

At the same time forestry staff and local villagers designated areas for forest protection. An area of forest around the hamlet became a scenic forest, where nothing could be cut. The team also acknowledged the existing cemetery forest and watershed-protection forest. Each of these sites had been protected by customary rules for many years, but now came under state regulation. The state was effectively co-opting the Akha ancestors' role of protecting woods. Rules and enforcement now came from the state forestry station rather than from village elders, and indeed villagers look to the forestry station for punishment of infractions. This is an instance of state formation in Agrawal's sense of "the internalization of rule by villagers" (2001:14), although in Xianfeng enforcement came from the forestry station rather than from a hamlet committee, as was the case in Agrawal's study of Kumaon, India.

The Reemergence of Landscape Plasticity

With newly allocated land, households in Xianfeng could make their own production decisions, within certain limitations. Each household now had to fulfill a grain contract quota for the state, for which they would be paid at a set low price. In 1996, the quotas in Xianfeng were set at 56 kilos of grain per person. In addition, each household paid taxes on wet-rice fields and on the amount of shifting-cultivation land actually planted. In 1996, the tax amounted to 10–15 yuan (US$1.20–1.80) per household, depending on the amount of land. As of that year, villagers could pay part or all of their contracts and taxes in cash, but in the past all of these payments were required in rice or corn. Accordingly, each household had to figure out how to produce enough grain each year to fulfill state obligations and to feed household members and livestock. To meet all these needs, Akha men and women realized that they could now begin to plan.

In interviews with numerous villagers about this transition, I got a sense of exploration, as people combined memories of practices from previous times with new possibilities for production and marketing. This was not a return to pre-1949 land uses, but a reworking of practice and opportunity. A tendency to use the landscape in multiple ways resurfaced, together with deployment of wage laborers in several directions. The realm of flexible landscapes came to include wage labor.

Understanding changes in household labor allocation and land use at the hamlet level requires a further brief policy overview for the 1980s and 1990s. National policies over this period gradually opened up the prices on fruits, vegetables, herbs, medicinal plants, mushrooms, and other wild edible products to encourage farmers to produce for the market. At the same time, related policy directives shifted the financial burden for maintaining local infrastructure and administration to the local level. Additionally, the cost of education and medical care, which had been free during the collective period, was transferred from the state to the household.[6] While opening up the price of agricultural products might have led farmers to sell some of their goods, forcing villagers to pay for education, health care, and the projects undertaken by local government ensured that farmers looked for a variety of income-earning possibilities. Household strategies during this period became more complex, as family members had to produce grain, feed the family, earn increasing incomes, and bear a wider variety of expenses.

Another long-term goal of both forestry and agriculture departments beginning in the early 1980s was to bring shifting cultivation to an end. FAO and United Nations Development Programme teams during those early reform years convinced Chinese policy makers that shifting cultivation was destructive to the environment. In Xishuangbanna, policies thus encouraged upland farmers to open wet-rice terraces to replace swidden fields as the site of grain production. These policy directives intended to make grain production more efficient per area of land as well as more sedentarized.

Farmers in Mengsong responded readily to new policies, although not always in ways that policy makers and local officials would have predicted. Those households who had been given shifting-cultivation lands at lower elevations, on gently sloping land with access to water, opened wet-rice terraces in their swidden fields. Their reason for opening terraces was not efficiency of space, however, but efficiency of labor time. Villagers said that wet-rice required peak periods of labor for planting, weeding, and harvesting, but at other times freed up labor for other purposes. Upland-rice fields, by contrast, required some labor almost year-round. Once households had switched to wet rice, women spent more time tending vegetables to sell, as well as collecting mushrooms, medicinal herbs, and wild fruits and vegetables prized in lowland markets. Men engaged in paid labor, either locally in mining or in jobs in Damenglong or Jinghong. By planting wet rice, households could spend more time increasing their cash incomes.

Another local response to the opening of markets was the production of more livestock. With changing policies toward minority nationalities allowing villagers to practice their unique cultures, both Akha and Tai households resumed using cattle and water buffalo in ritual sacrifices and feasts. Additionally, more Akha were eating meat from domestic animals in place of the wild game they preferred in the past. By 1989, most households had stopped opening swiddens in their shifting-cultivation fields. With the gradual increase in numbers of livestock, Xianfeng farmers began to burn large stretches of their upper-elevation shifting-cultivations fields each year to provide sweet new grasses for grazing animals. By 1996, almost all of the higher-altitude swiddens had effectively reverted to collective use, in spite of their earlier allocation to households. By that time, Mengsong as a whole supported three times the livestock it did in 1982, and sale of livestock constituted a major source of household income, second only to mining.[7] To extend the available pasture area, many people ranged their animals in adjoining areas of Burma as well. While the use of swiddens in Xianfeng for pasture was breaking land-use regulations, extending that pasture into Burma moved beyond any notion of allocated property areas or regulated uses altogether.

Another hamlet in Mengsong had the reverse experience with respect to shifting-cultivation land. In 1982, that hamlet had been allocated a collective pasture along the road leading to town. The hamlet fenced the pasture, but later stopped using it when these farmers, like those in Xianfeng, began to send their cattle and water buffalo over the border to graze. In recent years, a few households have begun opening swiddens inside the fenced area, turning what had been collective land into household fields. This was not done with official approval, but as a response to household need for more grain.

In Xianfeng, too, several households were feeling the pinch in their ability to produce enough grain. The tin mining in one area of wet rice had seriously undermined grain production for some households. In other households, sons had married and added wives and children to the household since the time of land allocation in 1982, but the available land area had not increased.

To address this shortfall, many older women in Xianfeng began opening swiddens in a new site (see fig. 12). The former people's militia member told me one morning that all households in Xianfeng had stopped using shifting cultivation in 1989. He stated firmly that everyone relied on wet rice for grain. That afternoon, when this man had a malaria attack, I followed his wife out to her shifting-cultivation fields, a site that had apparently escaped her husband's notice. This site had been designated as a common area shortly after 1950 for anyone in Xianfeng. During the collective period it had been used to plant vegetables. After land was divided to households, no one used this land and it regenerated into trees. In the late 1990s, after people had cut these trees for fuelwood, older women started planting upland rice and corn there. They had gradually planted saplings as fences along the edges of their new fields, informally claiming for individuals all the once common land.

In this area, Deuleu, the wife of the former people's militia member, planted 4 *mu* of upland rice and 4 *mu* of corn (about 0.25 hectare each). In her upland-rice fields, she planted two varieties of rice. One variety she intercropped with sunflower and planted in April. The second variety, without sunflower, she planted at a slightly lower elevation in May. With the higher-elevation upland rice, she also planted cucumbers, cassava, sesame, and eggplant. In the lower-elevation fields she intercropped sesame, cotton, watermelons, and green beans with the grain. Her corn fields were also planted with tea, tobacco, cassava, and ginger. Deuleu grew corn to feed livestock and to help pay taxes. Her upland rice could serve as the staple grain and also pay taxes. The vegetables in her plots could be both eaten and sold. This kind of diversity of production and purposes suited her vision of what land use and landscapes should be.

Another of these older women harvested not only grain and vegetables, but also the plethora of medicinal herbs that appeared in regenerating swiddens. She claimed to know medicinal uses for all but three of the plants and trees in Mengsong, and to be able to cure diseases in both people and livestock. She liked the common-area swiddens because they ensured the ongoing availability of certain medicines.

Other women found another means to extend available land area beyond what had been allocated. They opened areas in what was called the "lower hamlet," where they had lived until 1968, when state cadres forced them to move upslope. On sites that had once been their homes and surrounding

FIG. 12. Mother and son in swidden field

gardens, these women informally claimed the land to plant vegetables, fruit trees, and even some grain. Some of these women simply needed more vegetables to feed their families, but most were selling their fruits and vegetables in growing markets. Their strategies, like those of the women planting in the common area, were not holdovers from the past, but were firmly grounded in present concerns. All of these women were stretching available land in sites that were invisible to men and unallocated to households.

This kind of flexibility, or plasticity, of the landscape increased household security in ways that men in Xianfeng apparently did not notice.

Akha men, meanwhile, continued to hunt wildlife, but they now crossed into Burma to shoot deer, leopards, and smaller animals.[8] These wild animals had disappeared from Mengsong with the general move away from shifting cultivation, since there were no longer many areas of regenerating swiddens where wildlife liked to browse. Clearer landscapes that separated agriculture from forests, the landscapes introduced by state plans, had contributed to the loss of wildlife. Additionally, some of these animals, such as leopards, were by the 1990s on the endangered species list in China. Hunters from Mengsong slipped easily across the border to sites where wildlife was still abundant and the Chinese state could not restrict or punish them.

Household shifts from upland rice in swiddens to wet rice in terraces freed up household labor to engage in income-earning activities that ranged from growing more vegetables to mining. At the same time, many shifting-cultivation lands became pastures for increasing numbers of livestock, or, alternatively, collective pastures changed into household swiddens. These changes in land use and access were not necessarily planned by government agents, although they were all responses to policies that encouraged villagers to produce more grain and to participate more fully in the market economy. These shifts represent Akha farmers' operating in what Arun Agrawal calls the "crevices" in state power (1999:11), in this case in the maneuvering room opened up between state regulations for set plots of land and state requirements to produce for markets. Alongside these activities on state-allocated land, older women opened new fields on unallocated and seemingly invisible land areas, the common land and former home sites. Additionally, Xianfeng farmers pushed across the border into Burma to extend the arenas for herding and hunting, and as the story of Seuzon's son shows, for wet-rice cultivation as well. Plastic landscapes were increasing the scope and diversity of products that farmers could raise, capture, and sell.

Upland farmers who practiced shifting cultivation were familiar with a dynamic landscape that rotated from clearing fields to forest and back again. Older Akha were also still used to extending land uses across the border, and younger villagers explored new ways to do this. In talking with various farmers, it was clear that in their minds fields could become forests and pastures could revert to cultivated fields, with rules of access changing accordingly. They could also contact friends and family in Burma to gain access to various kinds of land. These farmers did not see themselves as breaking rules or subverting state purposes, but rather as being entrepreneurial with the various land-use possibilities available to them. This was not resistance to state plans, but rather a different vision of how to make best use of complicated social and physical environments.

By the late 1990s, though, villagers' practices of landscape plasticity were coming into conflict with state land-use regulations, which sought to set and quantify how various parcels of land would be managed. The forestry station staff in Damenglong informed me that the shifting-cultivation fields that were burned every year for pasture would be reclassified as collective forest. These foresters, including the Akha chief of the forestry station, claimed that, "local people's thinking hadn't achieved their expectations." According to state foresters, Mengsong Akha did not limit their tree cutting to allowed sites. In opening swidden fields, they said, Akha "only think about eating and plant large areas." State foresters mentioned that in Xianfeng, the primary forest near the hamlet had all been cut before land was divided to households. This was the same forest that state cadres had instructed Yah Teh to clear in the 1960s, but by the late 1990s, the clearing had become evidence of Akha backwardness. "We told them to protect the forest and they didn't listen. They only think to plant the mountain and eat the mountain (*zhong shan, chi shan*)." These foresters were pointing to incidents where their instructions were seemingly not followed. They were dismayed that plans to demarcate various kinds of forest areas had not resulted in clear, legible landscapes. This lack of legibility, in turn, was evidence of Akha backwardness and different thinking.

The head of the forestry station mentioned the need to have a permit to cut in the state forest, a permit that would often refer to specific trees. He also noted that the state timber cut limit was set separately for areas of state forest, collective forest, and household forest. All of these rules sought to bring control to cutting in the mountains and to make tree cutting more visible, or legible, to foresters in the township. To address the immediate problem of shifting-cultivation lands that were used for pasture, the forestry station decided that land not used as designated by the state (as swiddens) would revert to woods. The land would still belong to Xianfeng, but would have to be allowed to regenerate.

Forests Since 1984

Chinese foresters point to three periods of particular forest loss (*sandafa*) since the People's Republic was founded—the Great Leap Forward, the periods emphasizing local self-sufficiency in grain in the late 1960s and early

1970s, and the time right after the allocation of forestland to hamlets and households. In talking about this last instance, foresters invariably mention it as a period of *luan*, of uncontrolled local cutting. A Chinese forester would call what happened in Mengsong a prime example of *luanfa*. The word *luan*, literally "chaos," describes a situation outside government planning or control. The cutting in Xianfeng, from villagers' perspective, did not seem uncontrolled or chaotic at all. Villagers were cutting trees of carefully selected size and species to build wooden houses. Throughout the 1980s, beginning even before the state allocation of a collective forest, every household in Xianfeng constructed a new house.

The construction of wooden houses deserves a moment of reflection. As long as anyone could remember, and in legends purporting to have some antiquity, Akha had built houses of bamboo, with wood used only for posts and beams. Indeed, in Burma and Thailand, Akha still build houses of bamboo, with roofs of woven *Imperata* slats. The new houses in Xianfeng were modeled on the bamboo version, but were much larger and more solid in appearance. Contributing to the solidity were fired-clay roof tiles that Akha bought from lowland Tai.

With the allocation of property rights, Akha in Mengsong realized not only that the forest was theirs to use, but also that the state would not relocate their hamlets. One result was that many people decided to build stronger houses, a complex decision representing a somewhat favorable response to state policies. Although Akha had lived in Mengsong for more than 250 years, numerous hamlets had moved sites during that time, all within the area called Mengsong. As of 1984, hamlets could no longer move so easily, but neither were they threatened with relocation to lower elevations. Another reason for cutting trees for houses was that villagers feared that state policies would change again. If the state later decided that Akha could not cut anything, villagers would still have cut timber.

The Xianfeng collective forest, according to several informants, looked like the Sanpabawa in 1980, before people began building houses. In addition to timber for houses, however, the Xianfeng collective forest had also provided construction materials for the Mengsong school and new military barracks. Unsurprisingly, the Xianfeng collective forest in the late 1990s was in stem-exclusion stage, a young forest with many skinny trees growing close together. In discussing the condition of this forest, township foresters tended to forget the official projects (the school, the barracks) over which villagers had no control and to focus on the chaotic building of new houses.

The areas of household freehold forestland in Xianfeng were adjacent to

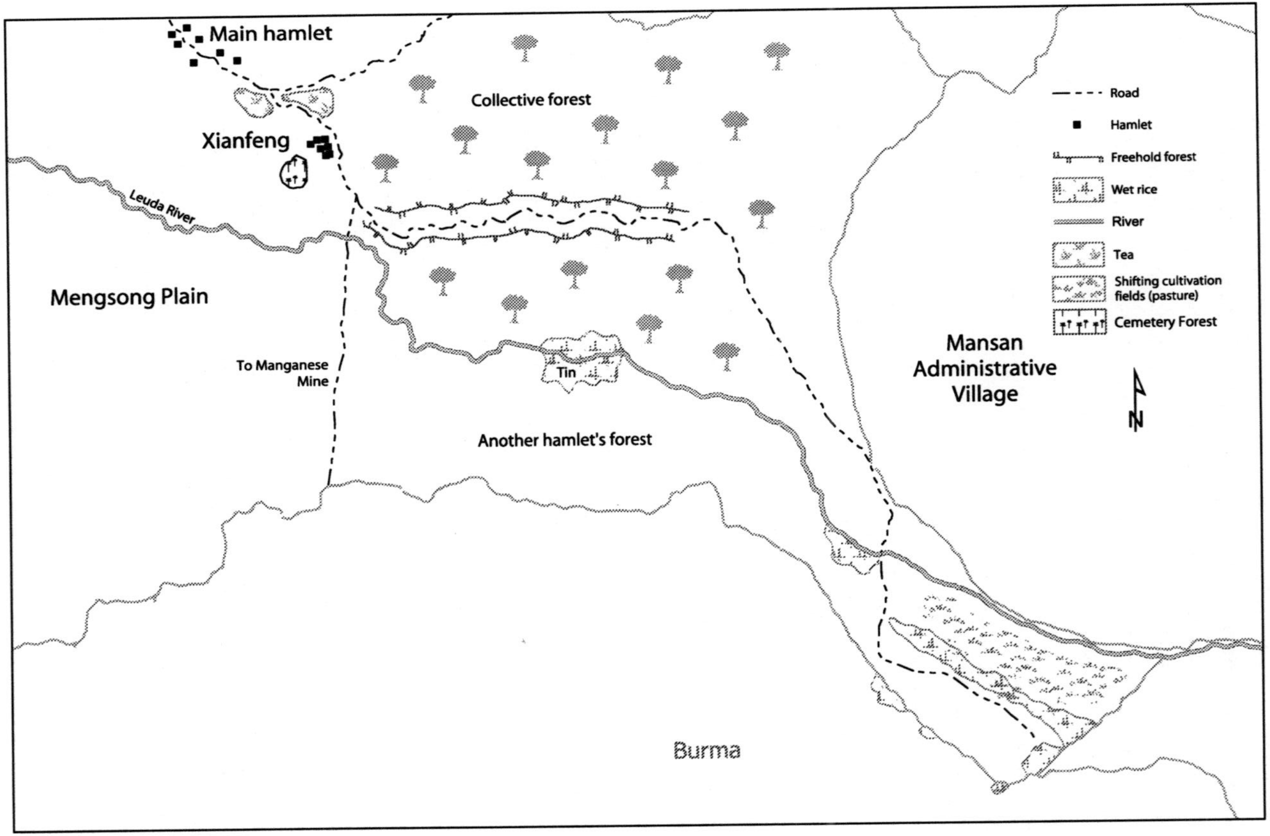

Legend:
- Road
- Hamlet
- Freehold forest
- Wet rice
- River
- Tea
- Shifting cultivation fields (pasture)
- Cemetery Forest

N

Mansan Administrative Village

Main hamlet

Collective forest

Xianfeng

Another hamlet's forest

Tin

To Manganese Mine

Leuda River

Mengsong Plain

Burma

FIG. 13. Xianfeng in 1997

the collective forest. Each year in January and February, households cut most of the fuelwood needed for the coming year from their freehold forest, their tea fields, and from any remaining regenerating swiddens. Because the collective forest had lost its large trees to house building, households started protecting tree species preferred for construction, such as chestnut (*Castanopsis argyrophylla*), in their freehold forestland. As of 1996, it was easier to find large trees on household forestland than in the collective forest. In fact, to acquire the large trees needed for house construction, many villagers drew on their connections in Burma—kin or even government officials—for permission to cut trees across the border. Through social networks and in some cases through patron/client relations, villagers gained access to trees of a size no longer found in Xianfeng.

Akha use of designated forest areas was more complicated than the state vision, with its neat allocation of areas for cutting and protection. Farmers left the collective forest largely untouched, since the trees there were too small to use for posts and beams. Instead, farmers protected particular species, especially chestnut, in their freehold land to grow straight and tall for future use in houses. These shifts in the use of forested areas were based on an intimate knowledge of particular species and specific wooded sites. Akha farmers knew the woods almost tree by tree and made plans based on known processes of regeneration. Akha saw both standing forests and regenerating swiddens as in transition, moving from current patterns and uses to future ones. Villagers remarked on the condition of the collective forest, but they could also imagine what it would be like in twenty to thirty years. They could adjust to new possibilities, but also make long-term plans.

In the late 1990s, Mengsong as a whole showed remarkable diversity in the products collected by Akha. There were more than fifty kinds of wild fruit, several of which were popular in lowland markets. There were also ten kinds of large bamboo, many kinds of small bamboo, and three kinds of rattan. In addition to diversity of uses across the land area at a given time, there had also been dramatic shifts in the landscape over time. The climate in Mengsong was warmer than thirty to forty years earlier, enabling farmers to plant upland rice, peanuts, and certain vegetables at 1,600 meters instead of at 1,000 meters, as in the past. Certain land uses had gradually moved uphill, changing the patchwork of upland land uses. For hamlets other than Xianfeng, the collective forest areas had all been cut before 1949, but by the late 1990s had high species diversity and more than one canopy, indicators of mature forests. This contrasted with the Xianfeng collective forest, which had earlier been primary forest and by the late 1990s was a new forest with many slender trees. The overall landscape in Mengsong showed itself to be highly variable over time, with forests cut and then regenerating for varying lengths of time and agricultural crops moving upward as the local climate grew warmer.

Walking through the land area of Xianfeng (see fig. 13), Agu (a hamlet official in Xianfeng) pointed to a thirty-year-old forest that had been *Imperata* grass when he was young. He also showed me different pastures that had not been burned for two, five, and twenty years—all now regenerating forests in various stages. Walking through the forest also brought out the stories embedded there: here is where Communist troops hung Nationalist soldiers in 1950; here is where we used to plant sweet potatoes for the Nationalists; here is where we opened tiny swiddens when we were in hiding in the 1940s. Memories of these past land uses and events were planted in the landscape. The histories and lessons of the ancestors were also embedded in specific places. The ancestors were still invoked in harvest and burial rituals, invisible to state officials. Additionally, the ancestors' ranks continued to grow. The former hamlet accountant, a Communist Party member, died during my stay in Xianfeng. When he was buried with full ritual, he too became an ancestor. The Akha ancestors now include former members of the Communist Party of China.

For Akha, the plasticity, or flexibility, of planning came to include households sending out people in multiple directions to sell cash crops and to engage in wage labor. The meaning of landscape shifted to include paid labor in various sites, some local, some not. In a variety of ways, and with diverse strategies, individuals, households, and larger groupings continued to produce livelihoods and landscapes that were more complicated than what state agents had in mind. Even the conflicting strategies between men and women added to overall landscape diversity. Villagers were aware of property lines and regulated land uses. They could map out their allocated land areas, even if actual uses tended to flow beyond these designated zones. The outcome as of 1997 was that state property lines combined with Akha complexity. This was a negotiated legibility, with Akha farmers and state agents in conversation with each other, even though state plans constituted the dominant force.

Contemporary Akha Livelihoods in Xianfeng

In March 1997, just before leaving Xianfeng, I carried out a social survey. This was a chance to assess the contingent outcomes of the intersection of

TABLE 1. Xianfeng wet rice holdings

Household	1996 wet rice planted (mu)	Grain enough?
1	5	No
2	19	Yes
3	6	Yes
4	6	Yes
5	6	Yes
6	7.4	Yes
7	8	Yes
8	5.5	Yes
9	3	Yes
10	6	Yes
11	5	No
12	9.8	No
13	7	No
14	7	Yes
15	2	No
16	8.6	No
17	4	No
18	16	No
19	6	Yes
20	10	No

NOTE: 15 *mu* = 1 hectare

state plans and Akha practices in one place. I wanted to find out the degree of equitability of land- and livestock holdings, the range and sources of household incomes, and whether households produced enough grain or the income to buy grain. I selected twenty households out of the fifty-six in Xianfeng by having the hamlet head draw numbers out of a hat and check the resulting household list to make sure it was representative of the diversity of incomes. During the survey, household heads (men and women) responded to set questions. I did not measure land or cross-check answers— I was not interested in that degree of precision.

Table 1 shows wet-rice holdings for twenty out of the fifty-six households in Xianfeng. Eleven out of twenty households had enough grain. Differences in landholding for the most part represent differences in household size. In other words, landholding in 1997 was fairly equitable.

Table 2 shows shifting-cultivation lands in Xianfeng, including how many

TABLE 2. Xianfeng swiddens and their 1997 use

Household	1982–83 allocated swidden fields (mu)	1997 use of swiddens
1	7	pasture
2	29	pasture/wet rice
3	81	pasture/wet rice
4	22	pasture/wet rice
5	81	pasture/wet rice
6	34	wet rice/upland rice
7	16	pasture/wet rice
8	45	pasture
9	117	wet rice/upland rice
10	80	pasture/wet rice
11	60	pasture
12	30	pasture
13	6	pasture
14	30	pasture
15	117	wet rice/upland rice
16	4	pasture/wet rice
17	16	pasture
18	30	pasture/wet rice
19	9	pasture
20	11	wet rice

mu each household acquired in 1982–83 and how those lands were used in 1997. Many households had changed the use to pasture, a combination of wet rice and pasture, a combination of upland rice and wet rice, or entirely to wet rice. In less than twenty years' time, most households had switched land uses around considerably to suit emerging needs.

Table 3 shows household livestock in Xianfeng in 1996. Most people owned water buffalo and pigs. Household 2 specialized in cattle. Although some households owned more than others, the discrepancies were not large. Also, there were no households without livestock.

Table 4 shows household income sources for 1996. The two highest sources of income were tin and manganese mining, both local activities. The next highest source of income was livestock. As the table shows, most households derived income from mining and livestock. Other sources of income

TABLE 3. Xianfeng 1996 household livestock

Household	Water buffalo	Cattle	Pigs
1	3	0	1
2	4	13	4
3	8	0	6
4	3	0	4
5	0	3	3
6	2	0	1
7	1	0	2
8	1	0	1
9	2	0	2
10	4	0	4
11	5	0	2
12	1	0	4
13	4	0	1
14	2	0	3
15	2	2	1
16	2	0	1
17	2	0	2
18	1	0	1
19	4	0	1
20	2	0	1

included sale of fruits and vegetables, tea, wild plants, and bamboo. The household with the highest income (15,060 yuan; US$1,818.47) earned 9.4 times as much as the household with the lowest income (1,600 yuan; US$193.20). The differences in household income are certainly noticeable, but do not indicate huge discrepancies. Some people were doing quite well and others were struggling, but no one was desperately poor. Those households that did not produce enough grain (table 1) could afford to buy grain to eat. Table 4 also shows that there were numerous possible sources of income. The term "fruits/vegetables" obscures how many different kinds of goods were both grown and collected. There were dozens of different vegetables sold, and among fruits, the various wild fruits collected and sold was probably several dozen. Additionally, Akha women kept discovering a market for herbs and spices that they had been gathering all their lives.

TABLE 4. Xianfeng 1996 household income (¥)

| | Income sources | | | | | | | Total |
Household	Tin	Manganese	Livestock	Tea	Bamboo	Fruits/ vegetables	Wild plants	household income
1	3,500	500	900	30		10,130		15,060*
2	2,000	1,000	3,900	400	18	500	440	8,258
3	2,000	4,800		100		110		7,010
4	5,000	1,000		300		180	50	6,530
5	5,430		800		30		40	6,300
6	2,000	2,000	2,400					5,400
7	200	2,700	1,116	150	20	500	8	4,694
8	1,000	2,000	1,200	300		50	100	4,650
9	2,500	300	1,400	100			200	4,500
10	1,500		2,070	400	150		300	4,420
11	3,000	1,000		200				4,200
12	1,000	2,000		150		615	200	3,965
13	2,000	1,000	800	150				3,950
14	1,000	500	1,500	500		40	70	3,610
15			790			720	20	3,530**
16		2,000		300	200	300	200	3,000
17	190	2,000		300		210	200	2,900
18	1,000	1,000	480			80	30	2,590
19	1,000		500	100			100	1,700
20	400	650		300		200	50	1,600
Total	34,720	24,450	16,857	3,780	418	13,635	2,008	97,867

*10,000 from trade with Damenglong
**2,000 from salary working at reservoir

Sources of income were multiple and expanding, a sign of the flexibility and complexity of livelihoods and land uses.

Overall, the social survey and the household interviews show that households had enough to eat and that household incomes were gradually increasing. Most villagers had numerous income sources and could point to new sources that they wanted to try. Their livelihoods were diverse and flexible, responsive to new possibilities. Most people indicated that their livelihoods were improving.

Portents for Future Landscapes

Young people often spoke of the future, both for themselves and for Mengsong. Xiao Li, a young man from Mengsong with a college education from Kunming, predicted that in a few years' time there would be fewer livestock. Under the current five-year plan, swidden fields were to be converted to other uses—economic trees or cash crops—by 2000. Once this was accomplished, there would be nowhere for livestock to graze. He regretted this loss, pointing out how many services livestock provided to farmers, including income generation. Such a shift would result in considerable losses for plastic landscapes in Mengsong as well. Once the shifting-cultivation fields were converted to other uses, there would no longer be a constant supply of fields regenerating into forests. There would also be less land that could be used for new purposes. Meanwhile, Xiao Li planned to look for a job in Jinghong, either in a business or a government office. With his college degree, he was no longer satisfied with a farming life in Mengsong. In this he was typical of younger educated Akha. Parents spoke with pride of children in government offices, businesses, and teaching positions, seeing these achievements as making good in Chinese society and providing the household with connections in new domains.

Mipeh, a teenage girl in high school in Jinghong, enjoyed returning to Mengsong for holidays. She was meanwhile casting her eyes at young Han men whom she knew in town. Like other educated Akha girls, she was looking for a husband who had money. This was more likely to be a Chinese man in Jinghong than an Akha farmer in Mengsong. Her future, like that of Xiao Li, would probably be in town. For Mipeh, as for Xiao Li, there would be numerous choices of occupation in town. The official landscape of modernity in China that included Akha as minority nationalities also accepted them as educated citizens. Every government office, store, and school in Jinghong had Akha on its staff. In the wider society of China, however, her ID card indicating her nationality (Hani) would be a permanent marker of backwardness.

Akheu, the administrative village head, advocated future plans to increase agricultural productivity by replacing water buffalo with tractors to plow the fields. He also wanted to see two new roads, one along the border to the next town and one extending from Mengsong to Menghai. Both roads would improve trade and bring visitors to the new lodge (see chapter 4). He praised state plans to replace shifting-cultivation fields with terraces of fruit trees. He supported the plan to experiment with planting upland rice in fixed terraces in place of rotating fields. Another state plan called for planting clearly delineated wheat fields in the central Mengsong plain.

As a mediating figure between Akha expectations and state plans, Akheu was often the one who introduced landscapes of productivity and rule into Mengsong. In some instances, as in the wasteland auction (see chapter 4), Akheu welcomed a clear, monoculture land use that concentrated a substantial piece of land in one person's hands. In the wasteland auction, the arrival of a simplified landscape also played out to Akheu's advantage, increasing his leverage as patron controlling resource access. In other cases, Akheu was the purveyor of new knowledge about what modern landscapes should look like. In the case of tractors replacing water buffalo, Akheu disregarded the fact that water buffalo, together with other livestock, constituted a major source of household income. Almost every household had at least one. If villagers switched to using tractors, only the wealthiest would own the vehicles, with others having to pay for their use. Additionally, of course, tractors were unsuited in upland landscapes, while water buffalo roamed around them with ease. Tractors, though, would represent progress, brought in by Akheu's foresighted planning.

Akheu aligned himself with state plans and visions, since this generally increased his local stature and stood him in good stead with township and county officials. Akheu was also quick to criticize Akha for profligate use of forests, in line with the narrative propounded by the forestry station. For his part, Akheu was promoting the use of fuel-efficient stoves, a scientific solution to purported forest loss. Akheu's access to state information also enabled him to take advantage of new projects—he already knew where to get saplings of black walnuts and a new kind of pear tree to plant on his own lands.

As administrative village head, Akheu's role was to introduce the state landscape vision. Advising villagers on new plans and crops was part of his mandate. For Akheu, this also meant using his new knowledge to become more like a ruler in relation to landscapes of productivity and rule. He represented progress, science, and the development pathways toward simplified landscapes that would enable farmers to increase production of fewer crops on set areas of land. To the extent that Akheu implemented this vision, or even propounded it, he pulled himself closer to lowland officials and the realms of information and pockets of money to which county and township administrators were privy.

For other Akha in Mengsong, meanwhile, the extent to which landscapes became simplified and sedentarized was also the extent to which farmers would lose both the plasticity and diversity upon which they had depended. As we have seen in Xianfeng, Akha farmers used the multitude and flexibility of land-use possibilities to move land uses around, to change the modes of access, to discover new possibilities in former sites, and to extend land uses across the border in numerous ways. Villagers used this flexibility and diversity in the face of state extractions and Akheu's predations. They also took advantage of the variety of products generated in Mengsong to tap into new markets in the lowlands. This very plasticity and diversity of the landscape constituted their agency in withstanding successive political regimes and ever-changing definitions of what counted as modern agriculture. For them, simpler, clearer landscapes under state-determined rules of access constituted a loss of this agency. Clearer, simpler landscapes tended to benefit local elites and outside actors. For upland farmers, landscapes of productivity and rule generally played out to the advantage of the rulers, but not necessarily to the farmers themselves.

AKHAPU, 1973–97: DWINDLING ACCESS TO LAND

When fourteen Loimi Akha households arrived in Akhapu from Burma in 1973, it seemed to the Ulo Akha living there like a benign event. Indeed, the residents of Akhapu welcomed the newcomers and went with them to help plant upland rice. Shortly thereafter, fifty more Loimi households arrived, and more kept coming. Within the first two or three years, conflicts erupted over land. The Loimi, who had planted wet rice in Burma, went out in teams to open wet-rice fields for each household. Ulo Akha watched their new neighbors shaping terraces right along the river. By the time Ulo farmers realized the value of wet rice, most of the appropriate sites had already been taken. Then fights broke out over shifting-cultivation land. Households from either group would go out to their fields only to find that someone from the other group had taken them over. Some conflicts were settled locally, but others, especially those over wet-rice fields, required Yibaw (the hill tribe representative) or even the courts in the town of Chiang Rai to settle. In official thinking, conflicts between hill tribe groups were to be expected— hill peoples did not know how to get along with each other. Whether over swidden fields or wet rice, however, conflicts broke out because households could no longer produce enough grain to eat. Akha, as hill tribes, paid no taxes; the issue of grain was sustenance. Akhapu had become a landscape of conflict and reduced access to land.

To resolve the problems, land claims by the two Akha groups became more set. After three years, areas worked by each household in either group were clearly known to everyone. Whereas before Ulo villagers could open swiddens anywhere, now they returned to the same areas again and again. Because of diminished land area, households were forced to use swiddens four to five years in a row, fallowing them for only another four to five years. Farmers acknowledged that soil fertility declined precipitously, together with yields. From previous experience, they thought land needed ten to thirteen years of fallow before using it again.

In another bid to reduce conflict, Ulo villagers, who had been living right next to the Loimi, moved to a new site along the saddle of the ridge, dividing Loimi and Ulo Akha into two hamlets. As an Ulo woman said, their chickens and pigs had begun to run into each other's lands, so they wanted to move. The former Loimi village head stated that when they first arrived, they thought that Loimi and Ulo were the same people with the same language. After three years, they could not understand each other. Nevertheless, they did seemingly resolve many difficulties, in spite of official comments that hill tribes could not get along with each other.

Both Ulo and Loimi Akha said that the forest was "intact" when the Loimi arrived. Older Ulo said that there never used to be any sense of whose forest was whose. Under questioning, though, older men recalled that in addition to a watershed-protection forest and a cemetery forest, where cutting anything was forbidden, there was also a site where Ulo cut trees for house construction. They did not let outsiders cut there. This is the site where the tea estate is now located.

In the early 1970s, a group of ethnic Chinese moved to the Akhapu settlement and settled farther along the ridge from the Ulo, closer to the road extending from Hin Taek to the Burmese border. Since the Chinese did not use the same area for swiddening or wet rice, they did not come into direct conflict with the Ulo (see fig. 17 later in this chapter).

This influx of people from Burma was part of a larger pattern of people fleeing the increasing violence in the Shan State in the early 1970s. There was heavy fighting there between the Burmese army and Communist Party of Burma forces, as well as a Lahu rebel army declaration of war against Rangoon (Lintner 1994). Villagers fleeing for their lives knew little about the larger picture. In stories from many parts of the hills, villagers told of being robbed by government troops time after time. When Burmese and rebel armies fighting in their village killed their friends and relatives, hill villagers would finally try to escape. "There were streams of people coming down that road," said one observer, the head of an Akha village adjacent to the road stretching from the border to Hin Taek. For several years in the 1970s, he saw refugees every day.

These upland people were fleeing a war zone following years of oppression and violence. In Thailand, however, they were not granted official refugee status (see Alting von Geusau 1983). Although Thailand had not signed the United Nations protocol on refugees, there had been large refugee camps on its borders with Laos and Cambodia when people from these countries were fleeing communist regimes (Hyndman 2002:42). One reason refugee status was not considered for those fleeing Burma was that Thailand had ongoing trade relations with the Burmese government, no matter its political stripe, and did not want to offend Burmese officials by calling international attention to Burma's inability to bring order to its northwestern regions (45). A second reason was that the people in question had already been labeled "hill tribes" in Thailand, a category consonant with "not Thai" and indeed not quite human. Hill tribes were portrayed in the press as squatters wandering around in the hills and burning forests, not as people escaping from recurrent violence and insecurity in Burma.[9]

In 1976, Khun Sa took over the northwest corner of northern Thailand, controlling it as his domain until Thai and former Chinese Nationalist forces chased him out of Hin Taek in 1982. The U.S. Drug Enforcement Agency and the United Nations Drug Control Program had put pressure on the Thai government to get rid of drug lords within Thailand. Immediately following the ouster of Khun Sa, the second phase of the Thai-Australia Highland Development Project enclosed Akhapu within its bailiwick. The project quickly began to introduce the Thai landscape vision for hill tribes in the uplands: the production of cash crops on greatly diminished areas of land.

Highland development projects across the north set out to end shifting cultivation and to substitute other cash crops for opium. These international projects had a curious dual role: they were both forcing the Thai government to exert more control over the north and at the same time enabling state agents to introduce state landscape visions through the intervention of project activities.[10] During the Khun Sa era, the Thai government had tacitly condoned his regime and had even granted him citizenship (*Bangkok Post*, December 29, 2001). Those in the Thai government who benefited from the drug trade had a stake in keeping Khun Sa and poppies in place. Once Khun Sa was gone, however, politicians and administrators claimed that the Thai government was firmly opposed to narcotics and committed to developing the north. They introduced a new landscape for uplanders, the intensive production of cash crops in place of extensive cultivation of upland rice. From the onset of the highland development projects, landscape plasticity was under threat.

Cash Crops and Landscape Legibility: Two Kinds of Tea

The opium substitution crop for Akhapu was tea, which arrived in two guises. A tea company introduced expensive tea varieties, while the highland project taught villagers to plant local tea. Even before the arrival of the highland development project, a handful of Nationalist Chinese returned to Akhapu to discuss the possibility of opening a tea company. The government of Taiwan was ready to invest in tea production in Thailand's far north. Thai government officials encouraged this plan, thinking that tea would keep the former Nationalist soldiers in the north. In this indirect way, the Thai state could influence small-scale sedentarization of peoples and territorialization of northern lands. In Akhapu, Lawjaw as village head, Yibaw as hill tribe representative, and a handful of Akha leaders agreed to the tea company and allowed the entrepreneurs to use an area of forest where the Nationalists had lived for eight years in the 1960s. Older villagers described this particular forest site as the "best forest," where they used to cut trees for houses. For use of this land, which belonged to the Royal Forestry Department, the tea company began to pay a nominal rent to the RFD. In other locales in the hills, businesses, in most cases run by lowland Thais, set up golf courses, resorts, and other tourist attractions under the rubric of "economic development" (Anan 1996). In Akhapu, "economic development" involved a tea estate.

With funding from Taiwan, the tea company imported expensive tea varieties from Taiwan and Guangdong—wulong teas and other coveted varieties. The tea company hired local people to open the forest, build terraces, put in an irrigation system, and to plant tea on tea company land (see fig. 14). Villagers planted the seedlings in neat rows along the carefully tended terraces (see fig. 15). To allow the full sunlight required by these fancy teas, the tea company removed all the trees from the tea fields. By 1997, the main tea estate occupied 12 hectares, with a total of more than 150,000 tea plants and plans to expand. Akhapu villagers continued to work on tea company land as needed. Additionally, a group of some thirty Akha from Burma crossed the border to work in the tea factory every day. The tea estate brought in simplified monoculture production of a cash crop on what had been primary forest.

The highland development project, meanwhile, introduced villagers to

FIG. 14. Women working in tea company tea

the cultivation of the tea growing in their forest. In 1983, Yibaw, now a project official, sent an ethnic Chinese man from Mae Kham to teach people in the Chinese village and in Akhapu how to construct tea nurseries, plant tea seedlings, and later to transplant the tea to the understory of village community forest. Many people took part and gradually planted tea bushes throughout the adjacent forest.

The introduction of the tea company, together with village cultivation of tea, had a number of effects on village economic stratification, the local economy, access to land, and on the condition of the forest. First of all, by simultaneously introducing the production of two kinds of tea in Akhapu, the tea company and the highland development project produced two kinds of people. Tea company owners, in collaboration with a handful of wealthy Akha, sold high-quality tea for 1,000 baht per kilo (about US$40 per kilo in 1997) to Chinese communities throughout Southeast Asia. Villagers, meanwhile, cultivated local tea, which sold for 50 baht per kilo (about US$2 per

FIG. 15. Tea company tea

kilo), to a wholesaler in Chiang Mai. The tea was so poor in quality that the Thai government refused to package and sell it. The Chiang Mai wholesaler mixed the tea with leaves from elsewhere, packaged it, and sold it in Thailand as low-quality tea. The introduction of two kinds of tea resulted in a landscape of marked disparities in income.

The second outcome of tea cultivation was changes in land access. As households planted the tea in areas of forest next to their homes, they began to claim the tea land as well as the tea bushes as belonging to them.

FIG. 16. Local tea

Households also began to claim any trees growing on their tea land. In particular, households protected species valued for house construction, such as chestnut (*Castanopsis argyrophylla*), the same tree preferred in Xianfeng. If another household wanted to cut trees there, the household claiming the tea fields would allow two or three trees to be cut, but not the protected chestnut. People did not have to pay for the trees cut, but did pay 50 baht apiece for any tea bushes destroyed in the tree felling. Through tea planting, the community forest that had previously been accessible to anyone in the village was now divided into household plots. This step reduced the flexibility of both access and use.

A third outcome of the arrival of the tea company was that villagers began to pay for local labor. Since the tea company paid locals for their work, others needed to pay for labor as well. Previously households had exchanged labor, especially for working in swidden fields, but now people began to pay one another, including relatives, to open fields, weed, help with harvests, and even to pick tea. This change increased the need for cash incomes.

The fourth outcome of tea planting was a change in the quality of the forest. On tea company land, there were no longer any trees, since the fancy tea required constant sunlight. The once "best quality" area of forest was gone. In the community forest, villagers gradually cut many of the trees in the tea fields below the main houses in Akhapu. They took out large trees to allow for the right amount of sunlight, since the local tea liked partial shade. Aside from the coveted chestnut, villagers prevented all other regeneration. Where the tea was intensely managed, the tea fields looked like tea fields, not a forest (see fig. 16). As a result of this development project, an area that until recently had been primary forest became a tea plantation. In areas of the community forest farther from where people lived, the forest looked more intact. With increasing dependence on tea for income, it was likely that more households would take out the forest to improve the quality of their tea. The development project thus introduced the sedentarized production of a cash crop and at the same time the gradual elimination of a primary forest.

A Legible Forest: New RFD Rules

In planning for the north, the region centered on Chiang Mai, the RFD and its consultants used GIS maps, satellite images, and land-use maps showing watersheds, forest cover, and areas for reforestation. Foresters were mainly concerned about reductions in forest cover. From 1991 to 1993, the rate of forest loss in the region was 992,831 *rai* per year (158,852 hectares), and from 1993 to 1995, 646,403 *rai* per year (103,424 hectares). Although the rate of loss was declining, foresters continued to press for curtailment of forest use.[11] The solution, according to the head of the RFD office in Chiang Mai, was to end shifting cultivation and to move hill tribes out of the hills. Then agricultural and forest land in the north could be clearly separated and demarcated on the ground, and RFD staff could prevent any further forest loss. This territorializing approach to the north informed RFD actions in relation to highland villagers, including in Akhapu.

The international highland development project provided the avenue through which state agents could begin to control local land use. It was RFD staff who instructed village heads that, before cutting any trees, local people needed three levels of permission: from the village head, the Border Patrol Police, and from the Security Patrol. The state was defining what a forest was, whom it belonged to, and how it should be managed.

While villagers said that no one was refused permission to cut trees, they thought the approvals a nuisance. A few years earlier, Lawjaw held a meeting in which villagers agreed that anyone cutting trees in the tea fields, whether their own or another household's (with permission), should not bother to get permission from government agents. Tea had by then been planted throughout the contiguous community forests of the Loimi Akha, Akhapu, and Chinese hamlets, so that effectively villagers decided to manage the access to trees in the entire stretch of community forest. Their decision represented a secret counter-territorialization.[12] If RFD agents caught villagers cutting trees, villagers would still have to pay a fine.

When RFD officials announced the cutting permits, they also designated new areas of watershed forest. In allocating these protected sites, RFD staff failed to note that Akhapu already had a protected watershed forest. The RFD watershed forest was in a completely new site. The foresters did not acknowledge the cemetery forest and another sacred site as protected, and as an odd consequence, villagers did not think of themselves as protecting any areas of forest. Customary rules forbid cutting in these sites, but RFD officials did not recognize that as protection. Villagers were beginning to internalize some of the state's vision for forests.[13] The injunctions of the ancestors held meaning for villagers, but bounced off the smooth shield of official knowledge.

In other nearby Akha villages, farmers faced an even sharper contradiction in their use of forests. If they left land fallow for fourteen to fifteen years, the government would claim it as state forestland. If they cut trees to plant upland rice, they would not get full Thai ID cards. For farmers with no sites suitable to open wet-rice fields, their options in the hills were severely limited.

Two State Actions: Hill Tribe ID Cards and Reforestation for the King

Two further steps added to the means for the Thai state to govern the north more directly. One was the introduction of hill tribe ID cards, a move to sedentarize upland villagers, and the second was reforestation for the king, a major effort to territorialize the north under the control of the RFD.

The distribution of hill tribe ID cards by the Public Works Department affected villagers' status in Thailand, access to resources, and the scope for practicing landscape plasticity. From 1985 to 1988, the National Security Council, the Department of Land Development, and the Public Works Department carried out a census of all upland peoples in the north. They counted 550,000 people. Hill tribe ID cards were to be allocated to that many people, with an initial plan that these people could later become citizens of Thailand. Hill tribe ID cards were blue, to distinguish them from white full Thai ID cards. The hill tribe IDs were issued to control highland peoples' movement, both into and within Thailand, and to protect national security. The government was trying to limit highland people's movement on a larger scale, just as development projects and land-use regulations limited flexible practices at the village level.

Staff at the Hill Tribe Welfare Department in Chiang Mai emphasized that the Thai government was particularly concerned about hamlets along the border, such as Akhapu. Many state administrators were reluctant to allow hill tribe villagers to become citizens, and as teams began issuing hill tribe ID cards, officials found that more people had moved in from Laos and Burma. State administrators feared threats to Thai national security, calling up visions of hill tribes as potentially disloyal to Thailand or involved in the drug trade, consonant with the larger discourse on hill tribes.

The 550,000 hill tribe IDs were probably all distributed, village by village. The plan was for villagers to exchange hill tribe ID cards for full citizenship cards at a later date. In practice, however, hill tribe villagers have found this hard to do. According to the regulations spelled out in the *Chiang Rai Hill Tribe Development Report* (Chiang Rai Committee 1994), any upland person born in Thailand who reached the age of twenty and could read, write, and speak Thai could apply for a full Thai ID card. Villagers reported, however, that even if they qualified, there were frequent demands for extra fees, and even then a Thai ID card might not be forthcoming. The rules changed in 1997, requiring an upland person to have a high-school education in addition to the other qualifications (Achao, pers. comm. 1997). Since high schools did not grant diplomas to students with hill tribe ID cards, even if all the required courses had been passed, getting a Thai ID would be difficult. The view that hill tribes were "not Thai" was a strong justification for official inaction.

With a hill tribe ID a person could not get a driver's license, own a car or motor bike, own land in Thailand in either rural or urban areas, or work for the Thai government or a large company. Only Thai citizens could graduate from high school, go to university, become government bureaucrats, buy a house and car, and participate fully in the Thai society and economy. The material outcomes of the hill tribe discourse were quite clear.

Residents of Akhapu had not been Thai citizens in the past, of course, but before the advent of hill tribe ID cards they could travel anywhere in Thailand and work wherever someone would give them a job. With a hill tribe ID, travel had become more difficult, and the range of jobs was limited to menial labor—gas station attendants, cooks and waiters in small restaurants, construction workers, nannies, and house cleaners. Two teenage girls reported that they went outside the village to work as soon as they completed sixth grade. In Mae Chan or the town of Chiang Rai they could earn 1,500 to 2,000 baht (about US$60–80) a month. They came back every month or two, usually bringing some money home. Other young Akha pointed out that none of the jobs available to them provided benefits, and in their experience, those with a hill tribe ID were the first to be laid off. Teenagers, though, saw their futures in locales where they could speak Thai and stay out of the sun—markers of modernity they had learned in school. With reductions in possible jobs, villagers had lost some diversity in the kinds of employment for which they might qualify. In this landscape of diminished possibility, some young people got involved in prostitution and the drug trade, activities that entailed another set of serious risks.

Reforestation for the king became a major project in the 1990s. For decades the extent of forest cover had been the primary measure of success for the RFD. With the recognition in the early 1980s that forest cover had dropped precipitously (see chapter 2), measures were drawn up to protect remaining forests and to plant new ones. One of these efforts was a major reforestation effort to honor the fiftieth year of the king's reign (1996) that encompassed all of Thailand, including the north. The target for the north in 1995, when planting began, was to reforest 1 million *rai* (160,000 hectares). For 1996, the target was 1.5 million *rai* (240,000 hectares), and for 1997, the target was an additional 1 million *rai* of new trees.[14] To demonstrate their green sensibilities, corporations such as the Electric Authority of Thailand and the PPT (petroleum company) contributed funds to the project. With this funding, calculated at 3,000 baht per *rai* (about US$120 per 0.16 hectares at that time), the project hired local villagers to plant native tree species on forest reserve land.

According to foresters at the provincial RFD office in Chiang Mai, areas selected for reforestation were to be abandoned land. The targets were to be past shifting-cultivation sites that had become degraded and abandoned

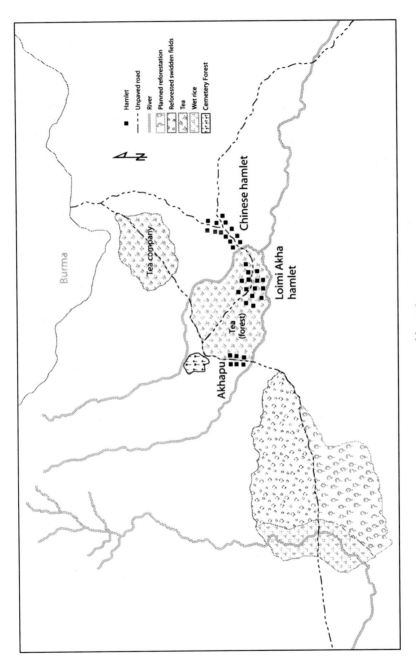

FIG. 17. Akhapu in 1997

Legend:
- Hamlet
- Unpaved road
- River
- Planned reforestation
- Reforested swidden fields
- Tea
- Wet rice
- Cemetery Forest

N

Burma

Tea company

Chinese hamlet

Loimi Akha hamlet

Tea (forest)

Akhapu

by hill farmers. Additionally, local farmers were to agree that they were not using the land and that they would be willing to plant trees. If farmers objected, the RFD would not use that land.[15]

Villagers in Akhapu, as well as in nine other Akha villages in the north, presented quite a different story about reforestation for the king. RFD officials appeared in their villages and told them that they were reclaiming village shifting-cultivation lands, which were on RFD reserve forestland. If villagers participated in reforestation, they would be paid 50 baht (about US$2) per day. Even elite villagers felt they could say nothing, since there was no room for local objection.

By 1996–97, about half of Akhapu shifting-cultivation lands along the river had been planted in tiny trees (see fig. 17). According to regulations in a 1996 RFD brochure on reforestation, 15 to 18 percent of trees planted were to be species other than pine. But the rows of trees in Akhapu looked like 95 percent pine trees. According to the Akhapu village head, the RFD would return with more seedlings and all of the shifting-cultivation lands were slated for reforestation. Villagers could continue to plant crops until the trees grew large, but they were not allowed to burn the fields. Farmers said planting without burning was too much trouble, and that they had stopped using their former fields.

Reforestation for the king brought several rapid changes in access, land use, and labor allocation in Akhapu. Many households were forced off their swiddens and faced a major loss of subsistence. A handful of wealthy households with sizeable wet-rice fields and large areas of tea were little affected, since they relied on wet rice for grain and on tea for income. For the majority of households with little wet rice land and little or no tea, this loss was devastating. They had suddenly been proletarianized and pushed off the land, similar to agrarian transitions to capitalism elsewhere (cf. Marx 1906; Scott 1985; Hefner 1990). People scrambled to find work for the tea companies, for others in the village, or in town. These jobs generally paid 40 to 60 baht (about US$1.60–2.40) per day.

Another result of reforestation was that most households sold off their livestock. As a result of tea in the forest, villagers could no longer let their livestock graze there without supervision. With reforestation, villagers could not pasture their cattle on swiddens in the off-season. Livestock, previously a major source of household income, rapidly became an encumbrance to unload. In the past, livestock had been used in important rituals, such as funerals. Now people could no longer afford to sacrifice a water buffalo for the newly dead to ensure good passage to the ancestors. This change eliminated both a source of income and the means of securing future prosperity by connecting with Akha in the past.

A final result of reforestation was that the RFD had taken the forest out from under Akhapu. The Akhapu community forest was well on its way to becoming tea fields among sparse, tall trees. Shifting-cultivation lands, meanwhile, were reclaimed and replanted in tiny trees by the RFD. The Thai state thus managed to separate forest-dependent people from the forest, literally. The RFD cut Akha off from the home of their ancestors and from the source of multiple potential livelihoods.

As a result of tea company and household tea cultivation and reforestation, Akhapu farmers experienced a serious loss of scope for the practice of landscape plasticity. There was no longer much room for villagers to adjust land uses to their own purposes as needed. The only flexibility open to households was for their members to find an array of arrangements for wage labor. An affinity for complex landscapes was translated into an affinity for a complicated patchwork of paid jobs. The time scale was foreshortened to immediate plans, and new livelihoods were delinked from forests, ancestors, and plastic landscapes altogether.

In the past, Akhapu farmers had exchanged labor with relatives in Burma and had traded goods to villages well into the Shan State. Ado, a man in his forties, recounted that he used to buy dried fish, salt, watches, radios, and tape recorders in nearby Thai towns and take them on horseback to sell in villages in Burma. In the late 1990s it was not safe to cross the border because of armed conflicts on the other side. Additionally, Thai government officials frequently cracked down on Akha crossing the border. On television most evenings there were images of police capturing Akha as they crossed the border with drugs. Akha farmers noted that many drug traders, including Thais, crossed the border every day, but the media seemed to focus on Akha. The state focus on Akha as drug traffickers contributed to the danger for Akhapu farmers in visiting Burma, even for routine purposes. Although traveling into Burma used to open up more possibilities for Akha livelihoods, now crossing the border might land an Akha in jail.

Contemporary Akha Livelihoods in Akhapu

In May 1997, when finishing my research, I carried out a social survey in Akhapu similar to the one in Xianfeng. I wanted to find out the contingent outcomes of processes that have shaped Akha land- and livestock holdings,

TABLE 5. Akhapu 1996 landholding:
Families in Akhapu four generations

Household	Swiddens planted (rai)	Wet rice planted (rai)	Tea fields (rai)
1	20	100	100
2	3	0	5
3	0	5	5
4	3	0	4
5	3	5	15
6	0	0	5
7	2	0	5
8	0	0	0

NOTE: 6.25 *rai* = 1 hectare

household incomes, and sources of income. For survey purposes, I divided
Akhapu into two different groups of households. Those families who had
lived in Akhapu for four generations had both the prestige of first arrival
and the advantage of longer establishment in the region. The village head
came from this group. A second group of households had arrived within
the past fifteen to twenty-five years (1973–97). All had fled the violence in
the Shan State of Burma. On their arrival, the village head allocated to them
shifting-cultivation lands from the dwindling land left.

In Akhapu, I interviewed eighteen out of seventy-six households, again
chosen by the village head drawing numbers out of a hat and evaluating
how well the list represented diversity in incomes. The proportion of all
households was fewer than in Xianfeng because the interviews were done
in May, which is the planting season when people are extremely busy.
Nonetheless, the respondents fall almost evenly into the two groups. Based
on other interviews and data sources, I am confident that these two groupings are representative of conditions for many households.

Table 5 shows landholding for families living in Akhapu for four generations. In 1996 the only household with substantial landholding or tea fields
was number 1, the village head. Among the others, only two households had
wet-rice fields. Areas of shifting cultivation were soon to be lost to reforestation.

Table 6 shows landholding for families living in Akhapu from fifteen to
twenty-five years. In 1996, two of these households planted 10 *rai* of shifting-cultivation fields, but the others planted less than that or in two cases
none at all. Only two of these ten households planted wet rice and only three
had tea fields. Areas for shifting cultivation would all be lost to reforesta-

TABLE 6. Akhapu 1996 landholding:
Families in Akhapu 15–25 Years

Household	Swiddens planted (rai)	Wet rice planted (rai)	Tea fields (rai)
9	5	5	5
10	10	0	0
11	5	0	3
12	3	0	0
13	2	0	0
14	10	0	0
15	4	0	1
16	2	0	0
17	0	0	0
18	0	1	0

tion. These numbers, plus information from interviews, show that land-holding was diminishing rapidly.

Table 7 shows livestock holding for fourth-generation families. In 1996, with the exception of one household with two water buffalo, no households had any water buffalo, cattle, or horses. All households had pigs, which they kept around the house.

Table 8 shows livestock holding in 1996 for families living in Akhapu fifteen to twenty-five years. In 1996, only one household (number 9) had one water buffalo. None of the other households had any water buffalo, cattle, or horses. Some households kept pigs around the house. By 1996, villagers' overall wealth in livestock was very limited.

Table 9 shows income sources for fourth-generation families. In 1996, households 1 and 2 had the highest incomes in all of Akhapu. Household 1, the village head, was involved in the drug trade. Household 2, the village head's brother, was the manager of the tea company. In 1996, only three out of the eight fourth-generation households derived income from livestock. In fact, these households had sold off most of their livestock in 1996 because there was no longer room to pasture or herd animals. Previous areas for grazing animals—fallowed shifting-cultivation lands and the community forest—had been lost to state reforestation and tea plantations. As table 9 shows, among these households the chief sources of income were labor and tea, with labor inside the village more common than labor outside the village. The highest-earning household among the fourth gener-

TABLE 7. Akhapu 1996 livestock holding:
Families in Akhapu four generations

Household	Water buffalo	Cattle	Horses	Pigs
1	0	0	0	3
2	0	0	0	3
3	2	0	0	4
4	0	0	0	3
5	0	0	0	12
6	0	0	0	3
7	0	0	0	3
8	0	0	0	1

TABLE 8. Akhapu 1996 livestock holding:
Families in Akhapu 15–25 years

Household	Water Buffalo	Cattle	Horses	Pigs
9	1	0	0	5
10	0	0	0	3
11	0	0	0	5
12	0	0	0	5
13	0	0	0	0
14	0	0	0	3
15	0	0	0	0
16	0	0	0	8
17	0	0	0	0
18	0	0	0	1

ation households (441,400 baht; about US$17,656) earned 73.5 times more than the lowest-earning household (6,000 baht; about US$240). Excluding the village head (household 1), but including his brother (household 2), the household with the highest income (70,000 baht; about US$2,800) earned almost 12 times more than the household with the lowest income (6,000 baht; about US$240). Economic stratification was pronounced. Additionally, income sources were diminishing. Most households had sold off almost all their livestock in 1996. The next year there would be little

TABLE 9. Akhapu 1996 household income:
Families in Akhapu four generations

Household	Income Sources					Total household income (baht)
	Livestock	Labor (I)	Labor (O)	Ginger	Tea	
1					x	441,400*
2		x	x		x	70,000
3	x	x			x	26,500**
4	x	x	x		x	21,800
5	x	x		x	x	21,000
6		x			x	16,000
7		x			x	9,000
8		x	x			6,000

Labor (I)=inside village   *had outside businesses
Labor (O)=outside village   **sold off all cattle

livestock income. Increasingly, even households among the somewhat more secure group of fourth-generation families depended on labor and tea for income.

Table 10 shows income sources for households living in Akhapu for fifteen to twenty-five years. In 1996, the predominant source of income for these households was labor inside the village. Four of these households had sold livestock in 1996, but as was the case in fourth-generation households, they had sold off most of their animals due to lack of pasture. Sales in 1996 might represent their final income from livestock other than pigs. The strong movement, discovered from surveys and interviews, was toward wage labor and away from livestock. Sources of income were quickly becoming more limited, and households were urgently seeking new wage-labor opportunities. The highest-earning household among this group (55,000 baht; about US$2,200) had an income 110 times greater than the lowest-earning household (500 baht; about US$20). For the highest-earning household, though, that income had come mainly from sale of livestock, a one-time event. If we compare the highest-earning household overall, number 1 (441,400 baht; about US$17,656), with the lowest-earning household overall, number 18 (500 baht; about US$20), the highest-earning household earned almost 900 times as much as the lowest-earning one.

Overall, landholding for all Akhapu households except the village head's

TABLE 10. Akhapu 1996 household income:
Families in Akhapu 15–25 years

| Household | Income sources | | | | | Total Household |
	Livestock	Labor (I)	Labor (O)	Ginger	Tea	Income (baht)
9	x				x	55,000*
10		x	x	x		30,000
11		x	x	x	x	26,350
12	x	x	x	x		18,500
13	x	x				13,000**
14		x		x		5,500
15		x				2,400
16		x				2,000
17		x				2,000
18	x	x				500

NOTE: Labor (I)=inside village   *Sold 6 (of 7) water buffalo
NOTE: Labor (O)=outside village   **Sold off all pigs

was declining and would diminish further once state reforestation of shifting-cultivation lands was complete. Few households, even among the fourth-generation families, had enough wet-rice and tea fields to provide sufficient grain and income. All households, with the exception of the village head, relied on wage labor, mostly within the village, to supply the cash to buy grain and other necessities. This tendency was increasing rapidly in concert with the loss of land. The diversity and mutability of land uses that Akha had relied on in the past was quickly disappearing, as household members became laborers for very low wages.

According to villagers, an income of 10,000 to 15,000 baht per year (about US$400–600) was needed to get by, depending on household size. Households with incomes below that level, which included three among the fourth-generation families and half of the more recently arrived, were falling through the cracks. The village head, meanwhile, had an extravagant income by village standards. Not only was his landholding huge compared to other Akha farmers, but also his outside businesses, in addition to sale of crops, ensured him an income far in excess of what other villagers could even dream of. Overall landholding was highly inequitable, and disparities in household income were even more striking. Aside from the village head, Akhapu villagers had lost their scope for managing flexible landscapes and had become wage laborers instead.

Assessment of the Past, Trajectories for the Future

Yibaw played a key role in the development of Akhapu over the past thirty-some years. He served as hill tribe representative, mediating between the Thai state and upland villagers in the implementation of security measures as well as state agricultural projects. He was a project officer for the highland development project, introducing tea, the cash-crop to substitute for opium. Villagers respected him as someone who spoke eight languages and was skilled in settling disputes. When I visited Yibaw in Mae Kham, where he headed a government project to get highland peoples to plant flowers for the cut-flower market, he expounded on the status of upland peoples in Thailand. Thirty years ago, he said, upland peoples had been free. They were wild people like wild animals. They opened land wherever they wanted. They burned and destroyed the forest. Now rain brings about massive erosion that threatens the livelihood of people in the lowlands. According to Yibaw, hill tribes must be stopped from destroying the forest.

Yibaw was presenting a perceived landscape of destruction, the very basis for state intervention to control highland people's agriculture, prevent their use of trees, and to circumscribe their movement. For a summary of the hill tribe discourse, RFD staff could not have done any better. Like RFD staff, Yibaw failed to recognize that the tea company, together with local tea cultivation, had removed much of the forest in Akhapu. Also like state foresters, Yibaw blamed forest loss on shifting cultivation. He had carefully positioned himself as a representative of the state, but also as a patron of people who, in the official vision, did not deserve land in Thailand. In spite of their backwardness, Yibaw would continue to help them. He was introducing the production of flowers for lowland markets, yet another means to sedentarize upland production on limited areas of land.

Lawjaw, the Akhapu village head, proudly confirmed that Akhapu had been declared an official village in January 1996. As a result, it was unlikely that the seventy-six households there would be resettled in the lowlands. According to the village head, Akha farmers would soon get permits granting them secure access to land planted in tea, perennials, and wet rice within a 3-kilometer radius of their houses. But they would not be allowed to plant upland rice or corn. The ecological plasticity of the shifting-cultivation landscape would be gone, supplanted by a set array of land uses on a much diminished land area.

Lawjaw saw the new land permits as a positive step, and indeed they represented a measure of security for villagers assaulted by huge losses from reforestation over a short period of time. At the same time, though, Lawjaw was complicit in the introduction of relatively permanent land uses on set plots of land. He was authorizing the loss of landscape plasticity for villagers, even as he served as the patron helping them to get land permits.

Lawjaw, meanwhile, had just bought fifty-two water buffalo and cattle in Burma to sell to Thais, and he continued to buy jade in Tachilek (Burma) to sell to a dealer in Chiang Mai who in turn had a market in Japan. Lawjaw boasted that he had more friends in Burma than in Thailand and that he made frequent trips to both Burma and Laos. As he spoke, he pulled out a new cell phone that had cost 50,000 baht (about US$2,000). Lawjaw's own enterprises extended across multiple borders, and his wealth continued to burgeon. In other words, even as he settled villagers on tiny plots of land for simplified production of cash crops, his own realms of business, especially those across the border, continued to expand.

In Thailand, the highland development project's introduction of new land uses and the loss of land to reforestation were actions in which ordinary villagers had no say. For their part, Thai foresters made no accommodation for Akha-protected forests, which RFD staff failed to recognize, establishing instead a watershed-protection forest in a different site. The introduction of simplified, set landscapes tended to benefit the village head and outside actors, at the same time that local people quickly lost out. To the extent that Akhapu became a landscape legible to state actors, state plans were implemented without discussion. This was an enforced legibility, implanting governance in an otherwise wild area.

Comparing data from Xianfeng and Akhapu forests shows outcomes of landscapes of productivity and rule in China and Thailand as of 1997. Data were collected in three different categories of sites: protected forests, used forests, and swiddens in various stages of regeneration. In each village, protected sites included the cemetery forest, the watershed-protection forest, and the forest right around the village warding off evil spirits. In China, the Sanpabawa was also included. Used forests included collective forests (*jitilin*) and household forests (*ziliushan*) in China and forests with similar uses in Thailand. Swiddens included sites that had been regenerating 2–3 years, 6–8 years, and 11–13 years in both sites. In 10-meter-diameter plots along north-south transects in each category, all trees with 10-centimeter

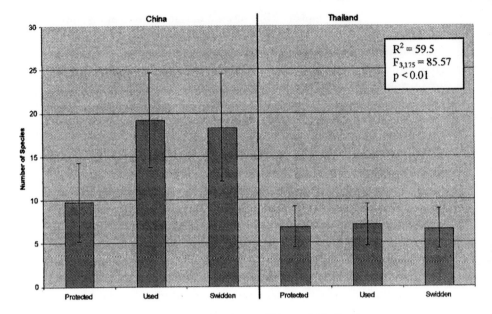

FIG. 18. Species richness, China and Thailand

NOTE: Comparison of tree and shrub species richness per plot in China and Thailand.
Plot area = 0.007854 ha, number of plots = 12 (China Protected), 26 (China Used), 16 (China
Swidden), 33 (Thailand Protected), 30 (Thailand Used), and 62 (Thailand Swidden). ANOVA
model R_2 = 59.5, $F_{3,175}$ = 85.57, p<0.01. Values are means; bars are +/- 1 SE.

or greater diameter at breast height (dbh) were measured and identified. In
a 2-meter-diameter plot nested within the larger plots, all trees and shrubs
were identified. Figures 18, 19, and 20 show a comparison of results.

The figures compare data from China and Thailand for species richness
(biodiversity), species dominance (degree of dominance by one species, and
kind of species dominating in each plot), and species density (basal area)
per hectare of measured area.

Figure 18 shows that land-use category (Protected, Used, Swidden) was
a viable predictor of species richness for variation in trees and shrubs as evident by using the ANOVA (analysis of variance) model, which revealed
significant differences in species richness by country (Chinese comparisons
were higher). Among the three dependent variables, species richness showed
the strongest sensitivity to land use. Figure 19 shows that for both Chinese
and Thai systems, species dominance varied only nominally among land-
use types and the overall ANOVA model explained insignificant amounts

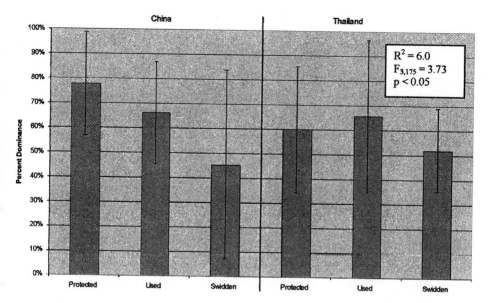

FIG. 19. Species dominance, China and Thailand

NOTE: Comparison of tree and shrub species dominance per plot in China and Thailand. Plot area and numbers are as in figure 18. ANOVA model $R_2 = 6.0$, $F_{3,175} = 3.73$, p<0.5. Values are means; bars are =/- 1 SE.

of variation. Figure 20 shows that for both Chinese and Thai systems, species density (as basal area per hectare) varied among land-use types, with swidden systems showing significant reduction. Nonetheless, land-use category was not a viable predictor of overall variation in tree and shrub density.

The findings on species richness, or biodiversity, point to the ongoing greater diversity of land uses in China as compared with Thailand. In Akhapu, where tea was replacing the forest around the village and many land uses had been sedentarized, the species richness was significantly lower than in Xianfeng. Given the similarity of the forest types in both areas, species richness in both places thirty years earlier might have been similar. Sedentarized, simplified land uses have reduced biodiversity in Thailand. The findings on species diversity support the case for land-use diversity in China and contribute to the argument for landscape plasticity. Plots in various stages of regeneration, whether former swiddens or not, contributed to the overall diversity of species found in China.

The data for Xianfeng on species dominance show that protected forests were dominated by fairly rare old-growth canopy species. This protection

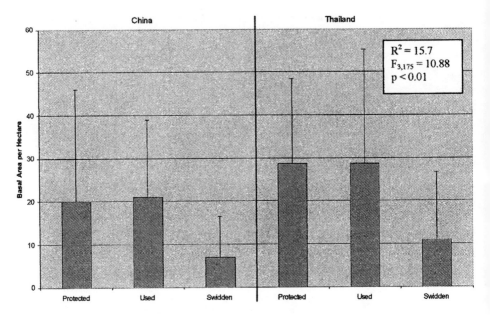

FIG. 20. Species density, China and Thailand

NOTE: Comparison of tree and shrub density as basal area per hectare for each plot in China and Thailand. Plot area and numbers are as in figure 18. ANOVA model R_2 = 15.7, $F_{3.175}$ = 10.88, p<0.01. Values are means; bars are + 1 SE.

resulted mainly from Akha customary rules, since state interest in forest protection appeared only in the past fifteen years. Even when foresters took over monitoring forest quality, they did so in conversation with local Akha over past uses of particular forests. The protected forests in China, especially the Sanpabawa, were in good condition.

In Akhapu, by contrast, the dominating species in protected forests were mostly pioneer species, those fast-growing trees that initiate a new forest stand. The dominance of pioneer species and relative lack of old-growth canopy species show that forest protection has not been very successful in Thailand. The protected forests were in poor and declining condition, as shown from the species-dominance data and from stories about trajectories of forest use. In Akhapu, villagers seemed unable to protect even the forests where their customary rules prohibited cutting.

The similarity of the results on swiddens for species dominance and species density in the two areas is not surprising. In China, most Akha farmers had switched to wet rice for grain, so that finding swiddens in early stages of regeneration was not easy. In Thailand, where the RFD had taken over many shifting-cultivation fields, there were also few sites in early stages of regeneration. The difference in species richness reflects the reopening of swiddens without enough fallow time in Thailand, whereas swiddens in China had fallowed for ten to thirteen years before reuse.

The forest data underscore the outcomes indicated in dozens of interviews in both Xianfeng and Akhapu. Taken together, the data results and the narratives of land-use change point to the ongoing diversity of land uses and species in China and the diminished diversity of land uses and species in Thailand.

COMPARISON OF BORDER LANDSCAPES, CHINA AND THAILAND

As of about 1950, land uses in Xianfeng and Akhapu were almost identical, relying on shifting cultivation and raising livestock in a largely forested environment. By 1997, land uses in the two sites were distinctly different. Akha farmers in China engaged with growing markets by producing and collecting increasingly diverse goods. Wage labor was a growing part of household income, as was local mining. Xianfeng households experienced rising incomes and opportunities for participating in the new market economy. Additionally, the flexibility, or plasticity, of the landscape was still largely in place.

In Thailand, by contrast, Akha villagers were losing land and related possibilities, such as raising livestock. The main cash crop, the tea introduced by a development project, was poor quality and a thin substitute for the array of crops they had grown in previous times. Wage labor brought in low and intermittent incomes. The plasticity of their landscapes had been eroded by forest policies and development projects, and their livelihoods were rapidly worsening.

Embedded in the modernizing landscapes of both Chinese and Thai states were notions of time, space, and productivity that conflicted with and threatened the practice of landscape plasticity. The desired and good future projected by either state vision, especially since the early 1980s, has not included shifting cultivation. Both states instituted policies to sedentarize and simplify land uses and to focus production on cash crops based on annual plans. In both cases, policies also separated forests from agricultural land. Taken as a whole, these state moves undermined complex landscapes based on mutable uses of multiple sites.

In China, state control over labor and grain production was later replaced by control over allocated lands through land-use regulations. Either way,

these were state attempts to govern areas considered to be on the periphery or border-as-margin of the nation-state, sites that needed to be included
under state rule. When allocating lands to households, state agents in
China worked with small teams of villagers to delineate both agricultural
and forest lands. While these processes were not exactly negotiated, they
involved discussion between villagers and state administrators. The allocation of household land freed up local farmers to decide where to spend their
energy, on what kinds of crops, and increasingly, with what forms of access.

Xianfeng villagers changed the uses and access rules for shifting-
cultivation fields and pastures and opened up fields on unallocated and invisible sites. They extended their livelihoods across the border for pasture,
timber, hunting, and even for wet-rice fields. Particularly in traversing the
border, farmers were operating within another meaning of border, the realm
of border-as-line with social relations across it.

Akheu, the Mengsong administrative village head, was meanwhile introducing settled, simplified agriculture through the wasteland auction, the production of fruit orchards and upland rice on settled terraces, and through
the promotion of tractors to replace water buffalo. He was ushering in not
only landscapes of productivity and rule, but also the border-as-margin of
the nation-state. His actions were turning Akha farmers into marginal people
in a way they had not quite been before—as farmers implementing forms
of lowland agriculture in an upland setting. By following this pathway, Akha
villagers would be operating on terms not quite of their own choosing, with
crops and implements not quite appropriate for their locale. They would
also lose, increasingly, the plasticity of land use and access that had allowed
them to endure border predators, excessive state extractions, and loss of
forests through state policies that focused on grain rather than trees. They
would be deprived of some of the agency that had enabled them to engage
with markets and policies in ways favorable to them.

In Xianfeng, though, the village land area in 1997 was the same as in 1958,
and there were still sites for shifting cultivation, wet rice, pastures, and tea,
as well as forest sites for both protection and use. Even within land-use regulations, which villagers tended to manipulate, there was still considerable
room for moving land uses around to suit new purposes. There was also
some room in the official administrative imagination for Akha to have useful knowledge about managing trees. This created space, not only for Akha
practices, but for discussion about how new government plans should be
implemented. The spatial and temporal scales of Akha planning were still
quite expansive, in spite of Akheu's plans.

In Thailand, the arrival of the Loimi Akha prompted the informal allocation of land to households, a form of sedentarization invisible to state agents. The highland development project attempted to stop shifting cultivation and to intensify Akha farmers' cultivation practices on much diminished plots of land. Through the introduction of tea, the highland development project effectively replaced a community forest with a low-value cash crop. In fairly rapid moves, both this project and the RFD took away most of the land area once managed by Akhapu farmers. In its place came a landscape of productivity and rule based on a vision of vast forests under state control and tiny areas on which upland farmers produced cash crops.

In Akhapu, the scope for use of Akha knowledge and practice of plastic landscapes rapidly diminished. The available land area in 1997 was less than a quarter of what it had been in 1980. For the most part, people were busy looking for wage labor to offset the loss of land. The spatial arena for cultivation had shrunk and the time scale had been reduced to immediate plans. In Thai official imagination, there was no room for Akha knowledge about managing forests and no room for discussion. Protected forests for the RFD were established on completely new sites with no reference to customary practices.

Lawjaw's role as village head, meanwhile, included negotiating with the RFD to allow his own shifting-cultivation lands to stay in place, even as state foresters required the reforestation of all other swidden lands. He maneuvered how forestlands became territorialized in Akhapu and benefited himself. More recently, he brought in electricity and water pipes through ensuring that Akhapu was an official village. His next step was to promise villagers that they would get land permits for sedentarized production of cash crops and wet rice. While escaping from state regulations himself, he helped all other villagers become firmly enmeshed in landscapes of productivity and rule in the border-as-margin of Thailand. Through his good offices, villagers enjoyed a modicum of security along the Thai border, but possibilities for landscape plasticity were gone. The forms of land use that had allowed Akha farmers a certain agency in dealing with changing markets and policies were gone as well. As a result of ongoing battles across the border, in addition to state suspicion of Akha involvement in the drug trade, extending livelihoods across the border was not nearly as possible as it had been twenty years earlier. The salience of border-as-line with social relations across it almost disappeared, forcing villagers back into the increasingly marginalized arena of border-as-margin of the nation-state.

In both of these cases, clearer, simpler landscapes benefited local elites and outside state actors, while local farmers tended to lose out. Where state policies and practices continued to enable landscape plasticity, as they did in China, both Akha and their forests fared well. Where state policies disabled landscape plasticity, as they did in Thailand, Akha and the forests around them fared poorly. The extent to which the introduction of landscapes of productivity and rule acknowledged and adjusted to Akha knowledge and practice, whether consciously or not, mattered a great deal for the quality of Akha livelihoods and the condition of the forest.

CONCLUSION

BORDERS ARE PROCESSES REPLETE WITH POLITICS, BOTH AS MARGINS OF the nation-state (border-as-margin) and as cross-border social relations (border-as-line). In the first meaning, border-as-margin, political centers have produced marginal peoples, spaces, and land uses by linking them together in national taxonomies at moments of state classification and then by devising policies based on images of backwardness in relation to state plans. In the second meaning, border-as-line, borders are sites that both join and separate people with a common social history, in which social practices both create and traverse borders. For Akha in China and Thailand, their means of gaining access to resources and managing upland environments were configured at the intersection of these two meanings of border.

Border landscapes have been sites of struggle and negotiation among land users, state agents, and local border chiefs over property rights, productivity, forest conservation, and a desired future, with the contingent outcomes of these negotiations legible in the resulting quality of livelihoods for Akha and in the condition of the forest. These landscapes can be understood as the complicated encounter between landscapes of productivity and rule and landscape plasticity.

Understanding these encounters has involved examining the tensions between two processes. The first process enclosed Akha and the forests around them within both national boundaries and state mental landscapes in China and Thailand, but in ways that located both people and their land

uses on national margins. The main source of difference in China and
Thailand lies in state definitions of Akha and forests. In China, for reasons
based on historical political practice as well as socialist logic, Akha were
classified within the Hani minority nationality, one of fifty-five officially recognized groups who became citizens (but not Han) as of the 1949 revolution. These peoples, their territory, and their forests, were included together
in the socialist polity, with plans to improve Akha culture as well as their
land use so that they could produce grain to meet state demands. Together
with other minority nationalities, Akha (or Hani) were at first judged to be
at a lower level than the Han on the scale of human evolution, or more
recently, to be in need of development. State means to educate and mold
Akha included the imposition of state-allocated property rights and land-
use regulations and the visits of extension agents to impart scientific knowledge for managing fields and forests. Under this scenario, the extent to which
Akha complied with regulations and adopted new cultivation practices made
Akha seem more developed but also redounded to the credit of the state,
and more broadly to the Han. The condition of the forests in Mengsong,
which was reasonably good, reflected well on Akha farmers and on the
forestry department. Through these processes, of course, the agency of
knowledge and good management slid in the direction of the state. But the
meaning of forests in China, from the 1950s onward, continued to be largely
as subsistence resources. In spite of a rapidly growing sense, among Chinese
foresters, that trees had both economic and environmental value, the bulk
of forested land in China as of 1997 still belonged to villages and households.
One result was that forests writ large had not taken on the same kind of heavy
symbolic value in China as they had in Thailand. For Chinese, forests were
important goods, but they did not represent the environment as a whole.

In Thailand, meanwhile, Akha as well as a number of other highland
peoples were designated as official "hill tribes." They were included in the
official imagination as "not Thai," interlopers on state territory, and criminal users of state (and more recently national) resources. Policies for property rights separated the forests, which belonged to the Royal Forestry
Department (RFD), from peoples who lived among and depended upon
the trees for livelihood. Among hill groups, Akha were thought to have the
most entrenched backwardness, stemming from their own culture with
its many rules for managing land and forests. These rules constituted an
impediment to learning scientific agriculture or forestry and were also a drag
on the national trajectory of progress. In counterpoint to the China case,
in Thailand the extent to which Akha continued to open shifting-cultivation

fields and to intercrop multitudes of vegetables with the grain, reinforced official conviction that Akha were close to hopeless in the realm of managing resources and becoming developed. The quality of the forests in Akhapu, which was poor and declining, reflected and reinvigorated the official view that Akha were forest destroyers. The official meaning of forests, meanwhile, shifted considerably over the past sixty years. In the 1930s, forests were dangerous realms where primitive people lived. By the 1960s, forests had been transformed into state economic assets to be exploited. As of the early 1980s, forests had again been recast, this time as environmental resources to be protected. In the time since, forests have acquired an enormous symbolic weight as national treasures belonging to future Thai generations. In the north, forests became a powerful representation for the environment under threat, mainly from hill tribe depredations. Forests sometimes seemed to stand for an embattled Thailand, surrounded by its enemies.

State definitions of peoples and resources have been key in determining their relative condition as of 1997. While ranking of various peoples was often based on historical power relations, state categorizations and evaluations solidified this hierarchy at moments of allocating citizenship and minority ethnicity. The state could then adjust the meaning of development, environment, and backwardness in relation to emerging needs. Rather than focus first on state policies, the important question becomes a prior one, what are mountain people and forests in relation to state plans? How do representations of upland people and forests inform state plans?

The second process producing border landscapes consisted of ongoing border dynamics, as small principalities and chiefdoms were transfigured into parts of major nation-states. These borders, whether swaths of territory among principalities or clear lines at the meeting point of larger entities, tended to be sites for the accumulation and distribution of resources as well as for mediation between larger political formations. Borders both divided and linked territories that had come to be defined as different, separate states. In the border sites of Mengsong and Akhapu, small border chiefs positioned themselves to exploit the dual nature of borders as dividers and links. The practices of small border chiefs both protected the border and enabled transgressions across it, serving to enrich themselves and further marginalize other Akha. Small border chiefs, meanwhile, always kept the state in view as they mediated between the state and its margin, between ethnic majority and minority peoples, and across international borders. As they cultivated political, economic, and cultural ties across the border, they positioned themselves as patrons in two senses: as the patron monitoring the border on behalf of the state and as local patron controlling access to resources needed by villagers. In some ways, small border chiefs recreated a mini version of a small border prince, but their role was bolstered and indeed sustained by state interests in both protecting the border and gaining access to people and products from the other side.

At the conjuncture of state formation and resilient border dynamics, small border chiefs such as the village heads in Mengsong and Akhapu set themselves up to accumulate resources for themselves and to control how other villagers gained access to such resources. Their modes of operation were remarkably similar, reflecting a common social history among regions that were until recently ruled by interrelated small princes. These village heads also both experienced the coercive small border polities in Burma, those who extracted products and labor at the point of a gun. But the context for operation of the two village heads was distinctly different.

In China, Akha villagers were citizens and recipients of state-allocated land and trees. Their subsistence was reasonably secure without help from the village head. The village head's maneuverings to control access to and distribution of resources as they became commodities were fairly successful, but encountered strong, public contention from other villagers. Hamlet heads had their own connections in multiple levels of state administration, officials to whom they complained about corruption. Although he was a skilled small border chief, Akheu in Mengsong was limited in the extent to which he could mediate the meaning of "Akha," property rights, development, and even the border. Other Akha also had strong voices in these definitions, voices that Akheu had no means to silence. He retained his mediating role, not because of local clients who depended on him, but because of state agents who needed his help in defending and negotiating across the Burma border.

In Thailand, by contrast, the village head long held a regional position as an accumulator of resources and dispenser of favors. His networks included former Nationalist soldiers, former drug lords, various kinds of traders, and government agents from many departments. As the only Thai citizen among a sea of hill tribe ID holders in Akhapu, Lawjaw represented the state for all those within his bailiwick who were officially "not Thai." Since other villagers were not citizens and had no formal property rights, Lawjaw held the key to their access to land, jobs, and even to residence in Akhapu. They were clients in his debt for everything that came their way, including any development from the state. When Lawjaw's actions resulted in his own enrichment and other villagers' impoverishment, villagers had no recourse against his predations. Lawjaw was well positioned to mediate not only access to resources, but also the meaning of "Akha," citizenship, resource use, and the border itself. He constituted the border, and he also enabled transgressions across it. He was a more complete embodiment of small border chief than Akheu, although the patronage practices were much the same. The arena of indirect rule in Thailand offered Lawjaw more scope for his role as border patron.

Considering the nature of international boundaries, the experiences of Akha in Mengsong and Akhapu confirm that borders are not separate from the lives of borderlands. On the contrary, borders are constituted by border power relations and livelihoods. In similar fashion, the state is not separate from border people, especially the small border chiefs who both protect and cross the border for their own purposes as well as the state's. The role of small border chiefs in creating transborder connections, though, does not include economic development for border peoples more broadly. The implications are instead for increasing wealth and influence for small border patrons and for increasing marginalization for farmers under their purview.

Akha villagers operated in both the nation-state in which they came to be located and on the border that they frequently crossed. In both China and Thailand, Akha participated in state formation, whether as citizens or not. In either case, Akha villagers wanted to be included in the largesse of the state: the allocation of property rights in natural resources; the provision of economic development, education, and a growing infrastructure. For younger people, the goods made available by the state seemed to include the trappings of modernity, including a national language and an urban lifestyle. Part of the context of Akha life, in either state, was a yearning toward the center.

At the same time, villagers in Xianfeng and Akhapu made frequent trips to Burma, when it was safe, for trade, rituals, labor exchange, tree cutting, hunting, and even for pasturing livestock. Crossing the border gave villagers access to timber, land, wildlife, labor, trade goods, and even to marriage partners, all of which might be in limited supply at home. Akha farmers made use of their complex, mountainous environments to produce a multitude of goods and to transform their landscapes into an ever-changing mosaic of uses. Their refashioning of the landscape allowed them to satisfy the demands of lowland princes, border chiefs, and their own ancestors. It also enabled them to respond to state extractions, growing markets, and different visions of the future in ways that reproduced complex livelihoods and diverse products. Akha practices of landscape plasticity tended to slide across set property lines, state regulations, and even national boundaries in creating dynamic, resilient landscapes in ways that fused marginal places and cross-border possibilities.

For Akha in Xianfeng, both the potential sites for new land uses and cross-border extensions were much more abundant and possible than for Akha in Akhapu. Chinese policies left Xianfeng with its land area intact and allowed upland minority nationalities to traverse the border without difficulty. Akha themselves, meanwhile, in differing and sometimes conflicting ways, changed swiddens to new uses, opened swiddens on commons and former home garden lands, adjusted the uses of forest sites, and spread across the border for herding livestock, hunting wildlife, and even for opening shifting-cultivation and wet-rice fields. Their land uses, means of access, and resulting products were much more diverse and dynamic than the settled agriculture that extension agents had in mind. As a result, the myriad products that people ate, sold, traded, and exchanged might shift over time but did not diminish in number. In various and sometimes contentious ways, Akha men and women in Xianfeng could feed their families and guests, sell goods in lowland markets, fulfill state demands, and reward the ancestors for keeping them safe. For most people in Xianfeng, livelihoods were secure and improving.

In Akhapu, by contrast, farmers remarked with some bafflement on the rapid loss of land for upland rice and the plethora of crops intercropped with the grain. They managed their tea lands but noted with dismay the low price for this borderline-quality tea. Most households had recently sold off all their livestock, since they had quickly lost grazing sites to RFD reforestation and their own tea. Men, women, and children fanned out to find wage labor to pay for household grain. Crossing the border from Akhapu was fraught with danger both from active rebel armies and from Thai enforcers catching hill tribe farmers returning from Burma, whether they brought back drugs or not. Akha experienced a sense of walls closing in, as options for diverse and flexible livelihoods were shut off in rapid order. Their household incomes, as well as room for maneuvering, were marginal and declining.

In China, the introduction of a governed landscape produced a negotiated legibility, with farmers paying taxes, producing grain, and managing recognizable forest areas. Their practices of land use and access, however, continued to be malleable and complex. In Thailand, the imposition of a governed landscape wrought an enforced legibility, with farmers producing low-value cash crops on tiny pieces of land. Their livelihoods shifted from cultivating a varied and extensive landscape to scrabbling for a grab bag of low-paying jobs. In both sites, small border chiefs promoted aspects of state landscapes of productivity and rule when those plans played into village heads' hands. For the long term in each case, simpler, clearer landscapes tended to benefit village heads and state administrators, to the disadvantage of other Akha farmers.

An analysis of changes in land use and livelihoods based on the concept of landscape plasticity opens up the understanding of Akha farmers' knowledge and practice, and the differing ways that state and Akha landscape visions encountered each other in China and Thailand. Landscape plasticity offered farmers a means of protecting themselves as well as participating in favorable markets and policies. The very flexibility of access and land use contributes to our understanding of property rights and of what is contended over in resource conflicts. Shifting access and use constituted Akha agency in contending with changing political economies; the loss of flexible landscapes, even in growing markets, marked a loss of scope for creating complex, mutable livelihoods with many choices left in Akha hands.

Border landscapes, then, were produced at the intersection of state plans to govern border peoples and land uses, and local actors, in various ways, seeking to make that governance play out on their own terms and to fashion landscapes that transgressed state categories. The outcomes depended on a complicated negotiation among state visions, local power relations, and Akha practices of plastic landscapes.

Tracing access to resources through all of these processes brings several elements under one lens: state-allocated property rights and state claims on rural resources, Akha farmers' means of access under the combination of state regulations and small border chiefs' machinations, and the ways that Akha farmers maneuvered among multiple patrons to stake their own claims. Staying close to access to resources through this complicated story revealed the complex ways that Akha extended land areas, reworked former land sites, and pushed across myriad kinds of borders and into unseen parts of the landscape to produce their livelihoods. The unexpected conclusion is that where there was a state net of household and village property lines and regulated uses, as in China, Akha played in and out of the net in ways sometimes to their benefit. In Thailand, where the state net was only for state property claims, scooping land and livelihoods away from Akha farmers, there was little room for Akha maneuver or play.

From the point of view of state policies or development thinking, accommodating Akha knowledge and practice into planning is thought to be a good thing—local participation. According to this view, the outcomes for the condition of Akha and their forests in China would be expected, since local participation leads to favorable outcomes. From a related point of view, however, granting secure and clearly defined property rights is also considered to be a good thing—leading to economic development. In Thailand, state plans did not include either Akha participation or granting Akha secure property rights. In China, the state granted property rights to Akha, but equally important, the intersection of state and local plans opened up some flexibility in practice. Where Akha retained some maneuvering room to shift around rules of access and use and to create landscapes more complicated than state plans, Akha livelihoods and forests were in good condition. Social relations and livelihoods that traversed boundaries, refashioned land uses, and re-created complexity were sources of agency for Akha in the interstices of state plans and border predations. Plastic landscapes resisted the mapping instinct, and for this reason increased the scope of Akha endeavors. Where plastic landscapes were enabled, as in China, Akha and their forests were in reasonably good condition. Where landscape plasticity was disabled, as in Thailand, conditions for both Akha and their forests declined. The convergence of Akha landscape visions, state plans, and border dynamics produced dramatically differing results in China and Thailand, illuminating the complex forces at work in the production of border landscapes.

APPENDIX 1

Trees and Shrubs of Mengsong, China

217 total species[1]

1. neev caiv[2]—*Stizolobium pruriens* (Linn.) D.C.
2. aqkaq savq—*Clematis fulvicosa* Rehd. et Wils. (Ranunculaceae)
3. qil guq—*Pueraria montana* (Lour.) Merr. (Papilionaceae)
4. naivq ssaq neev piav—*Atylosia mollis* (Willd.) Benth. (Papilionaceae)
5. wuq jil—*Imperata cylindrica* (Linn.) Beauv. (Agrostidoideae)
6. yal ka jeiq daovq—*Artemisia annua* Linn. (Compositae)
7. qaivq pal caq—*Eupatorium coelesticum* Linn. (Compositae)
8. yaiq ceevq—*Digitaria sanguinalis* (Linn.) Scop. (Agrostidoideae)
9. al laiq cev—*Microstegium ciliatum* (Trin.) A. Camus (Agrostidoideae)
10. al laiq haq—*Pogonatherum crinitum* (Thunb.) Kunth. (Agrostidoideaa)
11. tail sav—*Setaria palmifolia* (Koen.) Stapf. (Agrostidoideae)
12. wuq jil ma—*Themeda caudata* (Nees) A. Camus (Agrostidoideae)
    (same as 160)
13. gaq laq hhaoq saq—(1) *Blumeopsis flava* (D.C.) Gagn.; (2) *Conyza canadensis* (Linn.) Cronq.; (3) *Cyathocine purpurea* (Buch.-Ham.) O. Ktze.; (4) *Sphaeranthus africanus* Linn. (Compositae)
14. dul piul—*Bauhinia variegata* Linn. (Caesalpiniaceae)
15. puv haq—*Callicarpa arborea* Roxb. (Verbenaceae)
16. siq guq ma xel—*Ficus semicordata* Buch.-Ham. ex J. E. Sm. (Moraceae)
17. laiq oq—(1) *Rubus multibracteatus* Levl. et Vent.; (2) *Rubus ellipticus* Sm. dal laiv *Callipteris esculenta* (Retz.) J. Sm (Rosaceae)

18. hhaq baol ceevq kav—*Isachne globosa* (Thunb.) (Agrostidoideae)
19. pavq peel—*Blumea balsamifera* (Linn.) Kunth. D.C. (Compositae)
20. baol hel—*Triumfetta tomentosa* Bojer (Tiliaceae)
21. movq puq—*Ageratum conyzoides* Linn. (Compositae)
22. qul lu al baiv—*Cratalaria assamica* Benth.
23. mail laov—*Alpinia platychilus* K. Schum. (Zingiberaceae)
24. miq lai ju—*Maoutia puya* (Wall.) Wedd. (Urticaceae)
25. loq—*Kydia glabrescens* Mast. (Malvaceae)
26. al ganq—*Thysanolaena maxima* (Roxb.) O. Ktze. (Agrostidoideae)
27. xml qiq—*Pogostemon menthoides* Bl. (Labiatae)
28. dal piav—*Pteridium revolutum* (Bl.) Nakai (Pteridiaceae)
29. jaoq ba miq dovq—*Eupatorium odoratum* Linn. (Compositae)
30. naivq ssaq nmq xiq—*Rabdosia eroicalyx* (Dunn) Hara
31. nanl ma nanl yuvq—*Breynia rostrata* Merr. (Euphorbiaceae)
32. yal movq pil—*Crassocephalum cerpidioides* (Benth.) S. Moore
    (Compositae)
33. jeiq cml—*Measa indica* (Roxb.) A. D.C. (Myrsinaceae)
34. laol biml—*Bombax ceiba* Linn. (Bombacaceae)
35. hhaq ma naq pavq—*Boehmeria siamensis* Braib (Urticaceae)
36. qeq bavq—*Miscanthus floridus* (Labill.) Warb. (Agrostidoideae)
37. loq sav—*Kydia calycina Roxb.* (Malvaceae)
38. sanq du—*Eriolaena candollei* Wall. (Sterculiaceae)
39. laol taoq xeel—*Grevia calophylla* Kurz (Tiliaceae)
40. sml xil—*Stereospermum tetraganum* (Wall.) D.C. (Bignoniaceae)
41. qeevq miaivq yav haoq—*Laggera alata* (D.C.) Schultz-Bip.
    (Compositae)
42. byuq baivq—*Melastoma polyanthum* Bl. (Melastomaceae)
43. qil sav—*Schima wallichii* Choisy (Theaceae)
44. haq paq kuq cavq—*Viola angusti pulata* C. C. Cheng (Violaceae)
45. jaoq zevq—*Sperobolus elongatus* R. Br. (Agrostidoideae)
46. al laol zal maiv—*Hedyotis carymbosa* (Linn.) Lam. (Rubiaceae)
47. siq guq le tev—*Ficus hirta* Vahl (Moraceae)
48. byuq syuv—*Eurya groffii* Merr. (Theaceae)
49. haq laq baq ba—*Mussaenda hossei* Craib (Rubiaceae)
50. nii hav—*Stephania delavayi* Diels (Menipermaceae)
51. siq jaiv—*Parabarium tournieri* Pierre (Apocynaceae)
52. ssaq ma qyul kuv—*Cayratia trifolia* (Linn.) Domin (Vitaceae)
53. o piq daoq dyuq—*Disporopsis longifolia* Craib (Liliaceae)
54. hha qiq miq xail—*Piper polysyphorum* C.D.C. (Piperaceae)

55. danl laqma—*Cucurliago capittulata* (Lour.) O. Ktze.
56. haq ba—*Castanopsis calathiformis* (Skan) Rehd. et Wils. (Fagaceae)
57. pil pavq—*Lindera latifolia* Hk. f. (Lauraceae)
58. ceevq xail—*Castanopsis ceratacantha* Rehd. et Wils. (Fagaceae)
59. sanq anl—*Veronica volkameriaefolia* (Wall.) D.C. (Compositae)
60. sanq dao—*Symplocos paniculata* (Thunb.) Wall. (Symplocaceae)
61. yivq kanq—*Styrax fonkienensis* (Pierre) Craib (Styracaceae)
62. lavq qail—*Symplocos cochinchinensis* (Lour.) Moore (Symplocaceae)
63. sev mianq—*Pygeum henri* Dunn (Rosaceae)
64. siq bil—*Litsea cubeba* (Lam.) Pers. (Lauraceae)
65. laol miaol—*Saccharum arundinaceum* Retz. (Agrostidoideae)
66. aq keeq maiq lal tav—*Polygonum capitalum* Buch.-Ham. ex D. Don (Polygonaceae)
67. mail qyuv—*Alpinia kastumadai* Hayata (Zingiberaceae)
68. bu pavq teiq—*Aspidistra typica* Baill. (Liliaceae)
69. hmq tev le tev—*Smilax indica* Vitm. (Smilacaceae)
70. kaoq ya—*Decaspermum gracilentum* (Hce.) Merr. (Myricaceae)
71. qail zanl laiq oq—*Myrica esculenta* Buch.-Ham. ex D. Don (Myricaceae)
72. al ka dal hav—*Elatostema dissectum* Wedd. (Urticaceae)
73. dal ssaq oq dov dal pial—*Rungia henryi* C. B. Clarke (Acanthaceae)
74. mianq lal—*Baphicacanthus causia* (Nees) Bremek. (Acanthaceae)
75. bu pavq—*Phrynium capitatum* Willd. (Marantaceae)
76. sev xeel—*Calophyllum polyanthum* Wall. ex Choisy (Guttiferae)
77. hov tyuv—*Amneslea frangrans* Wall.
78. haq laq xaq yyuq—*Mischocarpus pentapetalus* (Roxb.) Radik. (Sapindaceae)
79. haol dml sev nav—*Litsea chinpingensis* Yang et Y. H. Huang (Lauraceae)
80. miq bev kaoq dul—*Monocelastrus monosperma* (Roxb.) Wang et Tang
81. nioq savq—*Millettia pachycarpa* Benth. (Papilionaceae)
82. sml pavq du miov—*Clerodendron serratum* (Linn.) Spreng (Verbenaceae)
83. nga baol—*Musa acuminata* Colla (Musaceae)
84. bil qai seq kal—*Helicia nilagirica* Bedd. (Proteaceae)
85. hov naq hov qil—*Sterculia lanceolata* Cav. (Sterculiaceae)
86. sanq piul—*Beilshineidia robusta* Allen (Lauraceae)
87. ganl bol xeel—*Xanthohyllum yunnanensis* C. Y. Wu (Xanthophyllaceae)

88. hmq qiq hmq hav—*Smilax perfoliata* Lour. (Simlacaceae)
89. jaq jul lul ma—*Callicarpa erioclona* Schau. (Verbenaceae)
90. al davq—*Canthium parvifolium* Roxb. (Rubiaceae)
91. al haq—*Pleiblastus amarus* (Keng) Keng f. (Bambusoideae)
92. hha mail—*Meliosma velutina* Rehd. et Wils. (Sabiaceae)
93. lavq byul—*Bauhinia claviflora* L. Chen (Casalpiniaceae)
94. ceevq kav—*Castanopsis argyrophylla* King ex Hk. f. (*mekongensis*)
    (Fagaceae)
95. aq nanq ju—*Saurauia tristyla* D.C. (Saurauiaceae)
96. lyul qyul—*Embelia ribes* Burm. f. (Myrsinaceae)
97. pan nii tev—*Craspedolobium schochii* Harms (Papilionaceae)
98. hha pyul baol dul—*Scleria chinensis* Kunth. (Cyperaceae)
99. jav hhaq qil haq—*Rauvolfia yunnanensis* Tsiang (Apocynaceae)
100. daq hovq—*Lithocarpus grandifolius* (D. Don) S. N. Bisw. (Fagaceae)
101. ceevq xail hhanl—*Castanopsis ferox* (Roxb.) Spach. (Fagaceae)
102. aq beevl—*Diaspyros kerrii* Craib
103. neev lyul—*Merremia hedracea* (Burm.) Hall. f. (Convolvulaceae)
104. lmq pial—*Macaranga indica* Wright (Euphorbiaceae)
105. lmq neil—*Wedlandia tinctoric* D.C. (Rubiaceae)
106. bimq niq—*Lindera caudata* Nees (Lauraceae)
107. dal gmq sav—*Pratia nummularia* (Lam.) A. Bret Aschers
    (Lobeliaceae)
108. qil hhaq qel lel—*Sinopyrenaria cheliensis* (Hu) Hu
109. ceevq gang—*Betla alnoides* Buch.-Ham. ex D. Don (Betulaceae)
110. hhaiq—*Prunus majestica* Koehne (Rosaceae)
111. ceevq niaivq—*Machilus rufipes* H. W. Li (Lauraceae)
112. ov qavq lavq sanq—*Embelia paraviflora* Wall. (Compositae)
113. zaq niyul—*Tricalysia fruticosa* (Mensl.) K. Schum. (Rubiaceae)
114. saoq laol—*Rhaphidophora decursiva* (Roxb.) Schott (Araceae)
115. pavq qail—*Santaloides caudatum* (Pl.) O. Ktze. (Connaraceae)
116. sanq hav byuq baivq—*Oxyspora vagans* (Roxb.) Wall.
    (Melastomaceae)
117. aq jil aq yo—*Elaeocarpus austro-yunnanensis* Hu (Elaeocarpaceae)
118. poq lanl—*Cryptocarya densiflora* Bl. (Lauraceae)
119. miav laol zaq biaivq—*Chasalia curviflora* Thw. (Rubiaceae)
120. aq jal—*Lithocarpus leucostachyus* A. Camus (Lithocarpus)
121. sanq anl pavq ssaq—*Blumea lanceolaria* (Roxb.) Druce
    (Compositae)
122. byul qanq—*Phoeba puwenensis* Cheng (Lauraceae)

123. pavq ja qul—*Cinnamomun tamala* (Buch.-Ham.) Nees et Eberm. (Lauraceae)
124. xaivq nii tev—*Melodinus tenuicaudatus* Tsiang et P. T. Li (Apocynaceae)
125. aq miov—*Cephalostachyum fuchsianum* Gamble (Gramineae)
126. yal saq hmq ma la hhe—*Ardisia tenera* Mez (Myrsinaceae)
127. pavq miav—*Engelhardtia spicata* Bl. (Juglandaceae)
128. yama o mianq—(1) *Robdosia coesta* (Buch.-Ham. ex D. Don) Hara; (2) *Dicrocephala intergrofolia* (Linn. f.) O. Ktze.
129. dal gmq ma—*Hydrocotyle nepalensis* Hk. (Umbellieferae)
130. pavq buq ma—*Alseodaphne andersonii* (King ex Hk. f.) Kosterm. (Lauraceae)
131. pavq buq ssaq—*Litsea monopetala* (Roxb.) Pers. (Lauraceae)
132. pavq maoq—*Ficus fulva* Reinw. (Moraceae)
133. avq miq—*Cyanotis vaga* (Lour.) Roem. et Schult. (Commelinaceae)
134. laiq guq laiq nii—*Gnetum montanum* Markgr. (Gnetaceae)
135. aq gan ngov—*Toddalia asiatica* (Linn.) Lam. (Rutaceae)
136. dal piav bao oq—*Alsophila costularis* Bak. (Cyatheaceae)
137. sev aovq—*Scleria laevis* Retz. (Cyperaceae)
138. alka pavq sav—*Baphicacanthus cristata* Linn. (Acanthaceae)
139. lmq pial pavq sav—*Mallatus macrostachys* (Miq.) Muell.-Arg. (Euphorbiaceae)
140. pavq mianq—*Viola philippica* Cav. ssp. munda W. Beck (Violaceae)
141. aq taiq maoq laq—*Stemona tuberosa* Lour. (Stemonaceae)
142. haq hhml daiq qiq—*Clerodendron japonicum* (Thunb.) Sweet (Verbenaceae)
143. yama ov lo—*Salacia polysperma* Hu (Hippocrateaceae)
144. iq mavq—*Rhus chinesnsis* Mill. (Myrtaceae)
145. siq bil—*Cinnamomun charatophyllum* H. W. Li (Lauraceae)
146. kaoq ya ma—*Syzgium cumini* (Linn.) Skeels. (Myrtaceae)
147. kaoq laiq—*Melia toosenden* Sieb. et Zucc. (Meliaceae)
148. lmq pial neil—*Macaranga henryi* (Pax et Hotfm) Rehd. (Euphorbiaceae)
149. kaoq ya tev—*Medinella septentrionalis* (W. W. Sm.) H. L. Li (Melastomaceae)
150. pavq ja—*Cinnamomun bejolghota* (Buch.-Ham.) Sweet (Lauraceae)
151. sanq dao—*Styrax suberifolia* Hk. et Zucc.(Styracaceae)
152. keeq seeq—*Polygala arillata* Buch.-Ham. et D. Don (Polygalaceae)
153. hov pail sev—not visible in March, short grass

154. qai caov—*Bidens pilosa* Linn. (Compositae)
155. dal gmq—*Centalla asiatica* (Linn.) Urb. (Umbelliferae)
156. qeevq miaivq zal dovq—*Evodia lepta* (Spreng) Merr.
157. mail qail—*Themeda caudata* (Nees) A. Camus (Agrostidoideae) (same as 12)
158. laol baoq pavq mevq—*Camellia confus* Craib (Theacae)
159. ssai—*Prunus acuminata* (Wall.) Dictz. (Rosaceae)
160. haq hhml qeiq dev—*Pithecolobium bigeminum* (Linn.) Benth. (Mimosaceae)
161. haol dml avq laoq—*Randia* spp. (Rubiaceae)
162. haq zeil lavq sanq—*Uncaria laevigata* Wall. (Rubiaceae)
163. sanq hav dal laiv—*Allantodia maxima* (Don) Ching (Athyriaceae)
164. miq jiv lml—*Sarcosperma kachinensis* (King et Prain) Exell (Sapotaceae)
165. o baq wuvl haq—*Trichilia connaroides* (Wright et Arn) Bentv. (Meliaceae)
166. maol neil siq guq—*Ficus pisocarpa* Bl. (Moraceae)
167. aq juq naq lavq hhel—*Schizandra henryi* Clarke var. *yunnanensis* A. D. Sm. (Schizandraceae)
168. hov pil—*Cinnamomun* sp. (Lauraceae)
169. pan nii—*Spantholobus suberechus* Dunn (Papilionaceae)
170. sanq daovq—*Dendrobium chysanthum* Wall. ex Lindl. (Orchidaceae)
171. naivq ssaq siq jaiv—*Trachelospermum cathayanum* Schneid. (Apocynaceae)
172. qil jaq haq—*Machilus robuste* W. W. Sm. (Lauraceae)
173. byuq syuv baiv—*Eurya cerasifolia* Griff. ex Dyer (Theaceae)
174. kaoq ya pavq qil—*Syzygium oblatum* (Roxb.) Cowan (Myrtaceae)
175. lml bol—*Nyssa javanica* (Bl.) Wanger (Nyssaceae)
176. eel niq—*Olea matsumuranus* Hayata (Oleaceae)
177. hov tul—*Cryptocarya brachythyrsa* H. W. Li (Lauraceae)
178. siq nanq—*Cleistanthus* spp. (Euphorbiaceae)
179. bil qyul—*Cyclobalanopsis rex* (Hemsl.) Schott (Fagaceae)
180. dal hhml laiv—*Calamus rhabdocladus* Burret (Palmae)
181. haq geeq—*Dinochloa tenuiparia* K. L. Wang (Gramineae)
182. laol baoq—*Camellia sinensis* (Linn.) O. Ktze. var. *assamica* (Mast.) Kitam. (Theaceae)
183. bimq—*Nephelium chryseum* Bl. (Sapindaceae)
184. haq tuq pievq—*Lithocarpus fenestratus* (Roxb.) Rehd. (Fagaceae)

185. pavq peel—*Acer garrettii* Craib (Aceraceae)
186. aq jil aq yo pavq ssaq—*Elaeocarpus varunua* Buch.-Ham.
     (Elaeocarpacae)
187. mail ceevq—*Alpinia kwangsiensis* T. L. Wu et Seajen
     (Zingiberaceae)
188. mal he caol wuvq—*Solanum khasianum* C. B. Clarke (Solanaceae)
189. haq tuq—*Lithocarpus corneus* (Lour.) Rehd. (Fagaceae)
190. al xeel—*Dicranopteris dichotoma* (Thunb.) Bernh. (Gleicheniaceae)
191. aq geeq leeq ma—*Toxicodendron acuminatum* (Hk. f.) C. Y. Wu
     (Anacardiaceae)
192. aq keeq oq haq—*Paederia scandens* (Lour.) Merr. (Rubiaceae)
193. haoq tang tail laiv—*Elaeagnus gonyanthes* Benth. (Elaeagnaceae)
194. meel nee haq—*Ilex godajam* (Colebr.) Wall. (Aquifoliaceae)
195. niail banl sanq gevq—*Ligustrum sinense* Lour. (Oleaceae)
196. aq gan—*Photinia glaba* (Thunb.) Maxim. (Rosaceae)
197. mail laol jaoq jav—*Pinanga macroclada* Burret (Palmae)
198. ya ma danl hhaq—*Pithe colobium clypearia* (Jack) Benth.
     (Mimosaceae)
199. dal piav dal xail—*Cyclosorus aridus* (Don) Tagawa (Thelypteridaceae)
200. pil pavq ssaq yul—*Machilus* sp. (Lauraceae)
201. dal laiv dal haq—*Tectaria grossendentata* Ching et C. H. Wang
     (Aspidiaceae)
202. qail ma—*Begonia crassirostris* Irmsch. (Begoniaceae)
203. hha qiv maiq ngovq—*Schizandra plena* A. C. Sm. (Schizandraceae)
204. al jil zanq lavq—*Euodia trichotoma* (Lour.) Pierre var. *pubescens*
     Huang (Rutaceae)
205. mail yaiv ma—*Hedychium forrestii* Diels (Zingiberaceae)
206. ji yao—*Amorphophalus yunnanensis* Engl. (Araceae)
207. haq hhml maiq maoq—*Reevesia pubescens* Mast. (Sterculiaceae)
208. pan nii yaq—*Millettia dorwardii* Coll. et Hemsl. (Papionaceae)
209. xaivq nii—*Bousigonia angustifolia* Pierre (Apocynaceae)
210. sanq daovq pavq teiq—small plant that grows on trees
211. miq cev lev—*Mukia javanica* (Miq.) Cogn. (Cucurbitaceae)
212. taiq neil haq—*Ormosia yunnanensis* Prain (Papilionaceae)
213. hov pail—*Albizia chinensis* (Osb.) Merr. (Mimosaceae)
214. naivq ssaq nee ganq—*Rhynchosia rubescens* (Willd.) D.C.
     (Papilionaceae)

APPENDIX 2

Trees and Shrubs of Akhapu, Thailand

87 total species[1]

1. *Styrax benzoides* Craib (Styracaceae)
2. *Baccaurea ramiflora* Lour. (Euphorbiaceae)
3. *Stereospermum colais* (Buch.-Ham. ex Dillw.) Mabb. (Bignoniaceae) (same as 24)
4. *Litsea glutinosa* (Lour.) C. B. Rob. (Lauraceae)
5. *Castanopsis argyrophylla* King ex Hk. f. (Fagaceae)
6. *Phoebe* sp. (Lauraceae) (same as 46)
7. *Callicarpa arborea* Roxb. var. *arborea* (Verbenaceae)
8. *Aporusa wallichii* Hk. f. (Euphorbiaceae)
9. *Castanopsis armata* (Roxb.) Spach (Fagaceae) (same as 36 and 80)
10. *Diospyros glandulosa* Lace (Ebenaceae)
11. *Quercus semiserrata* Roxb. (Fagaceae)
12. *Litsea glutinosa* (Lour.) C. B. Rob or *L. monopetala* (Roxb.) Pers. (Lauraceae)
13. *Millettia pachycarpa* Bth. (Leguminosae, Papilionoideae)
14. *Heliciopsis terminalis* (Kurz) Sleum. (Proteaceae) (same as 98)
15. *Schima wallichii* (D.C.) Korth. (Theaceae)
16. *Glochidion sphaerogynum* (M.-A.) Kurz (Euphorbiaceae)
17. *Bridelia pubescens* Kurz (Euphorbiaceae)
18. *Decaspermum parviflorum* (Lmk.) A. J. Scott spp. *parviflorum* (Myrtaceae)

19. *Eugenia albiflora* Duth. ex Kurz (Myrtaceae) (same as 37 and 93)
20. *Arctocarpus lanceolata* Trec. (Moraceae)
21. *Ficus glaberrima* Bl. var *glaberrima* (Moraceae)
22. *Artocarpus lakoocha* Roxb. (Moraceae)
23. *Cratoxylum formosum* (Jack) Dyer spp. *pruniflorum* (Kurz) Gog. (Hypericaceae/Guttiferae)
24. *Stereospermum colais* (Buch.-Ham. ex Dillw.) Mabb. (Bignoniaceae) (same as 3)
25. *Semecarpus cochinchinensis* Engl. (Anacardiaceae)
26. *Ternstroemia gymnanthera* (Wight & Arn.) Bedd. (Theaceae)
27. *Turpinia pomifera* (Roxb.) Wall. ex D.C. (Staphyleaceae)
28. *Lithocarpus elegans* (Bl.) Hatus. ex Soep. (Fagaceae) ?
29. *Wenlandia tinctoria* (Roxb.) D.C. (Rubiaceae)
30. *Dillenia parviflora* Griff. var. *kerrii* (Craib) Hoogl. (Dilleniaceae)
31. *Protium serratum* (Wall. ex Colebr.) Engl. (Burseraceae)
32. *Dalbergia rimosa* Roxb. (Leguminosae, Papilionoideae)
33. *Garuga floribunda* Decne. (Burseraceae)
34. *Paramichelia baillonii* (Pierre) Hu (Magnoliaceae) (same as 68)
35. *Homalium ceylanicum* (Gard.) Bth. (Flacourtiaceae)
36. *Castanopsis armata* (Roxb.) Spach (Fagaceae) ? (same as 9 and 80)
37. *Eugenia albiflora* Duth. ex Kurz (Myrtaceae) (same as 19 and 93)
38. *Cinnamomum iners* Reinw. ex Bl. (Lauraceae)
39. *Phoebe lanceolata* (Nees) Nees (Lauraceae) (same as 86)
40. *Engelhardia spicata* Lechen. ex Bl. var. *spicata* (Juglandaceae)
41. *Colona floribunda* (Kurz) Craib (Tiliaceae)
42. *Ficus* spp. (Moraceae) ?
43. *Dimocarpus longan* Lour. spp. *longan* var. *longan* (Sapindaceae)
44. *Ilex godajam* Colebr. ex Wall. (Aquifoliaceae)
45. *Mischocarpus pentapetalus* (Roxb.) Radlk. (Sapindaceae)
46. *Phoebe* sp. (Lauraceae) (same as 6)
47. *Oroxylum indicum* (Linn.) Kurz (Bignoniaceae) (same as 91)
48. *Garcinia* sp. (Guttiferae)
49. *Saurauia nepalensis* D.C. (Saurauiaceae)
50. *Alangium kurzii* Craib (Alangiaceae)
51. *Mallotus philippensis* (Lmk.) M.-A. var. *philippensis* (Euphorbiaceae)
52. *Sarcosperma arboreum* Bth. (Sapitaceae)
53. *Albizia odoratissima* (Linn. f.) Bth. (Leguminosae, Mimosoideae)
54. *Croton robustus* Kurz (Euphorbiaceae)
55. *Colona flagrocarpa* (Cl.) Craib (Tiliaceae)

56. *Cratoxylum maingayi* Dyer (Hypericaceae/Guttiferae)
57. *Horsfieldia amygdaline* (Wall.) Warb. var. *amygdalina* (Myristicaceae)
58. *Schleichera oleosa* (Lour.) Oken (Sapindaceae)
59. *Vitex limoniifolia* Wall. ex Kurz (Verbenaceae)
60. *Dalbergia fusca* Pierre (Leguminosae, Papilionoideae)
61. *Phyllanthus emblica* L. (Euphorbiaceae)
62. *Archidendron clypearia* (Jack) Niels. spp. *clypearia* var. *clypearia* (Leguminosae, Mimosoideae)
63. *Alstonia scholaris* (Linn.) R. Br. var. *scholaris* (Apocynaceae)
64. *Melia toosendan* Sieb. & Zucc. (Meliaceae)
65. *Gmelina arborea* Roxb. (Verbenaceae) (same as 69)
66. *Beilschmiedia* sp. (Lauraceae)
67. *Macaranga denticulata* (Bl.) M.-A. (Euphorbiaceae)
68. *Paramichelia baillonii* (Pierre) Hu (Magnoliaceae) (same as 34)
69. *Gmelina arborea* Roxb. (Verbenaceae) (same as 65)
70. *Eurya acuminata* D.C. var. *wallichiana* Dyer (Theaceae)
71. *Kydia calycina* Roxb. (Malvaceae)
72. *Symplocos macrophylla* Wall. ex D.C. subsp. *sulcata* (Kurz) Noot. var. *sulcata* (Symplocaceae)
73. *Pavetta petiolaris* Wall. ex Craib (Rubiaceae)
74. *Litsea salicifolia* Nees ex Roxb. (Lauraceae)
75. *Matedina trichotoma* (Zoll. & Mor.) Bakh. f. (Rubiaceae)
76. *Elaeocarpus floribundus* Bl. (Elaeocarpaceae)
77. *Spondias pinnata* (Linn. f.) Kurz (Anacardiaceae)
78. *Sterculia villosa* Roxb. (Sterculiaceae)
79. *Bombax anceps* Pierre var. *cambodiense* (Pierre) Roby. (Bombacaceae)
80. *Castanopsis armata* (Roxb.) Spach (Fagaceae) (same as 9 and 36)
81. *Dalbergia discolor* Bl. ex Miq. (Leguminosae, Papilionoideae)
82. *Ficus altissima* Bl. (Moraceae)
83. *Ficus semicordata* Buch.-Ham. ex J. E. Sm. var. *semicordata* (Moraceae)
84. *Trema orientalis* (Linn.) Bl. (Ulmaceae)
85. *Ficus auriculata* Lour. (Moraceae)
86. *Phoebe lanceloata* (Nees) Nees (Lauraceae) (same as 39)
87. *Melochia umbellata* (Houtt.) Stapf. (Sterculiaceae)
88. *Apodytes dimidiata* E. Mey. ex Arn. (Icacinaceae) ?
89. *Vitex canescens* Kurz (Verbenaceae)
90. *Holarrhena pubescens* (Buch.-Ham.) Wall. ex G. Don (Apocynaceae)

91. *Oroxylum indicum* (Linn.) Kurz (Bignoniaceae) (same as 47)

92. *Clerodendrum infortunatum* Linn. (Verbenaceae)

93. *Eugenia albiflora* Duth. ex Kurz (Myrtaceae) (same as 19 and 37)

94. *Albizia chinensis* (Osb.) Merr. (Leguminosae, Mimosoideae)

95. *Ficus fistulosa* Reinw. ex Bl. (Moraceae)

96. *Engelhardia serrata* Bl. (Juglandaceae)

97. *Dalbergia cana* Grah. ex Bth. var. *cana* (Leguminosae Papilionoideae)

98. *Heliciopsis terminalis* (Kurz) Sleum. (Proteaceae) (same as 14)

NOTES

INTRODUCTION

1. The pseudonym "Akhapu" is used because of the alleged involvement of some villagers in the heroin trade. In China, where villagers are not involved in the drug trade, the real name "Mengsong" is used.

2. "Tai" is the name of a language group, whose speakers include the peoples of Xishuangbanna, the Shan State of Burma, northern Thailand, and Laos. "Thai" is the national language of Thailand as well as a citizen of that country. See glossary.

3. See Coward (n.d.) for an extensive treatment of Tai land use and political relations with upland peoples in China, Burma, Thailand, Laos, and Vietnam.

4. The "Shan States" formally became the "Shan State" when incorporated into Burma after Burmese independence. See glossary.

5. In the 1990s, there were a number of coalitions of upland farmers, most notably the Assembly of the Poor, which organized large demonstrations and protests in front of government offices to demand security of access to land and trees. The Assembly drew mainly on farmers in the northeast. Although northern farmers also joined, no one from Akhapu contributed to this movement. For greater detail on the Assembly of the Poor, see Pinkaew (2001), Baker (2000).

6. See Breyer et al. (1997). This study showed an overall prevalence of 2.13 percent among all hill groups in Thailand, varying from a high of 8.75 percent among Hmong to a low of 0 percent among Karen. HIV prevalence among Akha was 5.0 percent.

7. In China, Akha are subsumed under the Hani minority nationality. Hani language is similar to Akha, although the two languages are largely mutually unintelligible. Akha speakers call themselves Akha.

8. Altogether there are an estimated half million Akha speakers in China, Burma, Laos, Thailand, and Vietnam (Kammerer 1989; Alting von Geusau 1983), although this figure may be low. In Xishuangbanna, the Akha (Hani) population in 1990 was 156,000 (Statistics Office, Jinghong). Estimates of Akha speakers in Thailand vary from 29,000 to 50,000 (*Hill tribe population survey report* 1988; Tribal Research Center, Chiang Mai, 1996).

9. My Akha research assistant in China, who traveled with me to Thailand, confirmed not only that these people were Akha, but also that Akha in the two villages spoke the same dialect.

10. In selecting research sites, I visited thirteen Akha villages in Thailand and fourteen Akha villages in Xishuangbanna.

11. More complete reporting on data analysis is in chapter 6.

12. Appendix 1 lists all the sampled trees and shrubs in Mengsong.

13. Appendix 2 lists all the sampled trees and shrubs in Akhapu.

2 / THE PRODUCTION OF BORDER LANDSCAPES

1. The name of the country was changed from Siam to Thailand in 1939, when a military coup ended the absolute monarchy. Scholars use "Siam" to refer to the pre-1939 political entity.

2. Chinese imperial expansion into areas included in western China today was not predetermined or inevitable. Owen Lattimore (1988:39) argues that for centuries in early imperial times Chinese could not go beyond the Great Wall to control peoples of the steppe because the mode of governance was different. He judges that in Mongolia, where Han agriculturalists encountered "barbarian" pastoralists, "the 'barbarism' of these barbarians, instead off being overcome, was essentially emphasized" (57). In Xinjiang under the Qing, Han armies met adversaries with whom they were "well matched" (Perdue 2002:371) and as such the eventual Qing conquest was not inevitable.

3. In the official list of minority nationalities in China today, the Akha are subsumed under the Hani.

4. Chinese scholars, however, may still interpret "raw" and "cooked" as stages in civilization (see Yin 2001).

5. Karen are a hill group thought to have originated in Burma. Many migrated into northern Thailand centuries ago, and they now constitute the largest group among the official hill tribes in Thailand (McKinnon and Vienne 1989).

6. "Self-civilizing" is the term used by Thongchai Winichakul in a presentation at the University of California–Berkeley in October 1997.

7. As of 1985, minority nationalities constituted 7 percent of China's population and occupied 50–60 percent of China's land area (Grunfeld 1985:54).

8. The collective period ended at different times in different parts of China, spanning the years 1980 to 1983. In Yunnan, communes were dismantled in 1982.

9. See, for example, *China: Forestry Support for Agriculture*, in which the FAO recommends the "eradication of shifting cultivation" (FAO 1978:81).

10. In 1980, Thai troops fought the Battle of Batang in northern Thailand against forces of the Miao Communist Party. The Thai troops were in fact former Nationalist soldiers who lost this battle, but gained citizenship for defending the Thai motherland (Bo 1987).

11. Most shifting cultivators in the north, even in the 1970s, were in fact northern Thai moving up into the hills, not ethnic-minority farmers (Kunstadter et al. 1978). Pinkaew Laungramsri (2001:214) estimates that as of the 1970s only 10 percent of shifting cultivators were hill tribe peoples.

3 / THE PRODUCTION OF BORDERS

1. Recent studies critiquing the galactic polity model as based exclusively on the view from the center include Tooker (1996) and Reynolds (1995).

2. See also Leach (1960:59) for instances of hill chieftains proclaiming loyalty to several different valley princes at the same time.

3. Kengtung was later incorporated into Burma as part of the Shan State.

4. Charles Keyes (1995) confirms that during this time, Tai in China and Burma (as well as in the Lanna States and Laos) participated in a common community, reading Buddhist texts in the same script.

5. Following Sara Berry's approach (1993) and looking from the bottom up instead of from the overlord's perspective, the reverse would be that serfs acquire access to grain and protection by submitting to a lord.

6. Unless otherwise cited, data are from field research, January 1996 to May 1997.

7. Gao He's estimate is based on Akha genealogies and twenty years of research in Xishuangbanna.

8. The Muslim Rebellion broke out shortly after the Taiping Rebellion (1850–64) that racked central China. Nervous about a religious group that seemed threatening to the Qing dynasty (like the Taiping rebels), Han soldiers in Yunnan attacked Muslims, prompting a violent response. These widespread rebellions helped bring down the Qing, which was already crumbling (Garnier 1996; Hill 1998).

9. In Akha, the Nationalists are called the "yellow Han," based on the pea-green color of their uniforms, while the Communists are called the "black Han." When Akha farmers woke up in the morning, Mengsong was full of Communist troops.

10. Sipsongpanna in Dai or Thai means "twelve districts" (of the kingdom). Xishuangbanna, a transliteration, has no particular meaning in Chinese, helping to erase the old kingdom.

11. Before 1948, there were numerous small principalities called the "Shan States." Following unification, the area was officially consolidated as one "Shan State."

12. Aung San was the father of Aung San Suu Kyi, the Nobel Peace Prize–winning

leader in Burma. Martin Smith (1991:71–87) indicates that Aung San's role was ambiguous and that British failure to include the ethnic groups in negotiations leading to independence was more decisive than Aung San's death in producing their resistance to inclusion in the Union of Burma.

4 / SMALL BORDER CHIEFS
AND RESOURCE CONTROL, 1910 TO 1997

1. The names of both men are pseudonyms.

2. The Bulang, another of the fifty-six official minority nationalities in China, are mountain people living in China and Burma.

3. Akha in Xishuangbanna divide themselves into two groups, Udo and Uqie, based on genealogies that diverged many generations ago. Most Akha in Mengsong are Udo. Those who moved to Mengsong in the 1930s are Uqie Akha. Udo Akha in China speak a dialect very similar to Ulo Akha in Thailand, while Uqie Akha speak a dialect very similar to Loimi Akha in Thailand. I had no way of discovering if those with similar dialects considered themselves to be related.

4. Damenglong was one of the twelve districts in Sipsongpanna. As the nearest valley town to Mengsong, it later became the head of the commune to which Mengsong belonged and today is the local township.

5. Each of the eleven hamlets in Mengsong was given a revolutionary name at the beginning of the Cultural Revolution (1966–76). Each hamlet also has a Tai name as well as an Akha name. Local people use the older Akha names when speaking Akha and the Cultural Revolution names when speaking Chinese.

6. During the collective period, villagers received work points rather than cash for their labor. This system is explained in detail in chapter 6.

7. In Chinese, *shangmian* means the layers of administration above one's position. Although many policies originated at the national level, they would have been transmitted to Mengsong by commune-level cadres.

8. Every hamlet and village had a people's militia person for local security. These were local villagers, not military personnel, perhaps best understood as a citizens' militia.

9. During my research, the second-in-command of the military post was a Lisu—another mountain ethnic group—from elsewhere in Yunnan.

10. The hamlet head and head of administration for Xianfeng are from the two clans that settled Mengsong. Members of their clans were heads of Xianfeng up to the Cultural Revolution. After ten years out of office, they are now in charge again. There are similar histories of leading clans in other hamlets, as well as at the administrative-village level.

11. This land allocation process is covered in detail in chapter 6.

12. By law all minerals belong to the state. In practice, the state is only inter-

ested in rich deposits. In a case like Mengsong, where the amount of tin is limited, state agents are satisfied to let villagers mine and sell the tin, so long as the state collects a tax on it (Xu, pers. comm., 2000).

13. Mining involved digging holes in the fields, pumping water out of the holes, and separating the tin from other soil. The digging, as well as tailings from the operation, was destroying the wet-rice fields.

14. By 1989 the price of tin was fluctuating so widely that it was hard to make a profit.

15. The set of elected officers in a hamlet form the legal entity called the collective, which is able to sign contracts on behalf of the hamlet.

16. Data from social survey conducted by the author in March 1997.

17. For an extended analysis of wasteland auctions in Sichuan, see Grinspoon (2002).

18. These two strands reflect two definitions of development that often get conflated, as noted by James Ferguson (1994:15). Poverty alleviation and the development of a market economy are not the same thing. Akha farmers could tell the difference.

19. To illustrate his clout, when Akheu drove me across the border, at the checkpoint on the Burma side he eased our crossing by handing over two cigarettes.

20. In describing his role to me, Lawjaw still used the title of *pusaen*, as well as *phuyai ban*, the Thai term for official village head.

21. For a discussion of a similar phenomenon of the political eminence of the "first arrived" in frontier areas of Africa, see Kopytoff (1987).

22. Jane Hanks and Lucien Hanks (2001) refer to Yibaw as the regionally powerful "lord" of this area in the early 1960s.

23. The details of the tea company are explored in chapter 6.

24. I am grateful to Margery Lazarus for translating these displays for me.

25. Since tea is not really indigenous to Thailand, the presence of tea bushes indicates that previous residents must have planted them. I thank David Thomas for this insight.

26. Lawjaw was the *zoema*, the Akha leader responsible for external relations. The *boema*, or spiritual leader, was someone else. See Tooker (1996) for more detail on these customary Akha roles.

27. By "Americans" I assume Lawjaw meant CIA staff, based on descriptions of their involvement in the drug trade (Lintner 1994; McCoy 1991, 1972).

28. This was not an insignificant post, since agriculture involved all opium-eradication and crop-substitution projects.

29. Forestry staff in Chiang Rai and health-care workers in Chiang Mai knew Lawjaw and had enjoyed his hospitality.

30. This constraint would be true of other northern Thai villages as well. The village head is the local patron and sole representative of local views to state officials

(Hirsch 1989). Peter Vandergeest (pers. comm. 1999) reports that villagers in the south of Thailand complain frequently to government officials about their village heads, suggesting that practices may vary in other parts of the country.

31. Many villagers claimed that opium did not grow well in Akhapu. Those who grew poppies usually did so in fields across the border in Burma.

32. For further detail on the charisma of forest monks, see Tambiah (1984).

5 / PREMODERN BORDER LANDSCAPES
UNDER BORDER PRINCIPALITIES

1. The most useful book for birding in Xishuangbanna is Roland Eve's *The Birds of Thailand*, because of the area's climate and proximity to Southeast Asia.

2. Akha protected one water source to ensure that the water was the most ritually pure. This water was used in ceremonies, including those before opening swidden fields in the spring. To keep the water pure, farmers were prohibited from cutting anything in the watershed surrounding the water source. For Akha, the thinking was not the same as that of current watershed-protection advocates, but the outcome for protecting forests was similar.

3. For a more extensive treatment of the history of conservation in the Sanpabawa, including rules for collecting rattan, see Xu (1990).

4. Mengsong, at 1,600 meters, was once much colder then than it is now, making it unsuitable for growing upland rice or peanuts. Wet-rice fields used to freeze and frost covered the ground on many days in the winter. Mengsong became considerably warmer in the 1970s, when agricultural policies brought about extensive loss of forests.

5. This customary prohibition on, and the danger resulting from, opening primary forest is important when considering the forced opening of higher-elevation forests under Communist rule, discussed in chapter 6.

6. To avoid confusion I use the Cultural Revolution name, Xianfeng (vanguard), which is used by villagers and others when speaking Chinese. In speaking of the 1930s and 1940s, this is an anachronism.

7. The tea merchants represent an early instance of Han residing in Sipsongpanna. See Hill (1998:73–86) for a detailed examination of the political economy surrounding tea.

8. Unless otherwise cited, all data in this chapter are from fieldwork from November 1995 to July 1997.

9. Residents of other villages say Dongfanghong villagers have never opened any of their own wet-rice fields. The greater area per person in Dongfanghong than in any other Mengsong hamlet is confirmed by data in Xu (1990).

10. The shape of landforms in figure 10 differs from figure 13 ("Xianfeng in 1997," in chapter 6). The 1940s map was hand-drawn, whereas the 1997 map was based on a government topographical map.

11. The sixth hamlet, Dongfanghong, was all Uqie Akha who moved in during the 1930s.

12. Wa are an official minority nationality in China as well as an upland group in Burma. They are renowned for their hunting skills.

13. As for Akha in China, the watershed forest was protected so that this water source would be ritually pure.

6 / LANDSCAPE PLASTICITY VERSUS LANDSCAPES OF PRODUCTIVITY AND RULE

1. Unless otherwise cited, all data in this chapter are from field research, January 1996 to May 1997.

2. For an extended discussion of taking grain as the key link, see Shapiro (2001:95–98).

3. For more information about the destruction of forests during the Great Leap Forward, see Richardson (1990) and Ross (1988).

4. This designation also influenced what land was called "wasteland" under the wasteland auction policy. I thank Su Yongge and Elisabeth Grinspoon for pointing out these maps and their implication for current policies.

5. As Mark Selden notes, "'taking grain as the key link' (to the detriment of animal husbandry, forestry, and commerce), . . . hit hill and mountain regions particularly hard" (1993:151).

6. See Park et al. (1994) for a more extensive discussion of these policy shifts.

7. Data on the number of livestock is from Shuosan, the administrative village accountant.

8. Since the 1950s, the Chinese state had allowed Akha to keep their rifles, since Akha had to protect themselves from dangerous animals in the forest. Other citizens were not allowed to have guns.

9. See, for example "Highland development programme" (1975); "Thai war on opium: More than just a pipe dream," *New York Times*, October 18, 1984; "Hilltribes map out new way of life," *The Nation* (Bangkok), October 1, 1990.

10. For a study of how development projects depoliticize increased state intervention and control of rural areas, see Ferguson (1994).

11. These opinions and data are from forestry consultants at Chiang Mai University and the head of the RFD office in Chiang Mai.

12. See Peluso (1992) on local people mirroring state plans in claiming forests. See also Peluso (1995) on counter-mapping of forestland.

13. As in China, villagers internalized the state role in monitoring and protecting forests, a form of state formation (Agrawal 2001).

14. Altogether this amounted to 560,000 hectares (interview with a forester at Chiang Mai University, 1997).

15. Interview with a forester at Chiang Mai University, 1997.

APPENDIX 1

1. Identified by Tao Guoda, Forest Taxonomist, Xishuangbanna Tropical Botanic Garden, March 1997.

2. Akha names are in the official romanization devised in Jinghong, Xishuang-banna.

APPENDIX 2

1. Identified by J. M. Maxwell, Chiang Mai University Herbarium, May 1997.

GLOSSARY

administrative village In China, unit of administration below township and above hamlet during the period of research.

Akha Tibeto-Burman-language-speaking hill ethnic minority found in China, Burma, Thailand, Laos, and Vietnam. See also *Lisu, Lahu.*

Akhapu Pseudonym for the Akha settlement and the research hamlet in Thailand.

Akheu Administrative village head of Mengsong, 1992–98.

Bulang Hill ethnic minority found in China and Burma.

caw phaendin Overlord (in Thai and other Tai languages).

Dai Official minority nationality in China that includes Tai-speaking peoples in Xishuangbanna. Both the language and the minority nationality are romanized as Dai in China. See also *minority nationality.*

galactic polity Scholarly conception of rule in premodern Southeast Asia, in which the king's power radiates outward from the court, with rule involving hierarchical layers of patronage relationships in which the king is the patron controlling the most resources.

hamlet Lowest unit of administered community, used here in place of "village" to distinguish it from "administrative village" in China and the Akha settlement (of three hamlets) in Thailand.

Hani Official minority nationality under which Akha are subsumed in China. See also *minority nationality.*

hill tribe   Used in Thailand for nine officially designated upland ethnic minorities (*chao khao* in Thai); the term is considered pejorative.

Hin Taek   Town in Mae Faluang District of Thailand, where Akhapu is located. Purportedly established by Khun Sa, the "drug lord" from the Shan State of Burma, Hin Taek served as headquarters for Khun Sa's domain in northern Thailand from 1976 to 1982. See *Khun Sa.*

Hmong   Hill ethnic minority in China, Burma, Thailand, Laos, and Vietnam, subsumed under the minority nationality called Miao in China.

household   Unit of social organization used by modernizing states to identify people who share a hearth; a "legible" unit that oversimplifies Akha clan and work relationships in both China and Thailand.

Jinuo   An official minority nationality found only in Xishuangbanna, China.

Kengtung   Tai (Shan) principality, one of the Shan States of Burma.

kha   *Kha* (falling tone) refers to slaves, bondsmen, or subjects; *kha* (low tone) was used in premodern times in Siam and Burma to refer to all hill peoples (Tai and Thai). In the literature in English the two terms are sometimes conflated.

Khun Sa   Most famous among the "drug lords" in the Shan State of Burma; ruler of an informal drug-producing domain in northern Thailand from 1976 to 1982. See also *Hin Taek.*

Lahu   Tibeto-Burman-language-speaking hill ethnic minority found in China, Burma, Laos, and Thailand. See also *Akha, Lisu.*

Lanna States   Small Tai principalities north of Siam, now part of northern Thailand.

Lawjaw   Customary Akha head of Akhapu from about 1965 onward; state-designated village head (*phuyai ban*) of Akhapu settlement (including Akhapu hamlet) beginning in 1982.

Lisu   Tibeto-Burman-language-speaking hill ethnic minority found in China, Burma, and Thailand. See also *Akha, Lahu.*

Lua   Austroasiatic-language-speaking ethnic minority in Thailand, thought to be the original inhabitants of the north (also spelled Lawa).

Mengsong   Administrative village in China where Xianfeng hamlet is located. Mengsong currently includes eleven hamlets. See also *administrative village, township, hamlet.*

minority nationality   Socialist term used in China for ethnic minority groups thought to be products of past oppression (*shaoshu minzu*).

mu   Chinese unit of area; 15 *mu* equal 1 hectare.

muang   Political domain; also the people in a political domain (Thai).

rai   Thai unit of area; 6.25 *rai* equal 1 hectare.

RFD   Royal Forestry Department in Thailand.

saw-bwa   Shan prince (Burmese).

Shan   Term used for Tai-speaking people in Burma, most of whom live in the Shan State.

Siam   Kingdom for which the name was changed to Thailand in 1939, when a military coup ended the absolute monarchy.

Sipsongpanna   Tai principality in what is now southwestern Yunnan; earlier a tributary state of both China and Burma. Renamed Xishuangbanna when it was incorporated into China in 1950. See *Xishuangbanna*.

Tai   Language group, whose speakers include the Tai Lue of Xishuangbanna, the Shan of Burma, northern Thais in Thailand, and the Lao in Laos; also, Tai-speaking peoples.

Thai   Citizen of Thailand; national language of Thailand.

township   Administrative unit in China above the administrative village; commune headquarters during the collective period (1958–82).

tusi   Local non-Han chiefs appointed by Han rulers to keep order along the southwestern border of the Chinese empire.

Udo Akha   Subgroup of Akha in China, possibly related to Ulo Akha in Thailand. See *Ulo Akha*.

Ulo Akha   Subgroup of Akha in Thailand, possibly related to Udo Akha in China. See *Udo Akha*.

Wa   Hill people found in China and Burma.

Xianfeng   Akha research hamlet in China.

Xishuangbanna   Autonomous prefecture in southern Yunnan (previously Sipsongpanna), which the Communist government renamed Xishuangbanna (a transliteration) when it was incorporated into China in 1950. The name Xishuangbanna has no particular meaning in Chinese, helping to obscure the historical Sipsongpanna Tai principality. See *Sipsongpanna*.

BIBLIOGRAPHY

Achao. 1997. New Life Center, Chiang Mai, Thailand. Personal communication.

Agrawal, Arun. 2001. State formation in community spaces? Decentralization and control over forests in the Kumaon Himalaya, India. *Journal of Asian Studies* 60 (1): 9–40.

———. 1999. *Greener pastures: Policies, markets, and community among a migrant pastoral people.* Durham: Duke University Press.

Alting von Geusau, Leo. 1983. Dialectics of *Akhazan*: The interiorization of a perennial minority group. In *Highlanders of Thailand*, ed. J. McKinnon and W. Bhruksasri. Kuala Lumpur: Oxford University Press.

Anan Ganjanapan. 1996. State conservation policy and the complexity of local control in forest land in Northern Thailand. Paper presented at meeting of the International Association for the Study of Common Property, Berkeley, June.

Anderson, Benedict. 1991. *Imagined communities.* Rev. ed. New York: Verso.

Armijo-Hussein, Jacqueline. 1996. Sayyid 'Ajall Shams Al-Din: A Muslim from Central Asia, serving the Mongols in China, and bringing 'civilization' to Yunnan. Ph.D. diss., Harvard University.

Baker, Chris. 2000. Thailand's Assembly of the Poor: Background, drama, reaction. *South East Asia RESEARCH* 8 (1): 5–29.

Baud, M., and W. van Schendel. 1997. Toward a comparative history of borderlands. *Journal of World History* 8 (2): 211–42.

Baumler, Alan. 1998. Negotiating purity: The Chinese people and opium under the republic. Paper presented at meeting of the Association for Asian Studies, Washington, DC.

Bernatzik, Hugo Adolph. 1970. *Akha and Miao: Problems of applied ethnography in farther India.* Trans. Abis Nagler. New Haven: Human Research Area Files.

Berry, Sara. 1993. *No condition is permanent: The social dynamics of agrarian change in sub-Saharan Africa.* Madison: University of Wisconsin Press.

————. 1988. Concentration without privatization? Some consequences of changing patterns of rural land control in Africa. In *Land and society in contemporary Africa,* ed. S. Reyna and R. Downs. Hanover, NH: University Press of New England.

Bo Yang. 1987. *Golden Triangle: Frontier and wilderness.* Hong Kong: Joint Publishing Company.

Boserup, Mogens. 1963. Agrarian structure and take-off. In *The economics of take-off,* ed. Rostow.

Breyer, C., D. D. Celentano, S. Suprasert, W. Sittitrai, K. E. Nelson, B. Kongsub, V. Go, and P. Phanupak. 1997. Widely varying HIV prevalence and risk behaviours among the ethnic minority peoples of northern Thailand. *AIDS CARE* 9 (4): 427–39.

Brookfield, Harold. 2001. *Exploring agrodiversity.* New York: Columbia University Press.

Bunnag, Tej. 1977. *The provincial administration of Siam, 1892–1915.* Kuala Lumpur: Oxford University Press.

Cameron, Meribeth. 1931. *The reform movement in China 1898–1912.* Stanford: Stanford University Publications.

Cao Guangxia and Zhang Lianmin. n.d. Innovative forest management by local communities in Yunnan Province, Southwest China. Working paper prepared for Southwest Forestry College, Kunming, China.

Chiang Rai Committee. 1994. Chiang Rai hill tribe development report: Legislation, regulations, resolutions, measures and directive policy of government sectors in solving highlander problems and exterminating the narcotic drug cultivation. Chiang Rai, Thailand: Office of Administration for Solving Hill Tribe Problems.

China forestry yearbook, 1949–1986. 1987. Beijing: China Forestry Publishers.

Chinese Academy of Geological Sciences. 1976. *Geological map of China* [in Chinese]. Beijing: Geological Map Publishing House.

Chusak Wittayapak. 1996. Tenure insecurities in protected areas of Thailand. Paper presented at meeting of the International Association for the Study of Common Property, Berkeley, June 1996.

Cohen, Morris. 1927. Property and sovereignty. *Cornell Law Society* 8:8–28.

Conklin, Harold C. 1957. *Hanunoo agriculture: a report on an integral system of shifting cultivation in the Philippines.* Rome: Food and Agriculture Organization of the United Nations.

Connor, Walker. 1984. *The national question in Marxist-Leninist theory and strategy.* Princeton: Princeton University Press.

Coward, Walt. n.d. Tai Valley–based polities and the uplands. Unpublished manuscript.

de Carne, Louis. 1995. *Travels on the Mekong: Cambodia, Laos and Yunnan.* Bangkok: White Lotus.

Diamond, Norma. 1995. Defining the Miao: Ming, Qing, and contemporary views. In *Cultural encounters on China's ethnic frontiers,* ed. Stevan Harrell. Seattle: University of Washington Press.

Donnan, Hastings, and Thomas Wilson. 1999. *Borders: Frontiers of identity, nation and state.* Oxford: Berg.

Dove, Michael R. 1999. Representations of the "other" by others. In *Transforming the Indonesian uplands: Marginality, power, and production,* ed. Tania Murray Li. Amsterdam: Harwood Academic Publishers.

———. 1996. Center, periphery, and biodiversity: A paradox of governance and developmental challenge. In *Valuing local knowledge: Indigenous people and local property rights,* ed. S. Brush and D. Stabinsky. Washington, DC: Island Press.

———. 1985. *Swidden agriculture in Indonesia: The subsistence strategies of the Kalimantan Kantu.* New York: Mouton Publishers.

Eve, Roland. 1996. *The birds of Thailand.* Trans. Patricia Arnold. Bangkok: bookSiam.

Feder, Gershon, and David Feeny. 1991. Land tenure and property rights: Theory and implications for development policy. *The World Bank Economic Review* 5 (1):135–53.

Feeny, David. 1989. The decline of property rights in man in Thailand, 1800–1913. *Journal of Economic History* 49 (2): 285–96.

———. 1988. Agricultural expansion and forest depletion in Thailand, 1900–1975. In *World deforestation in the twentieth century,* ed. J. Richards and R. Tucker. Durham: Duke University Press.

Ferguson, James. 1994. *The anti-politics machine: "Development," depoliticization, and bureaucratic power in Lesotho.* Minneapolis: University of Minnesota Press.

Fiskesjö, Magnus. 1999. On the "raw" and "cooked" barbarians of imperial China. *Inner Asia* 1: 139–68.

Fitzgerald, C. P. 1972. *The southern expansion of the Chinese People.* Bangkok: White Lotus.

Food and Agriculture Organization (FAO). 1978. *China: Forestry support for agriculture.* FAO Forestry Paper 12. Rome: Food and Agriculture Organization of the United Nations.

———. 1948. *Report of the mission for Siam.* Rome: Food and Agriculture Organization of the United Nations.

Forsyth, Timothy. 1995. Tourism and agricultural development in Thailand. *Annals of Tourism Research* 22 (4): 887–900.

Fortmann, Louise. 1995. Talking claims: Discursive strategies in contesting property. *World Development* 23 (6): 1053–63.

Gao He. 1995. Member of the Yunnan Provincial Folk Literature and Art Council.
Personal communication, July.

Garnier, Francis. 1996. *Further travels in Laos and in Yunnan: The Mekong exploration commission report (1866–1868)—Volume 2.* Bangkok: White Lotus.

Giersch, C. Patterson. 1998. Qing China's reluctant subjects: Indigenous communities and empire along the Yunnan frontier. Ph.D. diss., Yale University.

Gladney, Dru. 1991. *Muslim Chinese: Ethnic nationalism in the People's Republic.*
Cambridge, MA: Council on East Asian Studies, Harvard University.

Grinspoon, Elisabeth. 2002. Socialist wasteland auctions: Privatizing collective
forest land in China's economic transition. Ph.D. diss., University of
California, Berkeley.

Grunfeld, A. Tom. 1985. In search of equality: Relations between China's ethnic
minorities and the Han majority. *Bulletin of Concerned Asian Scholars* 17 (1):
54–67.

Grunfeld, F. 1982. *Wayfarers of the Thai forest: The Akha.* Amsterdam: Time-Life
Books.

Guha, Sumit. 1999. *Environment and ethnicity in India, 1200–1991.* Cambridge:
Cambridge University Press.

Guldin, Gregory. 1994. *The saga of anthropology in China: From Malinowski to
Moscow to Mao.* Armonk, NY: M. E. Sharpe.

Hafner, J. 1990. Forces and policy issues affecting forest use in northeast Thailand
1900–1985. In *Keepers of the forest: Land management alternatives in Southeast
Asia*, ed. M. Poffenberger. West Hartford, CT: Kumarian Press.

Hall, D. G. E. 1960. *Burma.* London: Hutchinson University Library.

Hanks, Jane Richardson, and Lucien M. Hanks. 2001. *Tribes of the north Thailand
frontier.* Monograph 51. New Haven: Yale University, Southeast Asia Studies.

———. 1999. Tribes of the north Thailand frontier. Unpublished manuscript.

Hanks, Lucien M. 1975. *Gazetteer for 1964, 1969, and 1974. Maps of ethnic settlements of Chiangrai Province north of the Mae Kok River, Thailand.* Ithaca:
Cornell University Southeast Asia Program.

———. 1962. Merit and power in the Thai social order. *American Anthropologist*
64:1247–61.

Harkness, James. 1998. Recent trends in forestry and conservation of biodiversity
in China. *China Quarterly* (Winter): 911–34.

Harrell, Stevan. 1995. Introduction: Civilizing projects and the reaction to them.
In *Cultural encounters on China's ethnic frontiers*, ed. Stevan Harrell. Seattle:
University of Washington Press.

Hart, Gillian, Andrew Turton, and Benjamin White, with Brian Fegan and Lim
Teck Ghee, eds. 1989. *Agrarian transformations: Local processes and the state in
Southeast Asia.* Berkeley: University of California Press.

Hefner, Robert. 1990. *The political economy of mountain Java: An interpretive history*. Berkeley: University of California Press.

The highland development programme in Thailand. 1975. *RIHED News* 2 (2) (April–June): 5.

Hill, Ann Maxwell. 1998. *Merchants and migrants: Ethnicity and trade among Yunnanese Chinese in Southeast Asia*. Monograph 47. New Haven: Yale University, Southeast Asian Studies.

Hill tribe population survey report. 1988. Chiang Mai, Thailand: Tribal Research Centre.

Hirsch, Philip. 1990. *Development dilemmas in rural Thailand*. Singapore: Oxford University Press.

————. 1989. The state in the village: Interpreting rural development in Thailand. *Development and Change* 20:35–56.

————. 1987. Deforestation and development in Thailand. *Singapore Journal of Tropical Geography* 8 (2): 131–38.

Hobsbawm, Eric. 1983. Introduction. In *The Invention of Tradition*, ed. E. Hobsbawn and T. Ranger. Cambridge: Cambridge University Press.

Hostetler, Laura. 2001. *Qing colonial enterprise: Ethnography and cartography in early modern China*. Chicago: University of Chicago Press.

Hyndman, Jennifer. 2002. Business and bludgeon at the border: A transnational political economy of human displacement in Thailand and Burma. *Geojournal* 55:39–46.

Kahn, Joel. 1999. Culturalising the Indonesian uplands. In *Transforming the Indonesian uplands: Marginality, power, and production*, ed. Tania Murray Li. Amsterdam: Harwood Academic Publishers.

Kemp, Jeremy. 1992. *Hua Kok: Social organisation in north-central Thailand*. Canterbury: Centre for Social Anthropology and Computing, University of Kent.

————. 1989. Peasants and cities: The cultural and social image of the Thai peasant village community. *Sojourn* 4 (1): 6–19.

Keyes, Charles F. 2002. Presidential address: "The Peoples of Asia"—Science and politics in the classification of ethnic groups in Thailand, China, and Vietnam. *Journal of Asian Studies* 61 (4): 1163–1203.

————. 1997. Cultural diversity and national identity in Thailand. In *Government Policies and Ethnic Relations in Asia and the Pacific*, ed. M. Brown and S. Ganguly. Cambridge: MIT Press.

————. 1995. Who are the Tai? Reflections on the invention of local, ethnic and national identities. In *Ethnic identity: Creation, conflict and accommodation*, ed. L. Romanucci-Ross and G. De Vos. Walnut Creek, CA: Alta Mira Press.

————. 1994. The nation-state and the politics of indigenous minorities: Reflections of ethnic insurgency in Burma. Paper presented at Tribal Minorities and the State, organized by the Harry Guggenheim Foundation, Istanbul, February 21–25.

Kipnis, Andrew. 1996. The language of gifts: Managing guanxi in a north China village. *Modern China* 22 (2): 285–315.

Kopytoff, Igor. 1987. The internal African frontier: The making of African political culture. In *The African frontier: The reproduction of traditional African societies*, ed. I. Kopytoff. Bloomington: Indiana University Press.

Kunstadter, Peter, E. C. Chapman, and Sanga Sabhasri, eds. 1978. *Farmers in the forest: Economic development and marginal agriculture in northern Thailand.* Honolulu: University of Hawai'i Press.

Lattimore, Owen. 1988 [1940]. *Inner Asian frontiers of China.* Hong Kong: Oxford University Press.

Leach, E. R. 1960. The frontiers of Burma. *Comparative Studies in Society and History* 3 (1): 49–68.

———. 1954. *Political systems of highland Burma.* Boston: Beacon Press.

Li, Tania Murray. 2001. Regional histories and the production of difference on Sulawesi's upland frontier. *Journal of Asian Studies* 60 (1): 41–66.

———. 1999. Introduction and chapter 1, Marginality, power and production: Analysing upland transformations. In *Transforming the Indonesian uplands: Marginality, power, and production*, ed. Tania Murray Li. Amsterdam: Harwood Academic Publishers.

———. 1996. Images of community: Discourse and strategy in property relations. *Development and Change* 27:501–27.

Li Xiwen and D. Walker. 1986. The plant geography of Yunnan Province, southwest China. *Journal of Biogeography* 13:367–97.

Lintner, Bertil. 1994. *Burma in revolt: Opium and insurgency since 1948.* Boulder, CO: Westview Press.

Locke, John. 1964 [1704]. *Two treatises of government: A critical edition with an introduction and apparatus criticus by Peter Laslett.* Cambridge: Cambridge University Press.

Macpherson, C. B., ed. 1978. *Property: Mainstream and critical positions.* Buffalo, NY: University of Toronto Press.

Marx, Karl. 1906. The so-called primitive accumulation. In *Capital, a critique of political economy*, ed. F. Engels. Chicago: Charles H. Kerr and Company.

Matisoff, James A. 1983. Linguistic diversity and language contact. In *Highlanders of Thailand*, ed. J. McKinnon and W. Bhruksasri. Kuala Lumpur: Oxford University Press.

McCoy, Alfred. 1991. *The politics of heroin: CIA complicity in the global drug trade.* Brooklyn: Lawrence Hill Books.

———. 1972. *The politics of heroin in Southeast Asia.* Singapore: Harper and Row Publishers.

McKinnon, John. 1997. Forests in Thailand: Strike up the ban? In *Development or domestication? Indigenous peoples of Southeast Asia*, ed. D. McCaskill and K. Kampe. Chiang Mai, Thailand: Silkworm Books.

McKinnon, John, and Jean Michaud, 2000. Introduction. In *Turbulent times and enduring peoples: Mountain minorities in the South-East Asian massif*, ed. Jean Michaud. Richmond, Surrey: Curzon.

McKinnon, John, and Bernard Vienne, eds. 1989. *Hill tribes today: Problems in change*. Bangkok: White Lotus.

Mekvichai, B. 1988. The teak industry in North Thailand: The role of a natural resource-based export economy in regional development. Ph.D. diss., Cornell University.

Meinzen-Dick, Ruth, Lynn R. Brown, Hilary Sims Feldstein, and Agnes R. Quisumbing. 1997. Gender, property rights, and natural resource. IFPRI Discussion Paper No. 29.

Menzies, Nicholas. 1992. Strategic space: Exclusion and inclusion in wildland policies in late imperial China. *Modern Asian Studies* 26 (4): 719–33.

Moore, Donald. 1993. Contesting terrain in Zimbabwe's eastern highlands: Political ecology, ethnography, and peasant struggles. *Economic Geography* 88:380–401.

Morgan, Lewis Henry. 1964 [1878]. *Ancient society*, ed. L. White. Cambridge, MA: Belknap Press of Harvard University Press.

Neumann, Roderick P. 1998. *Imposing wilderness: Struggles over livelihood and nature preservation in Africa*. Berkeley: University of California Press.

O'Conner, Richard. 1994. Professor of anthropology, University of the South. Personal communication.

Oi, Jean. 1989. *State and peasant in contemporary China: The political economy of village government*. Berkeley: University of California Press.

Ong, Aihwa. 1999. *Flexible citizenship: The cultural logics of transnationality*. Durham: Duke University Press.

Padoch, Christine. 2002. Spotting expertise in a diverse and dynamic landscape. In *Cultivating biodiversity: understanding, analysing and using agricultural diversity*, ed. H. Brookfield, C. Padoch, H. Parsons, and M. Stocking. London: ITDG Publishing.

———. 1982. *Migration and its alternatives among the Iban in Sarawak*. The Hague: M. Nijhoff.

Padoch, Christine, Emily Harwell, and Adi Susanto. 1998. Swidden, sawah, and in-between: Agricultural transformation in Borneo. *Human Ecology* 26 (1): 3–20.

Park, A., S. Rozelle, and F. Cai. 1994. China's grain policy reforms: Implications for equity, stabilization, and efficiency. *China Economic Review* 5 (1): 15–34.

Pasuk Phongpaichit and Sungsidh Piriyarangsan. 1994. *Corruption and democracy in Thailand*. Chiang Mai, Thailand: Silkworm Books.

Peet, Richard, and Michael Watts. 1996. Liberation ecology: Development, sustainability, and environment in an age of market triumphalism. In *Liberation ecologies: Environment, development, social movements*, ed. R. Peet and M. Watts. New York: Routledge.

Peluso, Nancy Lee. 1996. Fruit trees and family trees in an Indonesian rainforest: Property rights, ethics of access, and environmental change. *Comparative Studies in Society and History* 38 (3): 510–48.

———. 1995. Whose woods are these? Counter-mapping forest territories in Kalimantan, Indonesia. *Antipode* 27 (4): 383–406.

———. 1992. *Rich forests, poor people: Resource control and resistance in Java.* Berkeley: University of California Press.

Perdue, Peter. 2002. Fate and fortune in central Eurasian warfare: Three Qing emperors and their Mongolian rivals. In *Warfare in inner Asian history (500–1800)*, ed. N. di Cosmo. Leiden, The Netherlands: Brill.

Pinkaew Laungramsri. 2001. Redefining nature: Karen ecological knowledge and the challenge to the modern conservation paradigm. Chennai, India: Earthworm Books.

———. 1997. On the discourse of hill tribes. Paper presented at Workshop on Ethnic Minorities in a Changing Environment, Chiang Mai, Thailand, February.

Postiglione, Gerard. 1998. Ethnic minority education in China's market economy: Equality vs. multiculturalism? Paper presented at meeting of the Association of Asian Studies, Washington, DC.

Pragtong, K., and D. Thomas. 1990. Evolving management systems in Southeast Asia. In *Keepers of the forest: Land management alternatives in Southeast Asia*, ed. M. Poffenberger. West Hartford, CT: Kumarian Press.

Rambo, A. Terry, and Le Trong Cuc. 1995. The composite swidden system of the Tay and biodiversity in the mountains of northern Vietnam. Paper presented at symposium on Montane Mainland Southeast Asia in Transition, Chiang Mai, Thailand, November 12–16.

Reid, Anthony. 1988. *Southeast Asia in the age of commerce. Volume one. The land below the winds.* New Haven: Yale University Press.

Renard, Ronald. 1993. Civilized and uncivilized peoples. Paper presented at the International Conference on Thai Studies, London.

———. 1980. *Kariang:* History of Karen-T'ai relations from the beginnings to 1923. Ph.D. diss., University of Hawai'i.

Reynolds, Craig. 1995. A new look at old Southeast Asia. *Journal of Asian Studies* 54 (2): 419–46.

Richardson, S. 1990. *Forests and forestry in China: Changing patterns of resource development.* Washington, DC: Island Press.

———. 1966. *Forestry in Communist China.* Baltimore: Johns Hopkins Press.

Rose, Carol. 1994. *Property and persuasion.* Boulder, CO: Westview Press.

Ross, Lester. 1988. *Environmental policy in China.* Bloomington: Indiana University Press.

Rostow, W. W., ed. 1963. *The economics of take-off into sustained growth.* New York: St. Martin's Press.

Sack, Robert D. 1986. *Human territoriality: Its theory and history.* Cambridge: Cambridge University Press.

Sahlins, Peter. 1989. *Boundaries: The making of France and Spain in the Pyrenees.* Berkeley: University of California Press.

Santisuk, T. 1988. *An account of the vegetation of northern Thailand.* Geoecological Research, vol. 5, ed. U. Schweinfurth. Stuttgart: Franz Steiner Verlag.

Scott, James C. 1998. *Seeing like a state: How certain schemes to improve the human condition have failed.* New Haven: Yale University Press.

———. 1985. *Weapons of the weak: Everyday forms of peasant resistance.* New Haven: Yale University Press.

Selden, Mark. 1993. *The political economy of Chinese development.* Armonk, NY: M. E. Sharpe.

Shapiro, Judith. 2001. *Mao's war against nature.* Cambridge: Cambridge University Press.

Shipton, Parker, and Mitzi Goheen. 1992. Understanding African land-holding: Power, wealth, and meaning. *Africa* 62 (3): 307–25.

Sivaramakrishnan, K. 1999. *Modern forests: Statemaking and environmental change in colonial East India.* Stanford: Stanford University Press.

Smith, Adam. 1986 [1776]. *The wealth of nations.* In *The essential Adam Smith,* edited and with introductory readings by Robert L. Heilbroner. New York: W. W. Norton and Company.

Smith, Martin. 1991. *Burma: Insurgency and the politics of ethnicity.* London: Zed Books Ltd.

Sophon Ratanakhon. 1978. Legal aspects of land occupation and development. In *Farmers in the forest,* ed. Kunstadter et al.

Spence, Jonathan. 1975. Opium smoking in Ch'ing China. In *Conflict and control in later imperial China,* ed. F. Wakeman and C. Grant. Berkeley: University of California Press.

Steinberg, David, ed. 1987. *In search of Southeast Asia: A modern history.* Honolulu: University of Hawai'i Press.

Sturgeon, Janet C. 1997. Claiming and naming resources on the border of the state: Akha strategies in China and Thailand. *Asia Pacific Viewpoint* 38 (2): 131–44.

———. 1995–97. Unpublished fieldwork notes.

Tambiah, S. J. 1984. *The Buddhist saints of the forest and the cult of the amulets: A study in charisma, hagiography, sectarianism, and millennial Buddhism.* Cambridge: Cambridge University Press.

———. 1976. *World conqueror and world renouncer.* Cambridge: Cambridge University Press.

Tannenbaum, Nicola. 1999. Multiple sovereignty. Paper presented at meeting
of the Association for Asian Studies, Boston.

Tapp, Nicholas. 1989. *Sovereignty and rebellion: The white Hmong of northern
Thailand.* Singapore: Oxford University Press.

Taylor, J. 1991. Living on the rim: Ecology and forest monks in northeast Thailand. *Sojourn* 6 (1): 106–25.

Thongchai Winichakul. 1997. Professor of history, University of Wisconsin.
Personal communication.

————. 1994. *Siam mapped: A history of the geo-body of a nation.* Honolulu:
University of Hawai'i Press.

Tooker, Deborah E. 1996. Putting the mandala in its place: A practice-based
approach to the spatialization of power on the Southeast Asian "periphery"—
The case of the Akha. *The Journal of Asian Studies* 55 (2): 323–58.

Turton, Andrew. 1989. Local powers and rural differentiation. In *Agrarian transformations*, ed. Hart et al.

————. 1980. Thai institutions of slavery. In *Asian and African systems of slavery*,
ed. J. Watson. Berkeley: University of California Press.

Vandergeest, Peter. 1999. Associate professor of sociology, York University.
Personal communication.

————. 1995. Mapping nature: State territorialization of rights to the forest in
Thailand. *Society and Natural Resources* 9:159–75.

Vandergeest, Peter, and Nancy Peluso. 1995. Territorialization and state power in
Thailand. *Theory and Society* 24:385–426.

Wakin, Eric. 1992. *Anthropology goes to War: Professional ethics and counterinsur-
gency in Thailand.* Monograph 7. Madison: University of Wisconsin, Center
for Southeast Asian Studies.

Walker, Andrew. 1999. *The legend of the golden boat: Regulation, trade and traders
in the borderlands of Laos, Thailand, China and Burma.* Honolulu: University
of Hawai'i Press.

Wijeyewardene, Gehan. 1992. Rethinking the frontiers of Burma. *Thai-Yunnan
Project Newsletter* 19 (December): 2–7.

World Bank. 2001. *World development report 2002: Building institutions for
markets.* Oxford: Oxford University Press.

Wu, David. 1990. Chinese minority policy and the meaning of minority culture:
The example of Bai in Yunnan, China. *Human Organization* 49 (1): 1–13.

Wyatt, David. 1984. *Thailand: A short history.* New Haven: Yale University Press.

Xu Jianchu. 2000. Professor and deputy director, Department of Ethnobotany,
Kunming Institute of Botany, China. Personal communication, July.

————. 1990. *Research on a traditional agroecological system* [in Chinese].
Kunming, China: Kunming Institute of Botany, Academia Sinica.

Xu Jianchu, Pei Shengji, and Chen Sanyang. 1995. From subsistence to market-
oriented system and the impacts on agroecosystem biodiversity: The case

of the Hani (Akha) swidden cultivator in Mengsong, south China. In *Regional study on biodiversity: Concepts, frameworks, and methods*, ed. S. Pei and P. Sajise. Kunming, China: Yunnan University Press.

Yin Shaoting. 2001. *Yunnan swidden agriculture in human-ecological perspective.* Trans. Magnus Fiskesjö. Kunming, China: Yunnan Education Publishing House.

Zou Hengfang. 1994. Deputy director, Yangtze Shelterbelt Project, Yunnan Provincial Forestry Department. Personal communication.

Zuo Ting. 1997. Institutional constraints of social forestry development in Yunnan, China. Paper presented at the Regional Center on Forestry (RECOFT) seminar, Community Forestry at the Crossroads: Reflections and Future Directions in the Development of Community Forestry, Bangkok, July.

INDEX

aboriginal periphery, 28

Ado, 186

Africa, landholding in, 37

Agrawal, Arun, 10, 161

Agu, 166

AIDS, 12, 14

Akha people, 3, 7, 9, 11, 13, 15, 21, 36, 107; access to resources and, 4, 7, 39–40, 82, 100, 122, 125–26, 131, 135, 173, 192, 201; ancestors of, 11–12, 119, 121–22, 126, 131, 135, 140–41, 147, 152, 156, 166, 185–86; Burma border and, 16, 29, 83, 86, 99–100, 143, 161, 176, 186; Chinese citizenship and, 7, 11, 97; Chinese Communist guerrillas and, 76, 86; Chinese Nationalist army (China) and, 75, 76, 83, 99, 129–30; Chinese Nationalist army (Thailand) and, 78; comparative study of, 4, 16, 22–23; drugs and, 186, 199; forest condition and, 7, 41, 43, 174; forest management by, 14, 36, 125–26, 162, 165, 181, 196, 200; government offices and, 11, 14, 171; history and origins of, 12, 14, 120–41 passim; houses of, 84, 95, 124, 163; hunting by, 24, 161; landscape legibility and, 33–34; landscape plasticity and, 10, 25, 35, 40–41, 121, 130, 137, 140, 144–45, 158–62, 166, 173, 197, 199; landscape vision of, 24–25, 32, 36, 120; language of, 15, 17; Loimi Akha, 4, 135, 143, 173–74, 181, 199, 224; marginalization of, 7, 10, 40, 114, 198–99; migration of, 15, 74, 174–75; opium and, 58, 83, 128–31, 140–41, 147; Shan State and, 139–41; shifting cultivation and, 40, 120, 137, 153, 161, 199; small border chiefs and, 32, 86, 101, 116; small border principality and, 81–82; state-allocated identities and, 14, 27, 28; state plans and, 10, 14, 28, 36, 144–45, 167; tea and, 138–40, 147; tea company and, 104, 176–77; traders and, 83, 129, 139–40; Udo Akha, 83, 224, 231; Ulo Akha, 4, 173–74, 224, 231; Uqie Akha, 82–83, 129, 130–31, 141, 224, 227; village heads of, 10, 31, 40; wage labor of, 183, 191, 197

LIBRARY OF CONGRESSS CATALOGING-IN-PUBLICATON DATA

Sturgeon, Janet C.
Border landscapes : the politics of Akha land use
in China and Thailand / Janet C. Sturgeon.
p. cm.—(Culture, place, and nature)
Includes bibliographical references and index.
ISBN 0-295-98544-5 (hardback : alk. paper)
1. Akha (Asian people)—Land tenure.
2. Akha (Asian people)—Politics and government.
3. Akha (Asian people)—Social conditions.
4. Land use—China.
5. Land Use—Thailand.
6. Landscape assessment—China.
7. Landscape assessment—Thailand.
8. Indigenous peoples—Ecology—China.
9. Indigenous peoples—Ecology—Thailand.
10. China—Boundaries.
11. Thailand—Boundaries.
12. China—Politics and government.
13. Thailand—Politics and government.
I. Title. II. Series.
DS528.2.K37S78   2005
306.3'64'09513509152—dc22
2005016162

Breinigsville, PA USA
21 January 2010
231119BV00001B/2/A